0099296

LIBERALISM, MULTICULTURALISM AND TOLERATION

Also by John Horton

ASPECTS OF TOLERATION (*editor with Susan Mendus*)
JOHN LOCKE: *A LETTER CONCERNING TOLERATION* IN FOCUS
   (*editor with Susan Mendus*)
*POLITICAL OBLIGATION
TOLERATION AND INTEGRITY IN A MULTI-FAITH SOCIETY
   (*editor with Harriet Crabtree*)
TOLERATION: PHILOSOPHY AND PRACTICE (*editor with Peter Nicholson*)

Also published by Macmillan

Liberalism, Multiculturalism and Toleration

Edited by
John Horton

Lecturer in Politics
Director, Morrell Studies in Toleration
University of York

MACMILLAN

First published 1993 by
THE MACMILLAN PRESS LTD
Houndmills, Basingstoke, Hampshire RG21 2XS
and London
Companies and representatives
throughout the world

ISBN 0–333–57102–9

A catalogue record for this book is available
from the British Library

Typeset by Expo Holdings Sdn Bhd, Malaysia

Printed in Great Britain by
Ipswich Book Co Ltd
Ipswich, Suffolk

In memory of Deborah Fitzmaurice

Contents

Preface

This book issues from the Morrell Studies in Toleration based in the Department of Politics at the University of York. Several, though not all, of the papers were presented at one of a series of conferences on philosophical issues associated with toleration. This book and the associated conference are part of a wider programme of study supported by the C. and J.B. Morrell Trust aimed at enhancing the theoretical and practical understanding of toleration. My principal acknowledgement is of my debt to the trustees for their continuing generosity towards, and encouragement of, both the programme in general and this book in particular.

Peter Jones's essay first appeared in a slightly different form in the *British Journal of Political Science*. I am grateful to the editor and Cambridge University Press for permission to reprint it in this volume. I am also especially grateful to my colleagues Susan Mendus and Peter Nicholson for their considerable help and advice; to Rod Rhodes and Jenny Bradford for their support; to Clare Wace, an ever-patient editor; to Anne Rafique for her conscientious copy-editing; to Andrea Baumeister for compiling the index; and last but not least to Jackie Morgan for her work in preparing the manuscript.

Finally, it is also appropriate to record here the very sad loss of Deborah Fitzmaurice who died while this volume was in the final stages of preparation. Debbie was a vibrant presence at the conference on which the book is based, a generous person and a philosopher of enormous promise. The book is dedicated to her memory.

John Horton
York, 1992

Notes on the Contributors

Jonathan Chaplin is Tutor in Politics at Plater College in Oxford. He is currently completing his doctoral research at the LSE and editing two books on Christian political theory.

David Edwards is Lecturer in Politics at the University of York. He is co-editor (with Susan Mendus) of *On Toleration* (1987) and author of articles on J.S. Mill and blasphemy.

Deborah Fitzmaurice was Baring Foundation Fellow in Philosophy and Human Rights at the University of Essex. She was actively involved in introducing the philosophy of human rights into East European universities.

Peter Gardner is Lecturer in Education at the University of Warwick. He has published numerous articles on aspects of the philosophy of education including indoctrination, paternalism, personal autonomy, moral education, religious education, counselling mature students and ethical absolutism.

Jagdish S. Gundara is Head of the Centre for Multicultural Education at the Institute for Education, University of London. He has played a leading role in the development of multicultural education in the UK, and in addition to many scholarly articles he is co-editor of *Racism, Diversity and Education* (1986), co-author of *A Comparative Study of Adult Education in Australia, Britain and Canada* (forthcoming) and co-editor of forthcoming books on the history of black people and the history of racism in Britain.

John Horton is Director of the Morrell Studies in Toleration and Lecturer in Politics at the University of York. He is author of *Political Obligation* (1992); co-editor (with Susan Mendus) of *Aspects of Toleration: Philosophical Studies* (1985) and *John Locke: 'A Letter Concerning Toleration' in Focus* (1991); co-editor (with Peter Nicholson) of *Toleration: Philosophy and Practice* (1992); and co-editor (with Harriet Crabtree) of *Toleration and Integrity in a Multi-Faith Society* (1992).

Peter Jones is Senior Lecturer in Politics at the University of Newcastle. He is the author of numerous scholarly articles on political philosophy including democracy, freedom, neutrality, blasphemy legislation and the Rushdie affair. His book, *Rights*, will be published by Macmillan in 1993.

Susan Mendus is Senior Lecturer in Politics at the University of York. In addition to many articles in scholarly journals she is author of *Toleration and the Limits of Liberalism* (1989); editor of *Justifying Toleration* (1988); co-editor (with John Horton) of *Aspects of Toleration: Philosophical Studies* (1985) and *John Locke 'A Letter Concerning Toleration' in Focus* (1991); co-editor (with David Edwards) of *On Toleration* (1987); co-editor (with Ellen Kennedy) of *Women in Western Political Philosophy* (1987); co-editor (with J.M. Bell) of *Philosophy and Medical Welfare* (1988); and co-editor (with Jane Rendall) of *Sexuality and Subordination* (1989).

Tariq Modood is presently a Hallsworth Research Fellow at the University of Manchester, having previously taught in a number of British universities. He was Visiting Research Fellow at Nuffield College during 1991–2. He is the author of *Not Easy Being British* (1992) and of several articles on political theory. He is currently working on a book on the changing nature of the concept of race in contemporary Britain.

Glen Newey was a graduate student in the Department of Politics at the University of York. He successfully completed his doctoral dissertation on 'Rationality and Politics' and now works with Amnesty International.

Patricia White is Research Fellow in the Philosophy of Education at the Institute of Education, University of London. In addition to a wide range of articles and papers on ethical and political aspects of the philosophy of education, she is author of *Beyond Domination: An Essay in the Political Philosophy of Education* (1983) and editor of *Personal and Social Education: Philosophical Perspectives* (1989).

1 Liberalism, Multiculturalism and Toleration

John Horton

All modern liberal democratic societies are marked by diversity and difference – differences of ethnicity, culture and religion in addition to the many individual differences which characterise the members of such societies. Traditionally liberalism has been pictured as celebrating much of this diversity, or as at least tolerant of many differences which might not be thought valuable. Yet it has become clear that the relationship between liberalism, pluralism, especially multiculturalism, and toleration is much more problematic than this simple and comforting picture suggests. In particular, while not a new problem, it has become an increasingly urgent issue of theory and practice as to how tolerant liberalism is, or can be, of cultural and religious groups which do not themselves subscribe unreservedly or without qualification to what have been taken to be the basic values of liberalism.

However, to refer to the basic values of liberalism is itself to raise questions about the meaning and implications of modern liberalism. In fact liberal theorising has undergone a renaissance in the last two decades, but a renaissance which has perhaps created as many problems as it has resolved. Interpretations of liberalism have ranged from the libertarianism of Robert Nozick to the egalitarianism of Ronald Dworkin, and from the neutralism of Bruce Ackerman to the perfectionism of Joseph Raz.[1] At the centre of the evolution of liberal theorising meanwhile has stood the continually developing thought of John Rawls, the *éminence grise* of modern liberal theory.[2] Moreover, candidates for the status of liberalism's basic values have included liberty, equality, rights, neutrality, autonomy and sundry combinations of them. This internal diversity is perhaps itself symptomatic of the tensions and conflicts afflicting contemporary liberal theory as philosophers attempt to articulate it in a form which is adequate to the complexity of modern society. In this volume the arguments of several liberal theorists are examined and their implications explored specifically with respect to issues concerning the permissible limits and acceptable forms of cultural diversity. These focus on what has become known as 'multiculturalism'.

Multiculturalism too is a difficult concept, so much so that some writers eschew its use, preferring instead the older term 'pluralism'.[3] One ambiguity in the term, and in this respect pluralism is no improvement, is that it is used both descriptively and evaluatively. Sometimes multiculturalism simply refers to the existence of a plurality of ethnic or cultural groups within a society. Often when used in this way the term is employed to state a problem: multiculturalism is perceived as the problem of accommodating diverse and sometimes conflicting groups within a single society. However, multiculturalism is also used evaluatively to express an ideal. A multicultural society is a valuable end towards which policies should be directed. Of course these senses of the term are not unrelated and some would claim that the ideal of multiculturalism does no more than make a virtue out of a necessity (though liberals are characteristically likely to view it more positively). However, it is important to recognise that adopting the *ideal* of multiculturalism is not the only possible response to the *fact* of multiculturalism. Another possibility, favoured by many, but frequently criticised as culturally imperialist, is assimilation – a conscious and deliberate attempt to break down the distinctiveness of cultural groups within what is sometimes thought of as 'a melting pot' conception of society. Nor is it impossible to seek some kind of compromise between multiculturalism and assimilation although it has become clear that, while both in some sense aim at integration, the basic logics of the two processes are not merely different but ultimately contradictory.[4]

A further difficulty with the concept of multiculturalism concerns what is meant by a 'culture' or a 'cultural group'. Clearly cultural differences in a broad sense – that is differences in people's ways of life – can be more or less extensive. It is common to speak for example of working-class and middle-class cultures in Britain, but these involve differences which are not typically of the sort implied by references to multiculturalism. Yet it is very hard to define with any precision what sort of differences are implied. Most frequently the phrase 'ethnic or religious groups' is employed, and though it is obvious that some ethnic or religious differences are for most practical purposes unimportant, this probably best expresses what is meant. Where ethnic and/or religious groups share an extensive range of practices and values which separate them from other ethnic and/or religious groups then, in the relevant sense, they constitute a distinct culture. However, one persistent difficulty with this conception is that it is inclined to over-emphasize both homogeneity within cultures and separateness from other cultures. This is one of the principal reasons some people have for preferring the term pluralism, which lacks these implications. Yet for this very reason pluralism can be misleading precisely because it fails to distinguish the kind of differences implied by multiculturalism from the much more restricted and ethically often less problematic differences of tastes and pursuits which the term 'pluralism' also encompasses.

This last point perhaps helps us to understand the most crucial consideration in identifying and distinguishing 'groups', in the sense relevant to multiculturalism. Muslims or Jews, for example, are not groups of people who simply happen to share common interests or tastes, or even similar opinions. To be a Muslim or a Jew (or of course a Christian) is to understand one's identity as intimately bound up with membership of that group. It is to partake of a common history and to stand in a particular relationship with the group which is integral to one's sense of who one is. Inevitably the extent of this will vary, but even those who wish to make a complete break with their cultural community cannot but be cognizant of that with which they are breaking. Moreover, for those who continue to identify with their cultural community, group membership will be of the first importance; indeed where one's group is united by both ethnicity and religion it is hard to imagine anything more fundamental. None of this precludes extensive diversity within the group but it concedes that membership of this kind of cultural group plays a special role which to some extent distinguishes it from other associations such as sports clubs, trade unions, self-help groups or charitable bodies.

Multiculturalism becomes a problem when conflicts between groups about values or their interpretation cannot be comfortably accommodated within a particular social structure. Two such instances in contemporary Britain which are extensively discussed in this book concern education and the limits of free speech. Of course these conflicts should not be overstated and it is important to acknowledge that there is also considerable agreement on these matters. It is agreed, for example, that certain minimum standards of education should be achieved by all children and that free speech is an important value which should be protected by the law. But on both these issues there are also important disagreements, not merely about preferences but bringing into play moral values embodied in communal identity. Thus, for example, to put it very crudely, Muslims are concerned that the education of Muslim girls should reflect their place in Muslim society rather than the values of secular liberalism. And while Muslims have been outraged that 'free speech' should permit the vilification of the most sacred beliefs of an already socially disadvantaged group, liberals have been similarly outraged that many Muslims have been prepared to support the *fatwa* which condemns a man to death for writing a novel. Moreover, even to formulate matters in the way I have done is highly controversial since one of the issues at stake is about exactly how these disputes should be properly articulated. However, there can be little doubt that one of the issues at stake is the limits of toleration.

The practice of toleration is indispensable to any modern society marked by ethical pluralism, and especially to a multicultural society. The ideal of toleration has traditionally been one of liberalism's principal values.[5] As Steven Lukes has rightly said 'liberalism was born out of religious conflict and the attempt to tame it by accommodating it within the framework of the nation-state. The case for religious toleration was central to its development'.[6] Hence it might plausibly be thought that toleration should provide a particularly promising bridge between liberalism and multiculturalism: it is one of liberalism's most important ethical resources for confronting multiculturalism. At the heart of the idea of toleration – what might be characterised as the core conception of toleration – is a deliberate choice not to interfere with conduct of which one disapproves. Three components of this core conception of toleration can be identified. First there must be some conduct which is disapproved of (or at least disliked). Second, this disapproval must not be acted upon in ways which coercively prevent others from acting in the disapproved manner. Third, this refusal to interfere must be more than mere acquiescence or resignation. While each of these components gives rise to a number of questions – for example, about whether disapproval includes dislike, and about how intrusive or restrictive interference can be without becoming intolerant – it is the last component which has generated the most extensive discussion.

In part this is because there appears to be something very puzzling, even paradoxical, about toleration. This is most evident if we focus on instances where both the disapproval of conduct, and the justification for tolerating it, are moral. After all, on the face of it, is it not odd that the refusal to prevent conduct which is wrong should be regarded as morally required? It will be widely agreed that there may be a variety of prudential and pragmatic arguments for toleration, but the most interesting arguments are those which claim that in some circumstances toleration is a moral duty. This apparent paradox – that we should morally permit what is morally wrong – is considered by Glen Newey in his essay in this volume, but I shall not pursue his discussion here. What is clear though is that any liberal theory in which toleration has a central place must offer some account of why it is valuable. It is not an obvious or uncontroversial good.[7]

This volume is principally concerned with the philosophical exploration of the relationship between liberalism, toleration and multiculturalism. Not all the essays focus on all three concepts but all address issues of importance in trying to understand their relationship. Most of the essays therefore seek to pursue a variety of philosophical arguments as they bear on the questions which inform this book. However, the first essay, by Jagdish Gundara, adopts a different approach and situates the issues in a wider perspective. Gundara is concerned with how some groups within a state come to be marginalised and defined as alien or 'other'. He draws primarily on the work of social scientists to argue that multiculturalism is a more diverse and long-standing phenomenon within European states, including Britain, than is commonly supposed. States are not, for the most part, the culturally and ethnically homogeneous entities that they are frequently imagined to be. He argues that it is important to 'deconstruct' such fictions if excluded groups are to be properly understood, and if the interest of dominant groups in creating and maintaining mythical national identities is to be exposed. For Gundara myths of a unitary national identity serve to exclude disadvantaged groups (not always minorities, as in the example of women) from positions of power and also to circumscribe what passes for knowledge within a society. In short such myths are 'ideological' in serving the interests of dominant groups by excluding and disadvantaging other groups.

Gundara's essay provides a useful reminder of the social background which often underlies discussions of multiculturalism. In Britain, for example, racism is widespread and black people typically face in their day to day lives an extensive array of disadvantages and discriminatory behaviour which constantly reminds them that they are not members of the dominant cultural group. It is important to bear this in mind when considering the practical import of moral and philosophical arguments about liberal values such as liberty and toleration. However, Gundara's paper also indirectly shows the importance of the philosophical discussion of these issues, for instance in his frequent but undefined references to equality and rights. We need to know what is meant by these key values, how they hang together, and what they imply in terms of reasonably specific sets of social arrangements. Moreover, Gundara's emphasis on possible alliances between excluded groups, important as it is, neglects the potential for conflict within and between those groups, in addition to the conflict between excluded and dominant groups. Nor need the conflicts issuing from ethnic diversity be between dominant and disadvantaged groups. For example, as Deborah Fitzmaurice brings out in her essay, there may be very deep conflicts between women and certain religious groups which cannot be easily understood in terms of the arguments about dominant and subservient groups deployed in Gundara's essay. Hence while political philosophy needs to be more sensitive than it sometimes is to relevant sociological and historical considerations, these cannot simply substitute for the type of enquiry in which political philosophers characteristically engage.

Both Jonathan Chaplin and Deborah Fitzmaurice in their essays seek to explore and assess the claims of liberalism to be the political theory most hospitable to a genuinely tolerant multiculturalism. Chaplin in particular is deeply sceptical of such claims. He examines the arguments of Robert Nozick and Will Kymlicka, proponents of very different forms of liberalism, and he finds that both are less tolerant of cultural diversity than they purport to be.[8] Whereas Nozick's radically voluntaristic libertarian framework is held to undermine the range of cultures likely to survive and prosper within it, Kymlicka's attempt to protect minority cultures through allowing them special rights fails because it exploits two incompatible notions of the value of cultural membership. Both theories, therefore, despite their substantial differences, will incline towards a winnowing out of cultures which do not enshrine the principal values of liberalism, and in particular those which do not place a very high valuation on individual choice and autonomy. By contrast, Chaplin argues, it is the merit of Joseph Raz's 'perfectionist' version of liberalism that it clearly recognises the centrality of choice and autonomy, and in consequence explicitly accepts that liberals have no reason to protect or support forms of life in which autonomy is not prized.[9] Rather such cultures as do not value autonomy highly must either be allowed to wither and die or be significantly transformed through assimilation and absorption. Thus liberalism is argued to be tolerant only towards cultural and religious communities which are in substantial part microcosms of the larger liberal society; that is those which are themselves liberal.

Chaplin further contends that once we recognise that liberalism is itself a perfectionist political theory with its own conception of the good, then there is no reason to believe that it will necessarily be more tolerant than all other political theories. In his tantalisingly brief but most interesting conclusion, Chaplin suggests that we should reject 'the idea that there is any *independent* yardstick of toleration against which different theories could be ranked as more or less tolerant of cultural or religious pluralism'. Hence, he concludes, 'the liberal project of devising a universally valid conception of justice which is endorsable by all irrespective of their particular conceptions of the good is unattainable'. Certainly in so far as this is the aspiration of liberalism, and if Chaplin's arguments are sound, then this will appear a 'distressingly pessimistic conclusion' yet there may be more room for hope than Chaplin allows. First, not all liberals, and one thinks especially of the later Rawls, have such grand ambitions.[10] Secondly, in so far as we *share* yardsticks of toleration – though it is important to recognise that toleration is not universally valued – then the absence of an *independent* yardstick, even if Chaplin is right, need not be so serious. The existence of such shared yardsticks will mean that comparative evaluations about the extent of toleration are not precluded. Of course, conversely, in so far as they are not shared, this will lend support to his conclusion; and at the very least, Chaplin reminds us that there is no simple and universally accepted metric in terms of which toleration can be measured. And this is something of which any adequate liberal theory will need to take account; a conclusion further supported by some of the arguments in Glen Newey's essay.

Deborah Fitzmaurice is similarly critical of the aspirations of liberal political theorists to attain a neutral justification of liberal political principles. She too examines the consequent difficulty in construing the grounds of conflicts between the liberal state and traditional, especially religious, minorities in its midst. However, she explicitly dissents from the view that a non-liberal minority has as much reason to value its own institutions, which are non-autonomy supporting, as liberals have to value the autonomy-supporting institutions which they prefer. In this respect Fitzmaurice sharply parts company with Chaplin over the conclusions he draws from the failure of liberal neutrality. Rather she argues that the liberal has good grounds for sustaining an autonomy-supporting public sphere even in the face of opposition from non-liberal minorities; grounds which in fact should also be persuasive to non-liberals. Thus Chaplin and Fitzmaurice agree that liberalism cannot be neutral, even procedurally, between autonomy-valuing and non autonomy-valuing cultures, but Fitzmaurice rejects any claim that this leaves the liberal and non-liberal on a par or in a simple stand-off with each other.

Fitzmaurice's argument is a complex one drawing particularly on epistemological claims about the conditions of rationality in a modern plural society. The kernel of this argument perhaps lies in her claim that there is no acceptable alternative to public argumentation in a modern plural society, and that the very possibility of such public argumentation itself imposes conditions upon how it is to be conducted. These conditions are incompatible with certain paradigms of justification which do not admit of critical enquiry. This does not mean that traditional or non-liberal practices cannot be defended but that the only generally acceptable form of defence is through 'conversation, comparison and argument'. Such a defence is successful if those practices can be 'critically and reflectively affirmed'. However, this kind of defence in turn entails a commitment to the value of a public space in which autonomy is a necessary condition of participation. In consequence, as she puts it, 'if pluralism is acknowledged, then the value of the conditions of autonomy and of its exercise cannot consistently be repudiated' because the defence of any ethical view 'in conditions of cultural diversity, must involve the exercise of the capacity for autonomy, hence the acknowledgement of the value of the external conditions for the development of that capacity'. This is a powerful argument, but quite how powerful is not altogether easy to judge. In particular we need to know more about what 'the acknowledgement of pluralism' consists in, about the egalitarianism implicit in the argument, and about the nature of public justification; but above all we need to have a clearer sense of how extensive the commitment to autonomy must be for the non-liberal to participate effectively in a public process of justification. What does a commitment to the autonomy necessary for participation in the public process of justification amount to?

Some indication of Fitzmaurice's likely answer to this question is provided by her closing discussion of education in which she maintains that 'the argument for autonomy is a strong argument against unconditional parental rights and unlimited parental choice with respect to schooling'. More specifically, since 'some forms of religious schooling deprive the individual of autonomy' and are therefore harmful, 'such schools are emphatically impermissible'. Not surprisingly education has been one of the principal battlefields on which debates about multiculturalism and the limits of toleration have been waged. It forms a central focus of the essays by Patricia White and Peter Gardner, in addition to Fitzmaurice's briefer discussion. White is particularly concerned with the role of trust (and distrust) within a modern pluralist democratic society and with how the school, as the basic unit of institutionalised education within such a society, can contribute to the development of a proper understanding of it. Indeed, she suggests that considerations of trust may provide one reason for being sceptical about the desirability of separate schools for different ethnic or religious groups; and hence her argument supplies additional support for Deborah Fitzmaurice's conclusions on this point.

White maintains that the tasks of the school in a pluralist multicultural society are basically fourfold. First, it should instantiate what she calls 'social trust' in its own ethos; that is it should be an institutional embodiment of a context of trust. Second, the school should attempt to provide its students with an understanding of the meaning and role of social trust and distrust in a democratic society. Third, it should encourage students to apply that understanding not only to the wider society but to the school itself as one institution within that society of which they have a particularly intimate knowledge. Finally, the school should foster and maintain conditions for the development of personal trust between its members in addition to giving its students an understanding of trust within personal relationships. Through fostering trust, and an appreciation of its limits, the school can contribute to the development of a vital feature of the framework for a genuinely tolerant multicultural society; one which seeks to preserve civil and harmonious relationships between the cultural and ethnic groups which comprise it.

White's essay approaches issues of toleration indirectly via her concern with the question of trust; Peter Gardner's essay by contrast focuses exclusively on toleration. He is especially concerned to argue for a more extended conception of tolerance than is widespread. In particular Gardner claims that some kinds of toleration do not imply disapproval or dislike by the tolerant person. As he observes there is something rather perplexing in the common understanding of toleration which was outlined earlier, as (roughly) a refusal to restrict actions or practices of which one disapproves (or on some accounts, dislikes) where one has the power to do so. The perplexity arises from the fact that on this account a person may become increasingly tolerant by disapproving of more and more things but choosing not to act on that disapproval. This seems to imply an understanding of what it is to become more tolerant which radically conflicts with our ordinary sense of what it is to be a tolerant person. Thus Gardner suggests we should drop the condition that an act or practice must necessarily be disapproved of or disliked by a person if that person is properly to be described as tolerant of it. Rather, he contends that it is only necessary that an act or practice be, or be likely to be, disapproved or disliked by some people, not that it be disapproved of or disliked by the tolerant person. In this way the notion of tolerating something becomes separable from a negative judgement on the part of the tolerator: 'the tolerant person need not dislike, disapprove of or feel disgusted by what he is tolerant towards'.

The importance of this conclusion is, as Gardner states, that it undermines one of the common objections to toleration: that it always implies a negative attitude on the part of those exercising tolerance towards what they are tolerating. As he goes on to remark, 'With regard to education, this means that those concerned with encouraging children to be tolerant need not feel that they are in effect leaving prejudice or bigotry untouched and merely trying to stop children from acting intolerantly.' If tolerance does not imply disapproval then it is possible to see how trust and toleration can be mutually supporting. Toleration would be consistent with trusting others' judgements, and trust would imply tolerating people's acting on those judgements. Of course trust and toleration are not reducible to each other and remain importantly distinct values and may on occasion conflict. On the basis of White's and Gardner's essays, however, it becomes easier to see how they can reinforce each other, and how both are necessary to a genuinely liberal society within which ethnic and cultural pluralism flourishes without provoking hostility or antagonism, or inducing a sense of inferiority.

Neither White's nor Gardner's paper resolves, or attempts to resolve, problems about the scope and limits of toleration. These problems have proved among the more intractable within both the theory and the practice of liberal democracy. Despite a considerable measure of agreement about the failings of liberal theorising, Chaplin and Fitzmaurice ultimately arrive at very different conclusions about how the problem is to be formulated, and the effectiveness of the argumentative resources available to liberalism to resolve disputes about the limits of toleration at the theoretical level. It would be a further step to translate any theoretical resolution into practical policies. However, it may be that at a practical level it is better to begin by addressing the particular circumstances of a specific problem, rather than seeking to derive 'solutions' to such problems from high-level abstract theories (though this is emphatically not to suggest that such theories are without practical value). It may also turn out that attending to the details of a particular dispute about the limits of toleration will provide perhaps unexpected theoretical illumination of much wider significance and application.

The remainder of the papers in this volume all focus, to greater or lesser extent, specifically on what has become known as the 'Rushdie affair'.[11] My brief paper provides some background information about the dispute. It does not seek to make a substantive contribution to the debate, and it can be passed over by readers already familiar with the broad outlines of the events relating to the publication of Salman Rushdie's novel, *The Satanic Verses*, so I shall not therefore repeat this largely factual information here. The remaining essays, however, all make significant contributions to the philosophical discussion to which the Rushdie affair has given rise.

The contrasting essays by Peter Jones and Tariq Modood make for a particularly instructive debate. Though both are far from insensitive to the arguments and concerns of their opponents, they take largely opposed views of what ought to be the implications of the Rushdie affair. Jones provides a lucid, rigorous and powerful restatement of the value of free expression. After rejecting straightforward appeals to offended sensibilities as a basis for the restriction of the free expression of opinions he considers arguments from what he calls 'the principle of respect for beliefs'. What this principle amounts to is, roughly, the claim that some of people's beliefs should be protected from particular kinds of attack because 'the mutual respect which is required of citizens who form a plural society should be taken to include their not acting in ways which affront one another's beliefs'. The basis of this principle is not as such the mental distress caused by attacks upon cherished beliefs, but the idea of a right to a certain minimum of respect to which everyone is entitled. (Ultimately what is at stake is the meaning of respect for persons and whether the principle of respect for beliefs is an implication of it.) Jones then proceeds to argue that, in any strong form, entailing that some specific beliefs should be protected from criticism or disputation, this principle is unacceptable, given the importance of free enquiry and the nature of a plural society. This strong form of the principle does not seem to be seriously entertained by any of the major parties to the Rushdie affair – Muslims have not sought to claim that their faith, or any part of it, should be entirely immune from criticism or denial. However, Jones's discussion of it is useful both because it brings out the centrality of the value of free enquiry to religious believers as well as non-believers (a point David Edwards also emphasises in his essay) and because, as Tariq Modood reminds us, some states which would normally be thought liberal do appear to have adopted policies based on the principle. For example, it is a criminal offence to deny the truth of certain historical claims about the Holocaust in both France and Germany.

Jones also identifies a less stringent interpretation of the principle according to which what is to be protected is not the truth of any doctrine but the 'decencies of controversy'. On this interpretation any criticism and challenge is permissible but it must acknowledge 'the bounds of "decent" or "civilised" or "respectful" discussion'. This interpretation of the principle seems to be part of Modood's view. Jones, however, is sceptical about any attempt to enshrine such a require-ment in the law, though he is not entirely dismissive of it as a desirable condition of argument and disputation: it is more a matter of good practice than a compulsory requirement. However, he also maintains that the matter/manner distinction on which this interpretation of the principle seems to rest is often very difficult, and sometimes impossible, to make. One must agree that *The Satanic Verses* itself provides a very good example of these difficulties; difficulties of which Modood is not unaware but about which he is perhaps rather too sanguine. As Jones contends in his conclusion it is important not to expect too much from the law and to accept that sometimes 'legally, people should be entitled to do what, morally, they may be unjustified in doing'. This is a distinction perhaps surprisingly frequently ignored both by Rushdie's defenders and his critics. It is quite consistent to defend Rushdie's right to write and have published *The Satanic Verses*, while deploring its publication and criticising, or even despising, Rushdie for writing it. This is in fact typically the space afforded by the concept of toleration.

In my view any reader of Jones's essay would have to acknowledge that the case for free expression which he presents is a very powerful one. Yet some people, and certainly some Muslims, will feel that, at least in relation to the Rushdie affair, it is also a slightly unreal one. The idea that this controversy is principally about the free exchange of opinions in an enquiry after truth in the manner so lucidly described by J.S. Mill will appear to them an almost fanciful misdescription of what is at stake. Rather, from their perspective, as Modood vividly shows, what is happening is that an already oppressed and disparaged minority is suffering further public vilification and their oppressors are in effect, if not intention, being encouraged and supported. Jones gives some attention to this in his brief discussion of public order, where he, with obvious reluctance, concedes that the good of public order may sometimes override people's rights to free expression. In a sense this reluctance is appropriate – it is surely desirable in a liberal plural society that free expression should not occasion threats to public order - yet, as both Jones and J. S. Mill before him admit, there are undoubtedly kinds of expression which are 'unreasonably provocative'. Moreover, as Modood argues and Jones would agree, there are other values which even a liberal society must be concerned to preserve and protect which may, at least contingently, conflict with the maximal promotion of free expression. One such value may be the securing of self-respect for all the members of a society.

Tariq Modood's essay gives much more prominence to the circumstantial features of the Rushdie affair, though he too is concerned with its wider significance. For example, Modood draws attention to the injustice felt by many Muslims because they are excluded from protection by either the Race Relations Act or the laws of blasphemy as they currently obtain in Britain. Moreover, given the existence of this legislation, whatever its merits are judged to be, it is hard to deny that Muslim feelings of injustice are justified. These feelings have no doubt been further reinforced by some of the ignorant prejudice and suppressed racism that has been unleashed by the Rushdie affair. Much of Modood's essay is motivated by concern about the kind of hatred to which events such as the Rushdie affair gives rise and the consequent damage to race relations in modern Britain. It is partly for this reason that he believes that the iniquities of the present legislative position are best remedied not by the abolition of those laws which currently protect some groups from certain kinds of offensive utterance, but by extending legislation to provide a more comprehensive structure of legal protection. Modood's preferred way of achieving this is not, for example, through an extension of the existing law of blasphemy as Edwards advocates, but through legislation prohibiting group defamation.

The moral basis for such legislation, according to Modood, can itself be found in liberal principles. Liberalism is not libertarianism and it is wholly proper for liberals to be concerned with the requirements of public accountability and equality which should underpin legislation prohibiting group defamation. Modood himself points to several contexts, and one might especially mention that of feminist objections to pornography, in which some, though by no means all, liberals have been willing to accept restriction or prohibition of free expression on what are claimed to be liberal grounds. Furthermore, Modood clearly values free enquiry and recognises that 'one has to be very careful of course in distinguishing defamation from legitimate criticism for while freedom of expression is too gross a right and has to be seriously qualified by the protection of minorities and other civilised values, freedom of inquiry is too precious to lose'. However, there need be no serious conflict here so long as defamation is limited to 'threatening, abusive or insulting' language or images and does not preclude argument and disputation in a genuine context of inquiry. As he concludes, 'the ideal so far as free speech is concerned, ought to be to create the conditions for dialectical inquiry and to prevent those conditions which lead to the breakdown of rational discourse into eristical conflict', a conclusion echoed by Susan Mendus when she writes that 'where free speech is employed in such a way as to destroy the possibility of communication, and of mutual understanding, then its *raison d'être* is destroyed'.

Modood palpably succeeds in showing the unfairness of the present legislative position in Britain, but on this point most liberals (including Jones) would agree. Some may also accept as a temporary expedient that restrictions on free speech along the lines he recommends may be unavoidable; but many, including Jones, see such restrictions as a compromise of liberal values rather than a legislative embodiment of them. On this issue it seems that debate will centre around Jones's principle of 'respect for beliefs' – what it means and whether it has a significant place within liberalism. At a practical level many will share Jones's anxieties about the political process by which such legislation is to be decided and the judicial process of interpretation involved in its implementation. At this point they are likely to try to turn the tables on Modood by arguing that it is he, not they, who is being 'utopian' and unrealistic in his expectations of a law of group defamation. Indeed given recent experience of not dissimilar restrictive legislation, whether it be the law of blasphemy, the Obscene Publications Act or the existing libel laws, one cannot be too confident about the probable consequences of legislation in this area.[12] In the end I suspect no liberal can view with enthusiasm the prospect of imprisoning people for what they say or write – which is not to deny that it may sometimes be necessary – no matter how gratuitously insulting or offensive. In this respect not merely the conclusion of Modood's argument, but also its tone will strike many liberals as being too illiberal to accept with equanimity. Some rough and tumble, they will contend, cannot be separated from open debate and free expression in a liberal society.

David Edwards's essay focuses more narrowly on the specific issue of the blasphemy law in relation to the Rushdie affair. Much of his essay consists of a careful teasing out of the principal transformations that the English blasphemy law has undergone since the Middle Ages. This historical perspective is particularly useful in understanding how not only the extent, but also the basis, of the blasphemy law has changed. Whereas once it was central to the entire legal code, both because crime and sin were typically identical and because religious belief was regarded as the foundation of civil obligation, the blasphemy law is now an extremely restricted piece of legislation which provides very limited protection for Christians from the offence caused by extravagant desecrations of their faith. Indeed, it was only with the successful prosecution of *Gay News* in 1977 that it became clear that the blasphemy law remained an effective and functioning part of English law and was not, as many had supposed, a dead letter.[13] However, the additional discovery, if such it was, that the blasphemy law only applied to the Christian religion has generated further controversy about the coherence and justification of the law.

There appears to be widespread agreement that the present situation is unsatisfactory and inequitable. There seems no very compelling reason why, if the law is to protect religious believers against a certain kind of offence, this protection should be limited to Christians. However, there is no agreement about how this situation should be remedied. While some favour complete abolition of the law of blasphemy, seeing it as an inappropriate relic from a bygone age; others, including the Archbishop of Canterbury and very many Christians, have favoured its extension to include other faiths. It is this latter option that Edwards favours, though he is alert to the difficulties that this would involve. He is clear, for example, that such protection should not be extended to all religions, even allowing that we have arrived at a roughly adequate definition of what is to count as a religion. Rather, he contends that in order to merit circumstantial legal protection 'religious beliefs must advance a claim to be worthy of respect'. And 'the sort of respect which is involved in extending the sanction of the criminal law to the protection of a religion must surely imply a recognition of merit, esteem and value from those who do not share belief in the particular religion'. Moreover, the protection which the law should afford is not against contestation and counter-argument, however vigorous, but only against 'forms of expression which are not the advancing of an opinion, because no argument is presented, and no point of purchase is offered for counter-argument'. Edwards draws the lines around what the law should protect believers against more narrowly than Modood. What the law of blasphemy should protect, as it now in practice does (but only for Christians), is 'images of piety against obscene vilification'.

Edwards's argument shows a particular sensitivity to the distinctiveness of religious belief and sensibility, and he takes issue with the sharp distinction Peter Jones draws between offence and respect for beliefs as grounds for restriction. Yet there are at least two features of his argument which may give rise to scepticism about it. First, and perhaps most controversially, Edwards's argument appears to require us to make substantive judgements about the merits or 'respect-worthiness' of different religions. Not only is such a process theoretically obscure and practically daunting – how are such judgements to be made and exactly who is to make them? – it is far from obvious that it would result in the extension of the blasphemy law to non-Christian religions. For example, the majority of people in Britain know very little about Islam, and their image of it is in large part formed on the basis of tabloid headlines and TV pictures of Tehran; and many of the responses to the Rushdie affair indicate that this ignorance of Islam is extensive even among the more educated sections of the British population. In short the condition of 'respect-worthiness' is likely to prove highly contestable and may be very difficult to meet; and it may even result in exacerbating ill-feeling and resentment among those failing to meet the condition and hence lacking legal protection. Secondly, the sensitivity Edwards shows towards religious beliefs is less apparent in his treatment of the arts. He seems to assume that restrictions on artistic expression involve no real loss, since we can only learn from films, novels and poems if they are 'reduced to a merely didactic function'. This is not a view that would be shared by Rushdie or most creative writers. Glen Newey in his essay provides a useful corrective to Edwards's view and discusses an interesting example of a sculpture, the aim of which was certainly to make a statement about the cheapening of human life, but the point of which was inseparable from the shock and offence the sculpture was intended to provoke. Of course, this is not to claim, as have some of Rushdie's more enthusiastic supporters among the *literati*, that there can be no good grounds for restricting artistic freedom, that it cannot be outweighed in particular circumstances by other conflicting goods. However, Edwards appears not to weigh such a loss at all – in this he seems to me, perhaps paradoxically given their differing conclusions, to share with Peter Jones and many liberals a tendency to attach too much importance to a rather specific and narrow conception of argument and to neglect the value of other forms of expression. Do we perhaps here encounter the natural prejudice of the *philosophe*?

The issue of artistic censorship is more directly addressed in Glen Newey's essay. He claims that there is no necessary relationship between censorship and intolerance, and that the common presumption that toleration always favours a permissive attitude towards artistic censorship is mistaken. His essay provides some support for the arguments of both Chaplin and Modood. Newey argues that since toleration presupposes an attitude of disapproval – on this point he departs from Gardner's analysis of the concept – and since all such attitudes are historically and culturally contingent, there can be no entirely general principle of toleration. To tolerate is necessarily to adopt a contingent and contestable attitude to what is tolerated. The conceptual structure of toleration is tripartite: it includes: (1) a principle justifying disapproval of some act; (2) a principle inhibiting coercive restraint of that action (toleration); and (3) and explanation of when coercive restraint (intolerance) is justified. The relevance of this to the Rushdie affair is that liberals have too easily assumed that banning *The Satanic Verses* would be intolerant and have therefore unduly neglected counter-claims that permitting publication itself manifests a deep intolerance towards the Muslim minority in Britain. Newey shows that there are important gaps in the argument behind a liberal policy of minimal censorship which the identification of toleration with such a policy disguises. Moreover, he further claims that some standard arguments, for example the neutralist strategy of John Rawls's *A Theory of Justice*, cannot fill these gaps in a way that will necessarily result in the preferred liberal answer. By a different route, therefore, Newey's essay takes us back yet again to the issue of equal respect which lies at the centre of the Rushdie affair and several of the essays in this volume.

As Newey makes clear, his is neither an argument for nor against the publication of Rushdie's novel. Instead he is concerned to undermine the plausibility of some kinds of liberal defence of publication in terms of toleration, though he does not deny that a case could be made out in these terms. What he does deny is that we can assume that no case needs to be made because we can simply rely on some presumption of toleration which will necessarily favour publication. Many liberals, however, will object that Newey's argument is too narrowly drawn because it places too much importance specifically on toleration and its distinctive conceptual structure, and is insufficiently attentive to some of their justificatory arguments. But where the general direction of his argument dovetails with that of Modood is in moving the discussion away from appeal to simple general principles such as 'freedom of speech' or 'toleration' and towards an unavoidable engagement with *all* the values that are in play in the debate over *The Satanic Verses*. At the very least the Muslim case for prohibition has to be heard and assessed: it cannot be dismissed out of hand because it allegedly conflicts with some cherished liberal value. There is a dispute and there are (at least) two sides to it.

The polarisation of conflicting perspectives in the Rushdie affair is the principal focus of Susan Mendus's essay. Like Newey, but in more general terms, she denies that it should be understood as a 'battle between the forces of light and darkness; between the rationality and tolerance of liberalism, and the bigotry of fundamentalism; between the horses of instruction and the tigers of wrath'. Her aim is to seek some reconciliation between the factions, and through evaluating their claims at least narrowing the gap between them. She explores three apparent antinomies which lie at the heart of the debate: 'rationality versus sanctity, choice versus tradition, and the sovereignty of the individual versus the identity of the group'. Her strategy is to show that these apparent antinomies are less antagonistic than they are commonly presented as being; that it is less a matter of choosing one or the other of the terms than in recognising that each has to be accommodated within a society which is liberal, tolerant and multicultural.

One feature of Mendus's argument which is of especial interest in the context of some of the earlier discussions in this volume is that she attaches relatively little importance to the defence of free expression in terms of the pursuit of truth. She takes issue with the claim that in the areas of moral, political and religious debate truth is the most important justification of toleration and free expression (or indeed that it is necessarily best achieved through an unregulated market of ideas). She proposes 'an alternative account of the value of toleration – one which does not appeal to truth, to progress, or to individualist conceptions of rationality and choice, but which emphasises the individual's need to locate himself within a group. On this account the wrong which is done by tolerance is not the denial of rational decision making, or choice, but the wrong of exclusion'. In this way Mendus seeks to reconcile the central claim of liberalism – that people must be allowed to live their own lives in ways that they choose or believe to be valuable – with a recognition that such lives and choices need a context which supports and sustains people's sense of self-worth. Ultimately for Mendus free speech 'is important in so far as it increases the possibility of mutual understanding' and it is this which both justifies and sets limits to toleration in a liberal society.

At least two questions are likely to be suggested by Mendus's stimulating essay. First, is she right in her contention that liberalism should support free speech on the grounds of its promoting the possibility of mutual understanding rather than truth? Some liberals will undoubtedly contest this understanding of liberalism, but at the very least, she usefully draws our attention to the fact that there is no necessary connection between 'liberal values' and the kind of Millean account of intellectual progress which often happens to go with them. Moreover, in the context of an ethnically and religiously diverse society such as modern Britain her account of the basis of toleration provides a more accurate representation of why toleration in fact matters to people. The second question, however, is perhaps a more worrying one. This asks whether there do not remain important conflicts, for example of the sort identified by Deborah Fitzmaurice earlier about education, which Mendus's account of toleration provides us with little help in resolving? Indeed if one sees *The Satanic Verses* both as a work in which Rushdie profoundly explores questions of his own identity in relation to his Muslim and Western heritage, and also as a book giving deep offence to most Muslims, how far can 'mutual understanding' help to resolve the conflict? Additionally, in so far as Muslim anger at Rushdie was significantly influenced by the fact that he was a Muslim, a member of their group, and was hence a *murtadd* guilty of *riddah*, a kind of apostasy, is there not a real danger for the liberal in allowing that anger to have very much weight? In more general terms, notwithstanding her awareness of the issue, liberals are likely to see Mendus's emphasis on the importance of group identity as potentially subversive of liberalism's concern with autonomy and individuality.

That problems remain, however, should not come as a surprise. What all the essays in this volume bring out is the complexity of the relationship between liberalism, multiculturalism and toleration, both in general and in the context of the debate initiated by the Rushdie affair. It should by now be clear that there are no simple or straightforward answers. Yet the essays also show how, through careful attention to what is at stake and an honest acknowledgement of the merits of conflicting arguments and perceptions, it is possible for discussion to advance. Issues can be clarified and ignorance and misunderstanding dispelled. Even when it seems agreement cannot be reached, a better understanding of the nature and the basis of disagreement is still a worthwhile aspiration and a valuable achievement.[14]

NOTES

1. See Robert Nozick, *Anarchy, State and Utopia* (Oxford: Blackwell, 1974); Ronald Dworkin, *A Matter of Principle* (Cambridge, Mass.: Harvard University Press, 1985); Bruce Ackerman, *Social Justice in the Liberal State* (New Haven: Yale

University Press, 1980), Part Three; and Joseph Raz, *The Morality of Freedom*, (Oxford: Clarendon Press, 1986).

2. His *magnum opus* is John Rawls, *A Theory of Justice* (Oxford: Oxford University Press, 1971).

3. It is perhaps significant that while the philosophical literature on pluralism is extensive very little exists devoted explicitly to multiculturalism. It seems that multiculturalism has mostly achieved popularity with educationists. For a useful and wide-ranging discussion see S. Modgil, G.K. Verma, K. Mallick and C. Modgil (eds) *Multi-Cultural Education: The Interminable Debate* (London: Falmer Press, 1986).

4. These and other relevant issues are very interestingly discussed in Bhikhu Parekh, 'Britain and the Social Logic of Pluralism' in *Britain: A Plural Society* (London: Commission for Racial Equality, 1990).

5. For a helpful discussion of the relationship between liberalism and toleration see Susan Mendus, *Toleration and the Limits of Liberalism* (London: Macmillan, 1989).

6. Steven Lukes, *Moral Conflict and Politics* (Oxford: Clarendon Press, 1991), p. 17.

7. This discussion of toleration draws on my 'Toleration' in David Miller (ed.), *The Blackwell Encyclopaedia of Political Thought* (Oxford: Blackwell, 1987).

8. See Nozick, op. cit. and Will Kymlicka, *Liberalism, Community and Culture* (Oxford: Oxford University Press, 1989).

9. See Raz, op cit.

10. See John Rawls, 'Justice as Fairness: Political not Metaphysical', *Philosophy and Public Affairs* 14, 1985, and 'The Priority of Right and Ideas of the Good, *Philosophy and Public Affairs* 17, 1988.

11. Fuller references to the literature on the Rushdie affair can be found in note 4 to my essay and note 1 to that by Peter Jones in this volume.

12. See for example Eric Barendt, *Freedom of Speech* (Oxford: Clarendon Press, 1987).

13. Some of the issues arising from the *Gay News* case are discussed in Peter Jones, 'Blasphemy, Offensiveness and the Law', *British Journal of Political Science* 10, 1980.

14. I am very grateful to Susan Mendus for her helpful comments on a draft on this chapter.

2 Multiculturalism and the British Nation-State

Jagdish S. Gundara

One of the challenges posed to the social system in the British Isles by the anti-racist/multicultural movement has been to deconstruct the nature and relationship of cultures. There has been one fundamental problem for those who used terms like multicultural, multiracial and multiethnic, which is that they failed to resonate with the concept of the English nation/nationality, or the British nation/nationality, with which they are sometimes in conflict. The failure to engage with this basic construction of the British nation-state may have been responsible for setbacks to anti-racist/multicultural initiatives.

Dominant group hegemony is not a contemporary construction activated at the end of World War II when some immigrants came to settle. It has, in fact, a pedigree which has connections with the development of the British nation, which camouflages its modern unitary national identity from its earlier predatory origins. This hegemonic unity codifies the dominant group's legitimation of unequal socio-economic relationships.

In addition to disguising the pluralism in British society based on language, religion, social class and territorially-based nationalities, the nation-state has had to confront other divisive threats which emerged from capitalist industrialisation. In the first section of the paper it is intended to explore this issue.

Pluralism and State Survival

The assumption of this section is that the state as it emerged in Britain at the end of the nineteenth century was controlled by the bourgeois class, which recognised the importance of the state in preserving its interests as structured in society. It was felt that if capitalism was to survive it had to be maintained through the state, which included the taking of action to mitigate some of the harsher features of the new industrial system. The fear of disruption by the trade unions led to the rise of 'positive' liberalism and state intervention in the economy and the decline of *laissez-faire* or 'negative' liberalism.

The late nineteenth century in Britain and Europe was also marked by growth in the rise of nationalism, and subordinated groups were moulded and welded

18

into a seemingly coherent whole. These attempts at national unity led, for instance, in Germany to attacks by Bismarck on the Roman Catholic Church during the so-called *Kulturkampf*. Economic measures as well as educational policies to serve the interests of the state were activated in Britain and elsewhere. In England the emphasis on technical subjects and the natural sciences more than the humanities was supposed to strengthen the state. Actions by trade unions and others which were felt to disrupt the state were suppressed.

A series of élitist thinkers like Mosca, Michels and Pareto supported the oligarchic or élitist state, while a group of pluralists like Figgis, Laski, Cole and Russell argued for a participatory democratic framework. Pluralist thinkers in the United States have tended to believe that pluralist societies were in fact the best societies. Edward Shils in *The Torment of Secrecy* [1] for example claims this for the United States. However, a number of thinkers have argued that this form of institutional pluralism was in fact used as an intellectual justification of the status quo. C. Wright Mills in *The Power Elite* [2] makes the claim that a coherent élite group determined all the important decisions of government according to their narrow interests. H. Marcuse [3] has joined others in claiming that the United States is not a genuine pluralist society.

However, what neither European nor American thinkers have done is to look at Europe and the United States as plural societies in the way Furnival [4] has described such societies, after the European colonial enterprises intervened in Afro-Asian societies. L. Kuper and M.G. Smith [5] have used the concepts of social pluralism to describe the post-colonial nations of Africa and the Caribbean. By contrast many writers have tended to assume that countries like Britain are non-segmented societies. Like Figgis, they thought that Catholics, Protestants and atheists were also members of other social organisations such as trade unions. Hence denominational groups would have other societal affiliations which made societies like Britain cohesive and stable where the process of national integration was an accomplished fact. Therefore, if questions of minorities or national unity were raised, they were to apply only to those ex-colonial countries which needed overarching policies of 'national integration' and 'nation building'. In fact, there is an argument that such policies may be of questionable value in the ex-colonial Third World countries, and that some of the assumptions on which western states have been built may be false.

They may have excluded fundamental questions of diversity in their own 'nation building' in the nineteenth century: class interests, linguistic communities, religious affiliations, as well as territorially-based national minorities, are all important. The notion that these nation-states are homogeneous and cohesive may in fact rest on falsely constructed imaginations of national identities.

If, for the sake of argument, third-world countries ought to question their own processes of national unification to ensure that they do not construct national entities and identities based on the dominance of particular groups, then the same types of issue ought to be directed to European and other nation states, to ensure that such fundamental questions are raised in European contexts. On such a reformulation may rest the normally accepted issue of civil order and legally-binding codes accepted by society at large. If, as David Nicholls claims in the case of Trinidad, the belief 'that government must play an active and dynamic role in imposing or inculcating a single culture or set of values will lead either to totalitarianism or to civil war', [6] then the same question is as relevant for Britain or other European countries.

For Europe the problem can also be posed from another direction. If the British and other Europeans as members of their individual nation-states see their traditions, religious beliefs and social arrangements change or crumble, it is important to isolate where such changes may be coming from. The citizenry and governments of Europe may feel that the movement of other people of non-European origin may be the cause of crises in their societies, when, in fact, the real reasons may lie within the body politic. These may include the corporate onslaught on society with the continuous innovations which the state is not able to understand, ascertain, or challenge because of the need to preserve the stability of vested interests.

If, for instance, a range of groups who may be considered as minorities in Britain felt that, despite the democratic framework, they were disenfranchised, one effect would be to question the stability of the British state. In this case the sentiments of disenfranchisement may first and foremost be felt by the women who constitute at least half the population and are in no sense a minority. A large proportion of them, as well as the working-class interests of large numbers of people, may form a coalition of forces, particularly if they feel that their voice and their interests are being ignored. There are national minorities like the Scots and the Welsh who demonstrate another aspect of diversity which cannot be ignored by the British State. The linguistic and religious minorities who feel that their interests are ignored or feel alienated along with other groups, can establish alliances with other disenfranchised groups. The growth and development of such alliances and common interests can create powerful interests which can lead to the destabilisation of the established order of the state.

This larger alliance or grouping encapsulates the one category of a diverse group categorised by the state on the basis of 'race'. One of the consequences of the existence of racism is that large numbers of groups which include Celts, Jews, Blacks, Gypsies or Travellers, have been discriminated against and have been excluded from the European historical past and contemporary life. For this and other reasons, the establishment retains the masquerade of using this group as the only diverse group in British and European societies. In fact, the reality of diversity in these societies is of a very different order in qualitative terms given the other indices of diversity mentioned above. However, the establishment tends to use 'race' as a category, and to some effect, because of the way in which it has permeated the consciousness of all peoples (i.e. at all social levels). The use of 'races' as scapegoats for all social ills at times of crisis is a well-worn cliché.

It may well be argued that, for instance in the United States, constitutional rights are something for which all groups have had to struggle. However, the basic rights which the constitution seems to observe are the property rights of citizenry. The positive rights of liberty in terms of economic and social justice and the prevailing ethos of plurality of the state may only help in upholding the status quo within which the rights of the whites are predominant. [7]

As in the United States, so in the case of Britain, citizenship equality exists only as an individual right; particularly as entitlement to social and economic welfare is being eroded, and increasing disenfranchisement as opposed to enfranchisement becomes the order of the day. Other authors list other categories of heresies of the diffuse consensus of liberal-capitalist societies. As distinct from disenfranchisement, a number of modes of withdrawal have been identified by Moynihan: (a) the alienated in urban society suffering from an identity crisis and cross-pressures of this society's victims of technological innovation, mobility, rootlessness, family break-ups, inability to comprehend the system; (b) those who 'opt out' and live in communes and lead alternative life styles; (c) the New Left. The basic assumption is that because of stable political institutions backed up by effective law enforcement, the refusal, withdrawal or challenge to the established order is marginal and also ostensibly from a minority. There is, however, another basis on which the social diversity of societies can be analysed, the most basic being gender and class differences, which cannot be considered to be a minority issue, and through which large numbers of people and groups may feel that entitlements are denied to them by the state. In most societies social diversity is based on a range of indices, including religious, linguistic, regional or racial. The state may discriminate on single or multiple grounds and the intensity of discrimination may also differ. For instance, in Holland opposition groups, including young people and workers, have grown in numbers because of the lack of representation they feel within the system. [8] Harrison touches on a similar issue briefly, after referring to the situation of racial discrimination against blacks in the United States which has led to violence. He states:

> In Western Europe too, particularly in the UK and Western Germany, non-citizens of alien stock are relatively easy targets of community violence, first victims of unemployment and inadequate housing, most likely to be forced outside the law, which they have not had an opportunity to affect or consent to. [9]

While there is substantive truth to this statement in both countries, there is the additional problem in the British context where those who are citizens, yet happen to be black, also experience the same exclusion. Hence the implications for the political system of such issues are of major importance, because the issues do not revolve around 'aliens' and non-citizens, as for example the Turkish community in Germany. It is also critical in national contexts like Britain where blacks are legally resident or citizens of the state.

The pervasive discrimination against people in the working classes, women, languages other than the dominant language and members of racial and religious communities leads to their having diminished 'assets' or cultural capital to compete on fair or equal terms to attain not only equality of opportunity, but also equality of outcomes. Multiple disadvantages may compound the position of these groups and prevent them from competing within the political and economic frameworks of society. The linguistic cleavages in Belgium which have led to new party divisions is one example of this issue. [10] In constitutional terms the position of the dominant groups remains supreme:

> G.B. Shaw's comment on the constitution – that it was a guarantee to the American people that it never should be governed at all is an exaggeration drawing attention to the fact that at any time such dominant interests in society are in a good strategic position to resist any changes in the status quo which would diminish their dominance. [11]

Conversely, the distance from the centres of power of the groups which face discrimination or lack any 'assets' or cultural capital to participate or compete in the political and economic system remains ingrained. The development of 'corporatism' threatens further the rights of these peripheralised groups.

The increase of 'corporatism' and the strength of public and private bureaucracy has led to cynicism in society generally. In Britain, for instance, popular capitalism has not in any sense allowed the ordinary home-owners or shareholders to control their lives. This 'corporatism' and its rise virtually comes back full circle in undermining the consensus politics of the post-war groupings and the plurality of forces. The rise of the corporate state has immense implications for ordinary people because of the context in which this is happening. In Britain at a time when the claims for multiple voluntary, competitive and non-hierarchically ordered groups is the proclaimed governmental policy, the reality for ordinary people's lives is that participation, representation and accountability are being eroded.

It is not possible to test the validity of such developments rigorously, but hypothesis on the basis of these observations is possible. The concentration of power in the executive branches of governments and the weakening of representative governments is an observable phenomenon. Interestingly, Winkler [12] feels that 'corporatism' is 'an economic system in which the state directs and controls predominantly privately-owned business according to four principles: unity, order, nationalism and success'. A decade and a half after he wrote this the phenomenon seems to be still present, under a government pursuing an opposite tack for the running of the economic system. In a climate of so-called more participatory, less oligarchic and élitist environment precisely the same (i.e. opposite of what might be presumed) is happening. Hence, while the state might say that it has withdrawn from 'corporatism' and is not an actor but only an arbiter, this is only so because the vested interests and the corporate establishment are well in control of the heights of the economy. The executive branch of the government and the private corporate structure are still more powerful than the organs of representative government.

Nationalities and Nation: Core and Periphery

The pluralism of interest groups assumes that social cleavages in British society were subsumed within the various institutions with which the citizenry was associated. Yet, social cleavages remain despite the fact that they were seen as having reconstituted themselves into functional and specialised roles and positions.

Michael Hechter in comparing the black Americans and the Celts in Britain, makes one cardinal error. The Celtic nations are perhaps more akin to the Indian nations of the United States. The situation of black Americans, while large in numbers in the south or some northern states, because of the lack of their nationhood in territorial terms is perhaps more comparable in Britain with the black British community despite their urban rather than rural location. [13] On the other hand, the long historical links of the Celts in Britain and the Indians in North America establish stronger claims because of the national and territorial nature of their rights. The Indians are the original Americans. The recent initiatives of Indians in Canada highlight the issue of the denial of rights of territorially based national ties, not only in North America but in Europe as well. These groups include the people in northern Europe and the Corsicans and Basques in southern Europe.

In outlining the standard analysis of the nation-state in the metropolis, Hechter points out that the Durkheimian view that an increase in transactions between the core and the periphery acts like an osmosis is rejected by Parsons. The core, he argues, attempts in normative terms to impose symbols, cultural modernity and values to increase change in the periphery. Diffusion theorists argue that there is only a mismatch between core and periphery in the absence of mutual contact. The communication media for instance manipulates values and cultural symbols. These may include newspapers, radio, TV and the national school system, as well as other cultural institutions.

The structural diffusion theory argues that using economic integration, particularly through the structural differentiation of labour, leads to cultural integration. The question therefore is how does 'traditionalism' survive in a sea of modernity? The diffusion theorists, including structural diffusionists, may be misconstruing the core-periphery selections by assuming that the periphery accepts domination by the core without resistance. It is not as if there were agreement between core and periphery to accept willy-nilly the culture and institutions of the core.

In this paper, it is being argued that the periphery may not only exist in terms of territorially based national minorities like the Welsh and the Scots, but that within the core there are areas and groups of people who form a periphery. In the inner city areas where working-class communities and particularly racial minorities experience discrimination and domination, resistance is not totally dissimilar from that in territorially based peripheries. Hence regional peripheries face a similar predicament to peripheries within conurbations. It is this resistance of the dominated groups which leads to the examination of issues not purely from a diffusionist perspective, but also in terms of an alternative model of domination. What Hechter calls 'internal colonialism' may deserve further examination.

First, the question of a nation united as one people, either on the basis of one religion, language or race is not a matter of rule, but an exception in the way in which societies have emerged. While the core of many societies might have been dominated by one group, let us say on economic grounds with commerce and banking being in the core, a number of groups become peripheralised. While many metropolitan societies have constitutionally safeguarded democratic frameworks, there are nevertheless fundamental denials of economic, social, linguistic, religious and legal rights. The negation or denial of these rights and their articulation by dominated groups cannot be seen as a demand for 'ethnic pluralism' although that may be part of it. The fundamental issues here are not those of 'ethnicity' but of the denial of citizenship rights and justice in the way in which nation-states are structured. Hence, the persistence of 'ethnic' distinctiveness may itself be a function of the maintenance of an unequal distribution of resources between core and peripheral groups. As Barth states:

> the persistence of ethnic groups in contact implies not only criteria and signals for identification, but also a structuring of interaction which allows the persistence of cultural differences . . . a set of prescriptions governing situations of contact, and allowing for articulation in some sectors or domains of activity, and a set of prescriptions on social situations preventing inter-ethnic interactions in other sectors, and thus insulating parts of the cultures from confrontation or modification. [14]

Stratified polyethnic states may be of many kinds and utilise different mechanisms to perpetuate cultural divisions of labour. While these might be permitted by the advantaged group in society, at subsequent times the disadvantaged groups may themselves attempt to remain independent within a larger system seen by them as oppressive. There would thus be a *de facto* unequal distribution of power and resources between the two groups which would lead to differential access to institutions.

While metropolitan societies may have democratic frameworks, peripheral groups which also happen to be numerical minorities do not have the wherewithal to bring about a reallocation of political-economic power in their favour. Hence, they can remain un- or under-represented in the political economy of the nation. This complex phenomenon is misrepresented in many instances. Walzer, for instance, writes:

But ethnic pluralism as it developed in the United States cannot plausibly be characterised as an anti-state ideology. Its advocates did not challenge the authority of the federal government.[15]

In other words, the politics of the peripheralised groups is misrepresented by stating that theirs is not a politics which follows nationality, 'but rather that politics be separated from nationality – as it was already separated from religion. It was not a demand for national liberation, but for ethnic pluralism' [16]. In fact, the demands are more likely to be a call for democratisation of the nation-state. However, in the likelihood of this not materialising, there is bound to be a momentum for national liberation of the type Walzer assumes these questions are not about. Within Britain, the Welsh and the Scots look at events in Lithuania, Latvia and Estonia with more than a passing interest.

This marginalisation of certain groups is not new; it has a long history in the British context, and has been well illustrated by the work of Hechter. As his analysis suggests, the denial of a capacity to belong to the nation leads to marginalisation of groups which are so positioned; some because they can be 'racially' defined (as with black people in the British context) and others as 'different' (as in the case of the Irish). Developing from this analysis, it can be seen that this has clear implications both for British cities, within which live the great majority of Britain's black population, and for the education that is provided in them. This is because of the spatial consequences that can arise from the increase in intracollective communication and associated greater status solidarity that results from rejection by, and/or hostility from dominant and/or majority groups within British society. In other words, ghetto formation, in both its physical and spiritual manifestations, remains an active element in British urban society.

At one level, it is not surprising that immigrant groups in Britain, as elsewhere, are often placed in this marginal position by the dominant groups within the nation-state. Their socio-spatial marginalisation is reinforced by legislation concerning their status in British society. Thus, linking up with the earlier idea of 'Britishness', successive British governments have tied themselves in knots of ever more complex immigration and nationality laws, the purpose of which is to preserve the nation from being 'swamped' by alien (i.e. black) cultures. That this legislative framework is so is a serious issue, and one which few other nation-states either wish or are able to resolve in a satisfactory manner. Indeed, if the subordinated groups are defined out of the concept of the nation, and can only belong through a process of self-denial and rejection of their own identity, it is difficult to see how such exclusive states can do otherwise. What is perhaps surprising, and is most certainly a cause of equally serious concern, is the marginalisation of certain groups within the British nation-state who are not immigrant. In other words, many black British citizens remain as marginalised as their immigrant ancestors, unlike white British citizens with similar origins.

Thus, the consequent racist stratification in Britain, as in many other nation states, sustains and creates national divisions that result in advantaged and disadvantaged groups having unequal access to power and resources. And it is the reproduction of this through the education system that helps to ensure its inter-generational continuation.[17] An example of this process can be seen in the history and current position of the long-established black community in Liverpool. Still often regarded as in some way not British, primarily because they are black, they are economically and socially marginalised within a city that is itself in a similar position *vis-à-vis* the south-east dominated British nation-state. Furthermore, as a recent Government report indicates, their educational attainment continues to remain at a very low level, despite community efforts to make the education system more responsive to their educational needs.[18] Since the Liverpool blacks as a historically established community remain marginalised, it indicates that the issues that confront the British nation are not simply those of tolerating difference. The case of the Scots and the Welsh as peripheral within the British nation is further highlighted by the long-standing exclusion of Liverpool blacks. As an indication of the subordination of groups within nation-states, the more recent settlers in Britain demonstrate a few other aspects of the problems posed for centralised nation states by pluralism and multiculturalism within Britain and other European societies. To these issues this paper will now turn.

SECULARISM

The importance of involving social scientists in defining issues of pluralism in education is illustrated by the complexity of national populations, whether they include historic minorities or not. However, as modern states, European nations like other nation states also have another aspect. This is the issue of secularism which not only raises questions for the political system but has great significance for education and intergroup relations in both Britain and Europe. While religious tolerance is a facet of modern secular societies, their commitment includes the officially espoused French Republicanism entailing secularism within institutions. In Britain, the espousal is perhaps less clear and what we may observe is the phenomenon of lapsed Anglicanism. However, given religious diversity in European societies, is it not absolutely necessary to have clear definitions about the secular nature of such societies and the rights and obligations of various citizens and groups? Hence, if for example it was clear that issues of religious instruction were part and parcel of the private domain and played no role in secular societies, those who belong to religious groups would ensure that this remained the case. Similarly, issues of religious and spiritual knowledge and comparative study of religions can be part of the public domain and of the education systems. Recent events in various European countries have led not only to antagonism towards Islam but, because it is an issue tied up with history, have been dangerously conflated with issues of racism, sometimes directed at others who were not even Muslims. For instance, the rise of the French right is partially based on seeing the North African Muslims as not belonging to the body politic.

This raises questions at two levels. One is how can European nation states ensure that within their modern secular state contexts, Muslims and others of different faith communities will receive equality of treatment and freedom of speech, to be accompanied by duties and obligations as citizens. Secondly, for educators it does entail a much more serious issue of an accretion of feelings, ways of seeing and understanding by European nations of those who are classified as the 'Other' and whose voices are ignored. The notion of secularism therefore throws into much sharper focus our own understanding of what are the issues teachers and educators need to confront in intellectual terms.

The rise of theocracy in diverse societies in modern terms cannot be ignored. The rise even in secular societies of electronic churches (as in the United States) is a pointer to the type of fundamentalism which may need to be faced because of its implications for the multifaith nature of societies. Since the symbol systems of religions strike a stronger chord than the diffuse systems of secularism in societies, educators and social scientists need to reappraise the nature of secular education and its role in strengthening the legitimacy of all citizens in currently narrowly defined states. The exclusion of groups on linguistic, religious, class, gender or racial grounds poses major challenges for all involved in teaching. Similarly, fundamental beliefs about the economy or the market can have exclusive effects, and can give rise to religious fundamentalism.

Hence, the rise of such strong belief systems in modern secular states may be a reflection of how secular states have failed in providing a safe and secure framework for diverse faith communities. It may also be partly attributable to strong assertions of human rights which are not accompanied by effective measures to ensure their implementation. This is a challenge not only for European countries, but applies to countries of the Arabian peninsular, Asia, Africa, Latin America and the socialist countries – where there is currently the greatest turmoil and potential for change.

The major issue worth considering is what has caused this latent religious fervour to surface at the present time and to attack the very societal structures based on secular principles which have allowed faiths within multifaith societal contexts to exist. It is quite possible that failures of the secular state are partly responsible for the strengthening of belief and faith systems.

'THE OTHER' AND THE NATION-STATE

The most important barrier to better intergroup relations, particularly in the cultural and the educational domain, is the way in which immigrants are seen as the 'Other'.

Some European politicians have taken certain strident positions. Franz Schönhuber, head of Germany's Republican Party, for instance, makes this clear in the way in which the Turks are seen. He says that he is not against the Turks, and that not only is his daughter fluent in Turkish, but he also owns a villa on the Turkish coast. The Turks are hospitable and family-orientated people but they are an 'alien society'. [19] This virtually encapsulates the position of an orientalist and is to a certain extent connected with the issue of those who define issues of the 'Other' in European thinking. Another example of this kind of thinking is represented by a Belgian minister for the interior who, while cognisant of the fact that the very viability of the Belgian nation depends upon the Flemish and Walloon people cooperating on matters of bilingualism, attempts to sidetrack these fundamental questions and to scapegoat the immigrant community in Belgium as the cause of a malaise in Belgian society. This can be illustrated by the Minister for the Interior, Joseph Michel, who said in a speech in October 1987:

> We risk being like the Roman people, being invaded by *barbarians*, who are the Arabs, Moroccan, Yugoslavs and Turks. People who have come from far away and have nothing in common with our *civilisation*. [20]

This statement reflects the 'commonsense racism' of large numbers of European people. In opening up discussions about education or culture in plural societies it is important to explore how notions of 'our civilisation' have been constructed and how the 'Other' has been defined out of European historiography.

Joseph Michel's statement, while reflecting a narrow definition of a nation, does not rest on ignorance of European nationhood. It is a construction which is consciously created, recreated, manipulated, obscured.or mystified to enhance or to ensure the continuity of established nationalisms. Groups can be excluded, pathologised, dominated, marginalised or distanced by being referred to as 'barbarians', 'ethnics' or 'orientals'. It is therefore important, at this level, to explore the notion of 'our civilisation' and the distance or connections with groups considered to be uncivilised 'barbarians'. Modern nation states are complex and as they become even larger entities like the European Community, the governments of some states tend to retrench in order to reinstate their narrow national identities within the larger whole. [21]

The rise of narrow nationalisms is a major barrier against the recognition of the plural societies which exist internationally. One of the issues which requires some discussion is how such a narrow definition of nations and knowledge has emerged in Western Europe. This has implications not only for Europe, but for parts of the world where European nations have imposed their definitions of nation states.

Nation-states have tended to define themselves by generating a sense of the 'Other' as an outsider, who does not belong. They tend to generate this identity through myths and memories which may or may not be true. A range of definitions of the 'Other' have been articulated by Western thinkers and necessitates some discussion.

It is important that debates about society and the nation take place in broad frameworks which are informed by historians and social scientists. Otherwise a rather facile definition and discussion of multicultural or plural societies takes place. The role of historians and social scientists is likewise not to assist in the mystification of narrow nationalisms and fundamentalisms in currently structured nation-states, but to assist in their demystification. Social scientists and educators need to adopt a critical perspective and distance from narrow definitions of nations and not to aid and abet the implementation of narrowly based models in the name of 'fatherland', 'national unity' or 'national integration'.

The first task here is to undertake a very brief description of how the 'Other' has become defined in European thought, in the hope that it will shed some light on how to deconstruct it, using other systems of thought and historical frameworks. European nations may even deny the multifaceted and multifocal origins of the modern nation-states. The overwhelmingly centralised and dominant ethnicities of European nation-states need to be studied to enable the possibility of a clearer focus on the historical bases of knowledge and contemporary nature of these nation-states.

The use of European nationalism, particularly when it had overtones of Romanticism, tended to look on Greek and Hellenic culture as their points of origin. During the eighteenth and nineteenth centuries hostility towards the Egyptian and Phoenician civilisations was intensified, particularly to distance them from the Greeks.

In the 1880s the intellectual atmosphere was transformed by the triumph of racial anti-Semitism in Germany and Austria. Through imperialism, Europe and the Americas were also acquiring increasing control over vast parts of the world, and the indigenous people of America and Australia were exterminated while those of Africa and Asia were humiliated and subordinated. By 1885 the Indians and the Semites were both cast aside. The rise of Aryanism during this period is explained by a Belgian writer, Guy Bunnens, who argues that Europeans:

> maintained that it was unbelievable that nations so important today should have played no role in the past. It was therefore necessary to assert the "rights of Europe over the claims of Asia". The historical background at the end of the 19th century and at the beginning of the 20th century explains these new theories. For this was the epoch when the colonialism of the European powers was triumphant. There was another non-scientific factor. The end of the 19th century saw a great current of antiSemitism in Europe, particularly in Germany and France . . . this hostility against the Jews extended in history against those of the Semites, the Phoenicians.[22]

A critical reading of European thought is needed so as to reappraise the way in which knowledge is currently constructed. This different reading ought to involve a deconstruction of the way in which the diverse origins and developments of human history have been obfuscated. This would have a profound influence on how we construe the diverse origins and development of knowledge – which ought to assist in a reappraisal of what educators consider as legitimate and relevant knowledge. It might also assist in deconstructing 'commonsense' racism in Europe which is able to classify people as 'barbarians' or 'uncivilised'. The construction of these categories within European historiography and the denial of societal diversities within European nations requires further consideration.

The dominating group and élites have ignored the enormous contributions of all groups to the production and creation of knowledge. National boundaries tend to obfuscate not only the diverse origins of knowledge and peoples within the nation but also of those beyond its boundaries. The discussions and debates about a national curriculum in Britain are a case in point, particularly if 'national' were to be construed in narrow terms. As we approach the twenty-first century the thrust of educational debates ought to be towards international and universal perspectives on knowledge and not the reassertion of the outmoded national model which excludes certain peoples and bodies of knowledge.

National constraints not only structure knowledge, in terms of excluding contributions of the 'Other' who may include women, linguistic communities, religious minorities or non-believers but also of those who are considered to be racially different. Discussions and debate tend to demonstrate the better and lesser status of some groups. Hence, those in the 'developed' countries are able to talk of those in the developing countries – thus reinforcing their secondariness. The role of educators is to assist in the deconstruction of the dominant self wherever it may exist and however it is defined. This process would entail that educators are involved in assisting the 'Other' to speak for themselves and to articulate their cultures and histories. The 'knowledge industry', Edward Said maintains, has a responsibility to eliminate the maintenance of subsidiary and inferior geographical or intellectually constructed regions – at both international and national levels. [23]

In the context of discussions about pluralism and multiculturalism, these issues should be analysed at various levels within a range of academic disciplines. Academic social science based frameworks ought to allow a questioning of the state's hegemony which is better able to inform discussions about pluralism and multiculturalism within societies, including Britain.

NOTES

1. E. Shils, *The Torment of Secrecy* (London: Glencoe Press, 1956).
2. C. Wright Mills, *The Power Elite* (New York: Oxford University Press, 1957).
3. H. Marcuse, *One-Dimensional Man – Studies in the Ideology of Advanced Industrial Society* (Boston: Beacon Press, 1964).
4. J.S. Furnival, *Colonial Policy and Practice* (Cambridge: Cambridge University Press, 1948).

5. L. Kuper and M.G. Smith, *Pluralism in Africa* (Berkeley: University of California Press, 1971).

6. David Nicholls, *The Pluralist State* (London: Macmillan, 1975).

7. Derrick Bell, *And We Are Not Saved: The Elusive Quest for Racial Justice* (New York: Basic Books, 1987).

8. D. Nelkin, *Technological Decisions and Democracy* (Beverly Hills: Sage, 1977), p. 26.

9. R. Harrison, *Pluralism and Corporatism. The Political Evolution of Modern Democracy* (London: George Allen & Unwin, 1980).

10. Ibid., p. 144.

11. Ibid., p. 150.

12. J.T. Winkler, 'Corporation', *European Journal of Sociology*, vol. 1, 1976, pp. 100–30.

13. M. Hechter, *Internal Colonialism: The Celtic Fringe in British National Development 1536–1966*, (Berkeley: University of California, 1975) pp. xiii–xvii.

14. F. Barth (ed.), *Ethnic Groups and Boundaries* (Boston: Free Press, 1969), p. 16.

15. M. Waltzer, 'Pluralism in Perspective', in *The Politics of Ethnicity*, with E. Kantowicz, J. Higham, M. Harrington (Cambridge, Mass.: Belknap Press, 1982), p. 10.

16. Ibid., pp. 10–11.

17. This is not to argue for this form of stratification as being the factor in inequalities within society. Class/status and gender are clearly important areas for analysis.

18. Department of Education and Science, *Education for All* (London: HMSO, 1985) chaired by Lord Swann. See also G. Haydon (ed.), *Education for a Pluralist Society: Philosophic Perspectives on the Swann Report* Bedford Way Paper no. 30, (London: University of London Institute of Education, 1987).

19. *New York Times*, 26 November 1989, p. A4.

20. *New York Times*, 22 November 1987, p. 4 (my emphasis).

21. See J.S. Gundara, 'Societal Diversities and the Issue of "the other"' *Oxford Review of Education*, vol. 16, no. I, 1990.

22. Guy Bunnens, quoted in M. Bernal, *Black Athena: the Afro-Asiatic Roots of Classical Civilisation*, vol. 1 (New Brunswick: Rutgers Press, 1987), pp. 376–7.

23. Audio tape of E. Said's session at the American Anthropological Association Conference, Chicago, 1987.

3 How Much Cultural and Religious Pluralism can Liberalism Tolerate?
Jonathan Chaplin

INTRODUCTION

The purpose of this paper is to explore the question of the degree of cultural and religious pluralism which would be tolerated by a consistently applied liberalism. I shall do this by examining the views of three contemporary liberal political philosophers: Robert Nozick, Will Kymlicka and Joseph Raz. By assessing their varying conceptions of pluralism and the limits they each place upon it, some light can be shed on the liberal tradition as a whole.

To suggest that liberalism's capacity for toleration has some limits is not in itself a rebuke, since every political theory implies a limit on what is tolerable. However, since toleration is regarded by liberalism as one of its most fundamental principles, the question of where *it* draws the line is of special interest. Liberal pronouncements lead us to expect that liberalism will generally be more tolerant than any other theory. I shall try to show how certain important manifestations of cultural and religious pluralism would be undermined by the consistent application of a liberal policy. To this extent liberalism will be held to be culturally and religiously intolerant. I have in mind not only direct political intolerance through laws and government policies, but also the indirectly intolerant effects of such laws and policies, effects which make it more difficult to sustain some cultural and religious practices than would otherwise have been the case.

By cultural and religious 'pluralism' (a term I prefer to 'multiculturalism') I mean a condition in which two or more sharply contrasting cultural and religious communities exist within the same political community. Such pluralism creates a problem whenever the political community imposes obligations on its members which conflict with those arising from membership in various cultural and religious communities. It becomes more acute when the political community is, or is perceived to be, dominated by one particular cultural or religious community. It may become perilous if the dominant community *fails to recognise itself* as a community with a distinctive culture. This, I will suggest, is part of the problem with liberalism.

32

LIBERALISM AND PLURALISM

Liberalism understands itself as providing the foundations for a maximally tolerant society. In a liberal society, it is claimed, the greatest possible space is established for a diversity of beliefs and practices of all kinds. Many of these beliefs and practices compete with one another, sometimes fiercely, but the institutional framework of a liberal society ensures that each is permitted its maximum capacity for flourishing free from interference from its opponents. Moreover, a liberal state is one which adopts a position of neutrality with respect to competing conceptions of the good human life, such as those held or embodied by particular cultural and religious communities. It will thus be an equitably pluralistic state in which no cultural or religious community can complain of discrimination.

I shall explore the question of how accurate this liberal self-understanding is by examining the views of the three thinkers mentioned. Nozick has proposed a 'framework for utopia' which seeks to realise the liberal ideal of neutralist pluralism to the highest degree. I try to show that this framework will not establish the neutrality it proclaims. Kymlicka produces a very different conception of pluralism, charging liberals (like Nozick) with a failure to take cultural pluralism seriously, and proposing a theory of cultural membership which grounds a significant range of rights for minority cultural communities. I argue that Kymlicka's liberal premises undermine rather than support his theory of cultural rights. I then discuss Raz's comments on the position of cultural minorities within a dominant liberal culture, which shed light on the problem identified in Kymlicka's thought, and indeed on the nature of liberal toleration as such. I conclude with some brief general reflections on the concept of pluralism and toleration.

NOZICK'S PLURALIST UTOPIA

In *Anarchy, State, and Utopia,* Nozick proposes a libertarian vision of a pluralistic utopia. He takes as given the fact of a potentially limitless diversity of preferred ways of living. No single community or way of living could possibly satisfy all the aspirations of individuals as unlike one another as, for example, Wittgenstein, Elizabeth Taylor and Moses (309–10). What is required is a society in which each can best pursue their own way of life, one containing a 'wide and diverse range of communities which people can enter if they are admitted, leave if they wish to, shape according to their wishes....' In such a society 'utopian experimentation can be tried, different styles of life can be lived, and alternative visions of the good can be individually or jointly pursued' (307). Such a society would be a utopia in the sense of a 'utopia of utopias', or 'meta-utopia':

> Utopia is a framework for utopias, a place where people are at liberty to join together voluntarily to pursue and attempt to realize their own vision of the

good life in the ideal community but where no one can impose his own utopian vision upon others. (312)

Even if there *were* one kind of community which is best for everyone, the unfathomable complexity of human beings means that there is no way of knowing in advance what this might be. In searching for an ideal, all that could be done would be to propose and try out many variations, eliminating or modifying those that proved undesirable. The process of elimination would operate by means of a 'filtering process' (akin to Hayek's concept of 'migration'). This is essentially a process of critically evaluating those communities that had been attempted and proposing new ones in the light of knowledge thereby acquired. The filtering process does not involve any central agency, rather it operates as the outcome of voluntary individual decisions. Like the minimal state which Nozick derives in the first part of his book, the emergence of the utopian framework is understood in terms of an 'invisible hand explanation'. These 'explain what looks to be the product of someone's intentional design, as not being brought about by anyone's intentions' (19). 'No pattern is *imposed* on everyone, and the result will be one pattern if and only if everyone voluntarily chooses to live in accordance with that pattern of community' (316).

If there is one community that is best for everyone, the framework will discover it through the continuing operation of the filtering process (318). In any event, the framework is the best utopian scheme possible. All utopians would approve of it because it is 'compatible with all particular utopian visions, while guaranteeing none' (320). Even 'missionary utopians', those hoping to convince everyone to join their preferred community, will approve of the framework since, even though other undesirable communities will continue to exist, they can be sure theirs has at least an equal chance to compete for adherents. Only 'imperialistic utopians', those who would if necessary force everyone to join their community, would reject it (319–20).

Nozick's utopian framework thus claims to be neutral with respect to the prospects for any utopian vision (cf. 272–3). It is, however, neutral only in the 'negative' rather than the 'positive' sense (cf. Mendus, 1989:131ff; Raz, 1986:124). Negative neutrality implies refraining from acting in such a way that any particular conception of the good (utopian vision) is better off (stands a better chance of surviving or promoting itself) after the action than before, while positive neutrality implies 'establishing conditions of equality amongst individuals, conditions which "neutralize" certain factors that might otherwise enable one individual (or utopian vision) to fare better than another' (Jones, 1989:20). The fact that Nozick's neutrality is negative is consistent with his conception of the minimal state which is prohibited from any action having redistributive effects (e.g. 167–72).

Neutrality implies that no kinds of community are prohibited in advance (except those planning to coerce non-members). Indeed, particular communities may exist which are not themselves internally voluntaristic. They may be governed in ways that libertarians would reject if enforced by a state.

> In a free society people may contract into various restrictions which the government may not legitimately impose upon them. Though the framework is libertarian and laissez-faire, *individual communities within it need not be,* and perhaps no community within it will choose to be so. Thus the characteristics of the framework need not pervade the individual communities. (320–1)

A communist community, for example, may properly refuse to permit anyone to opt out of equal sharing. Nozick does not hold that every community must allow 'internal opting out'. For, as he rightly adds, 'sometimes such internal opting out would itself change the character of the group from that desired' (321). For instance, a Muslim girls' school would not be required to make wearing headscarves optional. Communities may also refuse someone entry if that person is deemed to threaten the character of the community (324, n. 11). The Labour Party, for example, would not be compelled to re-admit David Owen. In short, communities 'may have *any* character compatible with the operation of the framework' (323). None may be prohibited on paternalistic grounds, nor may restrictions be imposed whose purpose is to 'nullify supposed defects in people's decision procedures – for example, compulsory information programs, waiting periods'. No preferred internal structure for communities, for example one guaranteeing respect for certain individual rights such as the right to a fair hearing in disciplinary cases, may be imposed. Furthermore, communities may freely change their character even against the wishes of some members. No compensation obligation may be imposed by the state on communities whose changes damage the interests of some members. Rather, individuals ought to stipulate in advance arrangements for compensation in the contract into which they enter in joining the community (324).

The core of the framework is its voluntarism. Anyone can establish any community they wish, join any community prepared to admit them (they cannot force their way in), seek to modify (by voluntary agreement) any community of which they are currently a member, and leave any community at will. However, the voluntary character of the framework cannot *itself* be changed. Individuals may join non-voluntary particular communities (even sell themselves into slavery), but the framework as such must be 'fixed as voluntary'. As Jones puts it: 'individuals could become involved in forms of life which treated some individuals as of less consequence than others, or in which some individuals surrendered basic freedoms to others, *provided* that all concerned entered into those forms of life from the position of equal standing established by the neutral state' (1989:29).

Nozick does in fact raise the question of whether this does not lead to the exclusion of certain possible choices. 'Are we not saying in advance that people cannot live in a certain way; are we setting a rigid range in which people can move and thus committing the usual fault of the static utopians?' His reply is that, since the rigidity in the framework is purely 'general', the rigidity is acceptable. Who is to fix the framework? In the utopian framework some central authority ('protective association') will be required and this, we now discover, is equivalent to the minimal state. This will enforce the operation of the framework by, for example, adjudicating conflicts between communities or enforcing the right of individuals to leave a community (329–31, 333–4).

Nozick notes but does not resolve two problems regarding the task of the minimal state in his utopian framework. The first is whether the state can be required to compel individuals wishing to leave a particular community to fulfil obligations which have arisen from their membership (e.g. to work within the community which had contracted to educate him for that purpose, to fulfil family obligations, or to be disciplined for some offence). The second is how the state can ensure that children are informed of the alternative ways of life available to them, especially where parents wish to keep them in ignorance (330). As we have seen, compulsory information programmes are ruled out, though it is unclear whether this applies only to adults (cf. 307–8). Clearly Nozick would reject compulsory state education or any state regulations regarding the content of private education. How children are to be thus informed remains unclear (330–1). These problems are linked to a deeper ambiguity to which I return shortly.

In spite of such problems, Nozick claims that the minimal state is 'the one that best realizes the utopian aspirations of untold dreamers and visionaries'. It is, he concludes, 'an inspiring vision', fully respecting our right to the free pursuit of our chosen ends in free cooperation with others: 'How *dare* any state or group of individuals do more. Or less' (334).

Nozick's pluralistic utopia is likely to have strong initial appeal to anyone wishing to maximise toleration towards diverse cultural, religious and other kinds of communities. All are free to exist, to transform themselves, to govern their own affairs even to the extent of adopting internally authoritarian or other illiberal procedures. For instance, Muslim schools, it would appear, could do everything they do now. Indeed, they could do more, for Muslims would contribute nothing to a public education budget (since there wouldn't be one) and could use that portion of their income to finance their own schools, a possibility presently denied to them. Muslims could also establish their own banking system if they so wished (though they could not impose interest-free banking on non-members). Christians could run their own hospitals in which abortion was banned (though they could not ban abortion in other hospitals). So long as no community coerced non-members, or violated the rights of members not to be physically harmed or to leave, anything would be permitted. What could be fairer than that?

Numerous questions are raised by Nozick's prescription. I shall concentrate on just one, though from various angles. It concerns his assumption that particular communities whose internal structure differs from that of the framework as a whole will have the capacity to sustain themselves. How hospitable is Nozick's libertarian utopia to the realisation of non-libertarian communities? He raises this question himself, but answers it unconvincingly. 'How can small communities overcome the whole thrust of the society; aren't isolated experiments doomed to failure?' (326) We can generalise the point: isn't any community whose ethos is non-libertarian doomed to failure? Surrounded by myriad distracting alternatives and operating in a climate thoroughly permeated by a spirit of voluntaristic individualism, how could a Muslim or a communist or a Gandhian community survive?

His answer is that, in principle, they can overcome it by the power of sustained voluntary decision. For example, socialist workers could sustain a cooperative firm even in a society whose minimal state enforced capitalist rules of exchange and competition. If such firms were as efficient as competitors, no special problems would arise, but even if they were not there would be fully voluntary ways of overcoming their uncompetitive position without resort to state aid (250–2). Indeed, for any other community, 'there *is* a means of realizing various micro-situations through the voluntary actions of persons in a free society' (326–7).

The weakness of this argument begins to show on a closer examination of his discussion of workers' cooperatives. He notes the problems of operating such cooperatives efficiently once established (e.g. underinvestment or under-employment) but claims that these can be overcome if workers are committed enough to accepting lower wages in return for the compensating benefits of participation or solidarity. But he passes too quickly over the problem of how they could get started in a system that was already capitalistic. He simply says that 'if they were believed to be efficient, they could get some sort of support in a market economy'. It is not enough to say that, once they were operating successfully, they could repay any outside investment (254). The question is how to convince investors or indeed workers *in advance* that they will succeed. The 'whole thrust' of a libertarian society will have educated people to doubt the success of a socialist organisation of industry. Even heroic voluntary sacrifices by workers would be unlikely to sustain a cooperative in such an inauspicious environment. Thus while Nozick's libertarian utopia would appear not to be directly intolerant towards workers cooperatives – they would be legally free to exist – it would very likely be indirectly intolerant towards them. Parallel problems would face any communities characterised by strong moral, social or religious obligations, especially those in which no easy calculus of costs and benefits of the sort Nozick envisages individuals employing were possible. A libertarian framework would create a libertarian ethos in which the idea of open-ended or unquantifiable commitment to moral or religious values would be difficult to get off the ground or seriously eroded if it already existed. Indeed the very idea of regarding the communities which would populate the utopian framework as *experimental* militates against such commitments. Conducting an experiment on something implies taking distance from it. One cannot be wholly committed to something which is continually being tested. The desirability of at least some beliefs or practices can only be established after one has made a commitment to them (for example, as some would say, marriage or religion).

The question of the hospitality of Nozick's utopia to certain kinds of community is also linked to the ambiguity noted earlier regarding the state's duty to inform members of communities of the existence of other communities. As we have seen, Nozick does think that in some way 'it must be ensured' that *children* are so informed, but rejects imposing compulsory information programmes on communities. But why should the obligation to inform only apply to children? As hinted above, this may be because children have no easy access to the requisite information while adults might be expected to know their way around. It is clearly important to Nozick's utopia that individuals do know of the range of alternatives. The whole idea of a society based on maximal voluntary choice assumes that people's choices are informed. Otherwise the 'filtering process', by which undesirable communities were eliminated, would not work. The process operates by means of comparative evaluation and this cannot happen unless at least some people know what communities are to be compared. If the filtering process ground to a halt, a limited range of options would become entrenched and the whole point of the utopian framework would fail to be achieved. It appears that Nozick's radical voluntarism requires the kind of compulsory information programme he explicitly rejects. Let us suppose that such a programme were introduced. Marshall indicates the possible implications this would have for at least some religious communities:

> The priority of choice [would undercut] the ability of any community to shape its members and succeeding generations so that they will uphold the truth at all costs. One could imagine an Amish community where each member is advised (and informed enough so the advice means something) that they are and should be free to leave at any time: that the community respects this right and will not insist that communal solidarity comes before individual wish. Whatever such a community will become, it is no longer an Amish community in its heart, and it will soon cease to be an Amish community in its practices. (1989:11)

If we imagine applying this to certain Muslim communities in Britain, we can see the potentially intolerant consequences. I am not suggesting that Muslims seek the virtually complete isolation from their society that the Amish do from theirs. They do, however, complain of the corrosive effects on their religious communities of the necessity of sending their children to 'secular' state schools ('compulsory information programmes'?). I suggested earlier that, in Nozick's utopia, Muslims would be better off than they are now in the sense that they could divert what would otherwise be education taxes to fund their own schools. However, if Nozick's minimal state acted on its duty to inform children effectively about their guaranteed freedom to explore alternative lifestyles, utopia would no longer be quite as attractive to them.

The deeper ambiguity lies with the attenuated anthropology of Nozick's libertarian starting-point. Just as, in his derivation of the minimal state, he assumes a 'state of nature' characterised by right-wielding, equal individuals with no obligations to each other beyond respecting the same rights in others, so in his framework for utopia he assumes an initial condition comprising numerous unattached individuals in which no communities yet exist and in which no communal obligations have therefore arisen. The argument proceeds by asking how such hypothetical individuals in this condition might act, what communities they might join. Given this starting point, it is hard to conceive how communities in which members' moral, social or religious obligations were unspecifiable in detail in advance, as is typically the case in cultural and religious communities, could ever arise. But even if something like such communities actually succeeded in evolving out of voluntaristic experimental communities, they might soon be eroded by their members' offspring. Nozick's utopian individuals parachute into the world entirely unencumbered by moral, religious or cultural baggage, lacking any sense of obligation to whatever communities may have formed them (did anyone *ask* them whether they wanted to be so formed?). Such communities would self-destruct simply by trying to reproduce themselves.

KYMLICKA'S CULTURAL PLURALISM

In *Liberalism, Community and Culture*, Kymlicka seeks to overcome the neglect of the overwhelming reality of cultural plurality of which, not only Nozick, but also other liberals such as Rawls and Dworkin, are guilty. Rejecting the alternative 'communitarian' conception of culture associated with Sandel, Taylor, MacIntyre and others, he proposes what he believes is an authentically liberal theory of 'cultural membership' which provides the grounding for a robust conception of the rights of minority cultures and an ambitious policy of cultural pluralism. Kymlicka delves into the resources of the post-Millian liberal tradition (the 'new liberals' and their contemporary heirs) to rebut the charge that liberalism's focus on individual autonomy necessarily leads to the undermining of 'the very communities and associations which alone can nurture human flourishing and freedom' (2). The principal examples he uses are those of the aboriginal communities of North America, but his case clearly has much wider application.

The core of liberal political morality is the idea of equal freedom. Every individual has an equal interest in freedom, and governments treat people equally when they accord everyone such equal freedom. The aspect of freedom crucial to Kymlicka's theory of cultural membership is the freedom to revise our beliefs about what gives value to life. From this freedom can be derived not only civil and personal liberties but also the need for those cultural conditions, such as freedom of expression, which conduce to intelligent examination and re-examination of different views of the good life (13). Kymlicka denies that an abstract individualism (of the kind we criticised in Nozick) which supposes that the freedom to revise beliefs can be exercised apart from a conditioning social context, is a necessary part of modern liberalism (15–16). His theory of the rights attaching to cultural membership rests crucially on this denial.

Cultural membership is of value to individuals precisely because it provides an essential context of choice within which they can pursue and revise their conceptions about the good life. It is 'only through having a rich and secure cultural structure that people can become aware, in a vivid way, of the options available to them, and intelligently examine their values' (165). The beliefs between which free individuals can choose are presented to us by our cultural heritage. Choice can only take place between a given range of culturally-mediated options. We become aware that we have been born into a certain form of life and that others exist which we are free to endorse. 'We decide how to lead our lives by situating ourselves in these cultural narratives, by adopting roles that have struck us as worthwhile ones, as ones worth living' (165). It is worth observing here the similarity between this liberal conception and Nozick's utopia in which we freely evaluate and select from among various ways of life. Although Kymlicka does not envisage us simply innovating new forms of life, both he and Nozick regard the social or cultural context as of value not because it possesses any moral status of its own, but rather because it presents individuals with objects of choice (164–5).

It is doubtful, however, that this is an accurate characterisation of why most people value their cultures. Cultures are not valued primarily because they enable people to choose between different ways of living but rather because they relieve people of the constant need to choose how they should live. Being a member of a culture means that we tacitly endorse a certain way of living. If we have not endorsed it we are not a member of that culture, even though we may happen to be resident in it. Kymlicka's definition of the value of culture as such after all begins to look rather like a definition of the liberal idea of the good life, a point we explore further shortly.

Kymlicka accords to cultural membership the status of a Rawlsian 'primary good' (which Rawls does not). Since it is an essential source of a person's self-respect (which Rawls does acknowledge as a primary good), taking it seriously is imperative if we are to demonstrate equal concern for individuals. Cultural membership 'is a good in its capacity of providing meaningful options for us, and aiding us in our ability to judge for ourselves the value of our life-plans' (166).

Given this stress on the importance of cultural membership, what significance does Kymlicka attach to *particular* historical cultures? Puzzlingly, he appears to offer two quite different answers. I shall look first at the one which is promising for advocates of cultural pluralism. The primary good of cultural membership refers to 'the individual's *own* cultural community' (177) (my emphasis). People are 'bound, in an important way' to the cultural community in which they have been born and raised. It remains a 'constitutive part' of their social identity. They cannot be transplanted into another one without experiencing a disorientating and incapacitating loss of identity. Severance from the history in which one has been formed leaves one adrift and powerless. The tenacity of cultural affiliation usually makes assimilationist policies disastrous failures (175–6). Thus 'respecting people's own cultural membership and facilitating their transition to another culture are not equally legitimate options' (176).

Contemporary liberals like Rawls and Dworkin fail to acknowledge the importance of membership in particular cultures not because of a radical flaw in liberalism but rather because they assume an outdated model of the nation-state in which the political community is assumed to be coterminous with one cultural community (177–8). I will not explore here whether Kymlicka is right to exonerate liberals in this way, but rather go on to examine what he himself does with the theory of cultural membership he believes to be potentially derivable from liberal premises.

What would it mean for a liberal conception of justice if cultural membership were recognised as a primary good? His argument is that the theory justifies a *differential* distribution of liberties and resources as a way of redressing the *unequal* circumstances in which minority cultures find themselves. A 'colour-blind' (better: 'culture-blind') egalitarian distribution of primary goods would not be enough. *Special rights* for minority cultures will be required if their members' cultural membership is to be accorded equal respect with those of the majority culture (182–3). The argument assumes the moral significance of the distinction between the different choices people make and the different circumstances in which people find themselves. Since people are responsible for their choices they cannot expect special privileges to enable them to bear the costs of those choices. But people finding themselves with various natural or social disadvantages should not be expected to pay the costs arising from them. If the liberal commitment to equality is to be realised they should rather be compensated for such unequal circumstances (186). For example, aboriginal rights, such as those restricting the development of certain areas of land, can be seen as imposing extra costs on non-aboriginals in that they restrict the latter's rights. If the forms of life aboriginal rights seek to protect were regarded as the result of choices then granting such rights would violate liberal equality. But if such rights are conceived rather as ways of redressing unequal circumstances, then they in fact *realise* liberal equality.

Unlike the dominant French or English cultures [in Canada], the very existence of aboriginal cultural communities is vulnerable to the decisions of the non-aboriginal majority around them. They could be outbid or outvoted on resources crucial to the survival of their communities, a possibility that members of the majority cultures simply do not face. As a result, they have to

spend their resources on securing the cultural membership which makes sense
of their lives, something which non-aboriginals get for free. (187)

Special rights for minority cultures thus do not privilege the choices of their
holders but correct an unfair disadvantage facing them before they begin to make
any choices (189–90).

Kymlicka's idea of minority rights appeals to what we referred to earlier as the
'positive' meaning of liberal neutrality. It seeks to secure by political action
conditions of genuine equality of opportunity between different cultures, and it
does so by offering compensatory rights to minority cultures. On Nozick's
'negative' definition of neutrality, such an equalising or neutralising of the
conditions within which choices are made is illegitimate, because for him
differential initial circumstances are not a question of justice. For Kymlicka,
however, minority cultural rights 'can be seen as spelling out what it means to
treat [members of minorities] as equals, given their special circumstances' (191).
Affirmative action programmes for members of aboriginal or other minority
cultures will not be enough. These are programmes of positive discrimination
aimed at establishing genuine equality of opportunity in the competition for
scarce positions within the dominant culture. But they only benefit *individual*
members of such minorities, not the minority culture itself (190).

Protecting a cultural minority will require a package of measures. These will
include differentially (unequally) distributing some individual rights, such as
conferring special voting or property rights on members of aboriginal
communities. They will also include some collective rights, rights held by
communities as a whole. For example, the special aboriginal rights held by North
American Indian communities include the collective right to self-government
within a particular territory (a reservation) (138–9). Kymlicka rejects the
common liberal assumption that recognising collective rights is incompatible
with the liberal commitment to individual rights. On this assumption there is no
obligation to treat communities as equals so long as their individual members are
treated equally. 'Individual and collective rights cannot compete for the same
moral space, in liberal theory, since the value of the collective derives from its
contribution to the value of individual lives' (140).

Such an argument lay behind decisive liberal achievements like the *Brown* v.
Board of Education case in 1954, which overturned the 'separate but equal'
justification of racially segregated education in the American South, and provided
a model for a string of subsequent liberal reforms inspired by the idea of a
'colour-blind' constitution (141–2). It was this same idea which inspired
Trudeau's ill-fated attempt in 1969 to abolish the differential voting, property,
mobility and residence rights operative in Indian territories. The reservation
system was to be dismantled, but Indians would, like all Canadians, be free to
associate voluntarily with whomever they chose for whatever purposes they
chose. If they wished to preserve their culture, they could no longer rely on a

special constitutional status but could only resort to the classical liberal individual right to associate (142–4). The proposal was vigorously repudiated by the Indians. Had it been implemented, it would not, like the *Brown* v. *Board of Education* case, have *ended the exclusion* of a minority from a culture in which they wished to participate as equals, but would have *forced the inclusion* (assimilation) of a minority into a culture from which they wished to be separate (144–5). It failed to recognise that 'the viability of Indian communities depends on coercively restricting the mobility, residence, and political rights of both Indians and non-Indians' (146).

Kymlicka suggests that the question of cultural rights is not whether we should accord more respect to individuals or to groups, but rather how we should balance *two kinds of respect for individuals*. Respecting individuals as members of a particular cultural community may involve according them special rights, while respecting individuals as citizens, members of the same political community, requires according them equal rights. We are faced here with 'a genuine conflict of intuitions': 'the demands of citizenship and cultural membership pull in different directions'. Both matter, and 'neither [is] reducible to the other'. The consequence of recognising only equal political rights would be the reluctant assimilation of cultural minorities into a culturally uniform political community (151–2).

We have been following the logic of one of the answers Kymlicka gives to the question of the importance to individuals of *particular* historical cultures. It is people's *own* cultural community which is to be deemed a Rawlsian primary good. Differential rights for minority cultures are a way of compensating them for their unequal circumstances. Threatened cultural minorities throughout the world would appear to have found a powerful defence.

However, when we examine the second answer Kymlicka gives to the question of the value of particular cultures, a rather different conclusion emerges. This answer rests on the fundamental distinction between the *content* of particular cultural communities and the *existence* of cultural communities (168). Historical cultures, we are told, are worth preserving not because of any specific things we find intrinsically valuable in them (such as African hospitality or Japanese loyalty) but because without *some* cultural structures, the individual would be devoid of a subject-matter of choice. Whether or not a particular culture changes its character is not important, so long as it changes as a result of choices (166–7).

Thus the argument for the value of cultural membership cannot be invoked, as it is by conservatives and communitarians, in order to oppose proposals which would change the character of a particular cultures (168–9). 'Protecting people from changes in the character of their cultures can't be viewed as protecting their ability to choose. On the contrary, it would be a limitation on their ability to choose' (167). Against Devlin's case for retaining restrictive English homosexuality laws, Kymlicka claims that '[p]rotecting the homophobic character of England's cultural structure from the effects of allowing free choice of sexual life-style undermines the very reason we had to protect England's cultural structure – that it allows meaningful individual choice'.

Thus 'the very reasons we have to value cultural contexts argue against Devlin's claim that we should protect the character of a given cultural community' (169). The argument for recognising the importance of cultural membership is thus an authentically liberal idea since it derives from the priority of individual liberty.

Further implications of this argument become clearer when Kymlicka applies it specifically to minority cultures. He is constructing an argument for a defence of the cultural rights of individuals, but he now interprets this as meaning the preservation of the rights of individuals within cultural communities to choose whether or not they wish to protect or change the culture. Just as English people rightly asserted the right to sexual liberty, so members of minority cultures will need to assert similar kinds of rights within their own. It is apparently the task of liberals everywhere to do the same:

> Finding a way to liberalize a cultural community without destroying it is a task that liberals face in every country, once we recognize the importance of a secure cultural context of choice. That task may seem difficult in the case of some minority cultures. But if people respond to that difficulty by denying that we can distinguish the character of a cultural community from its very existence, then they have given up on the possibility of defending liberalism in any country. (170)

Kymlicka does accept that too sudden liberalisations of some minority cultures could destroy them. With the recent history of Canadian Indian communities in mind, he notes that the unregulated introduction of alcohol in certain formerly dry communities can have disastrous consequences. Refusing to let such communities impose restrictions of this kind would not be a 'victory for liberalism' but a 'deliberate act of genocide'. 'If certain liberties really would undermine the very existence of the community, then we should allow what would otherwise be illiberal measures'. But, he continues, 'these measure would only be justified as temporary measures, easing the shock which can result from too rapid change in the character of a culture ... helping the culture move carefully to a fully liberal society'; which is, of course, 'the ideally just cultural community' (170–1).

What has happened to Kymlicka's earlier insistence on protecting a diversity of particular cultures? His first reply to the question of the significance of such particularity led him to a robust defence of the rights of cultural minorities to govern their own affairs in ways potentially very different to those of the wider culture. Such minority cultures can organise their social, economic and political life differently from the majority culture and the state has a duty to secure their equal opportunity to continue to do so. Special property or voting rights were not there defended merely as 'temporary measures'. His second reply to the question, however, leads him to affirm the goal of the ultimate liberalisation of minority cultures. Regulations, such as on alcohol, are now described as 'illiberal' and 'temporary'. It is difficult to see how restricting property rights is different in principle to restricting the availability of alcohol. From the minority culture's point of view both are designed to protect the particular character of their culture.

Restrictions like that on alcohol are not the only measures regarded as undesirable by Kymlicka. The denial of religious freedom on certain reservations, for example, is ruled out in principle. Such a denial could not be defended on his account of minority rights because 'there is no inequality in cultural membership to which it could be viewed as a response'. Allowing different religions could not be regarded as any kind of threat to the character of a community (196). For, 'supporting the intolerant character of a cultural community undermines the very reason we had to support cultural membership – that it allows for meaningful individual choice' (197).

It is important to note that Kymlicka is now discussing the problem of minorities *within* minority cultures. Minority cultures may be granted different rights to those of the majority culture, but minorities within the minority culture may not be accorded different rights to those of the majority within their culture. Unlike Nozick, for whom communities need not be microcosms of the larger society, Kymlicka wants to bring them into line. His general point is that 'nothing in my account of minority rights justifies the claim that a dominant group within a cultural minority has the right to decide how the rest of the community will use or interpret the community's culture'. The theory 'supports, rather than compromises, the rights of individuals within the minority culture'. It may be that a minority culture claims that acknowledging some of the rights accorded to individuals by the larger culture would be corrosive of the character of their community – it might undermine tribal or clerical leadership structures, for example. The claim cannot be allowed to stand. The rights of individuals 'trump' it. The reason for protecting minority cultures against absorption by the majority culture is the same as that for protecting individuals within a culture against absorption by that culture, namely to protect the individual's right to choose her own way of life (197–8).

Okin, reviewing Kymlicka's book, correctly identifies the problematic consequence of this line of thought. Kymlicka's insistence that minority communities govern themselves by liberal principles 'clearly excludes many of the world's minority cultures from being eligible for collective rights, since they practice internal discrimination or restrict religious freedom, or both. Kymlicka says little about how this problem should be addressed' (Okin, 1991:128). But she fails to press home that this is not an incidental but a *fundamental* flaw in his case.

We can see where Kymlicka has led us. His claim that 'any liberal argument for the legitimacy of measures for the protection of minority cultures has built-in limits' (198), is in effect an argument for a conception of cultural plurality which has a *built-in liberalising tendency*. Cultural communities may preserve their distinctiveness, but only within the limits determined by liberalism. They can be distinctive so long as they are liberal (or on the road to becoming liberal). But the problem Kymlicka fails to address, or even notice, is that *if they become liberal, they may thereby have lost much of their distinctiveness.*

A striking feature of Kymlicka's discussion here is that he fails to recognise the fact that liberalism is *itself* a distinctive cultural community. For him, liberalism is merely a neutral framework for cultural communities parallel to Nozick's neutral framework for utopian communities. Thus attempting to liberalise a minority culture by requiring that it adopt the range of liberal individual rights is not regarded by him as involving the transformation of one kind of cultural community into an entirely different kind. He seems to assume (*contra* Raz) that a community can be liberalised without essentially changing its particular character at all (180, n. 3), but he can do so only be assuming that liberalism has no particular character of its own.

It thus follows that the only kind of culture Kymlicka really thinks is valuable is, after all, precisely a liberal culture. Other cultural communities are valuable to him in so far as they approximate the ideal liberal culture, one which is fundamentally structured around the notion of individual choice. To imply that this ideal liberal culture is not *itself* a particular historical culture is, to say the least, disingenuous. The failure to acknowledge the particularity of liberal culture enables Kymlicka to imply that the culture he envisages is inclusive while other cultures are exclusive (and so need liberalising). One might say that implicit in Kymlicka's view is the tacit assumption of a 'liberalizing mission'. Or, as MacIntyre puts it: 'The overriding good of liberalism is no more and no less than the continued sustenance of the liberal social and political order' (1988:344–5).

RAZ'S PERFECTIONIST PLURALISM

One of the many virtues of Joseph Raz's sophisticated re-statement of liberalism, in *The Morality of Freedom*, is that it appears willing to embrace the substance of MacIntyre's conclusion. Liberalism is indeed a 'perfectionist' theory of politics, a view Kymlicka is unwilling to concede. Raz also accepts that liberal culture is embodied in a distinctive cultural community. He avoids the relativism into which communitarians (who share this view of liberalism) fall, by arguing for the moral superiority of liberal culture over others. Liberal communities thus have the right to defend themselves against non-liberal cultures and indeed, if necessary, to liberalise them.

Part of Raz's case is the empirical claim that the central characteristic of modern Western society is the value it attaches to the possibility for autonomous individual choice. Whether we like it or not, this makes practices which rest on some principle of 'heteronomy' (or, we might add, on some non-liberal conception of autonomy) more difficult to sustain. 'For those who live in an autonomy-supporting environment there is no choice but to be autonomous: there is no other way to prosper in such a society' (1986:391). Those raised in such an environment will necessarily find themselves being educated into valuing autonomy. While such a position may allow considerable scope for diverse lifestyles based on autonomy, it does nothing to encourage and does much to discourage those lifestyles or practices (such as arranged marriages) based on heteronomy. And, conversely, autonomy 'cannot be obtained within societies which support social forms which do not leave enough room for individual choice' (395). Non-liberals could agree with this empirical claim, but alongside it is a powerful normative one following from Raz's acceptance that liberalism is perfectionist. This is that a liberal state has a duty to help create the conditions in which people can lead autonomous lives, to foster an autonomy-enhancing public culture (422–3).

What should be the liberal attitude to cultural communities which do not support autonomy? That depends on their 'viability'. A cultural community is viable if it offers its members a satisfying life. Where communities are viable and do not harm non-members, then their existence should, in general, be tolerated (423). Raz's acceptance of toleration is hardly enthusiastic, however. Affirming the moral superiority of the dominant liberal culture over non-liberal minority cultures within it, not only does he not recommend the kind of positive equal opportunity policies advocated by Kymlicka, he also holds that people in the dominant liberal culture are in principle 'justified in taking action to assimilate the minority group, at the cost of letting its culture die or at least be considerably changed by absorption' (424). He does caution, however, that suddenly wrenching members of minority groups out of their communities may be inhumane because such members are likely to be ill-equipped to lead an autonomous life, which is the life they will *have* to lead in the liberal culture if they are to prosper. For this reason the minority culture may often need to be tolerated. One should not normally take action which would lead to the rapid disintegration of such communities. However, some small cultural communities (regrettably he does not say which), supported by 'misguided liberals and conservatives', may act so as to 'condemn many of the young in [them] to an impoverished, unrewarding life by denying them the education and the opportunities to thrive outside the community'. If so, 'assimilationist policies may well be the only humane course, even if implemented by force of law'. In other cases, however, the appropriate course, where possible, is 'gradual transformation'.

This is simply the logic of Raz's 'perfectionist moral pluralism', a pluralism in which many conceptions of the good are recognised as 'so many valuable expressions of people's nature', but which nevertheless 'allows that certain conceptions of the good are worthless and demeaning, and that political action may and should be taken to eradicate or at least curtail them' (133). Raz's standpoint is instructive precisely because of its open acknowledgement of what I referred to earlier as liberalism's 'liberalising mission'. Raz does indeed endorse moral pluralism. But, as Mendus puts it: 'The pluralism and tolerance which this account of liberalism affords is only between and within life styles which place a high value on autonomy' (1989:107). (A position close to Raz's is also advocated by Debbie Fitzmaurice in her contribution to this volume.)

Raz's conception of cultural pluralism has a strong affinity to the second of the two lines of argument found in Kymlicka's case. That line of argument tacitly assumed the superiority of an essentially liberal definition of the value of culture as a context of choice. Kymlicka's ideal liberal culture would be a culture in which what Raz calls the 'conditions of autonomy' were dominant. Kymlicka's desire to urge this ideal liberal culture on non-liberal minority cultural communities is evidently much more restrained than Raz's, and this is because he also affirms the value to individuals of protecting the *particular* cultural communities within which they live (which may not be liberal). I do not think these two lines of argument can be fully reconciled and hence Kymlicka's case is an uneasy compromise between them. It advances a powerful argument in favour of distinctive minority cultural rights, but this is rendered precarious by its association with the idea of the ultimate goal of liberalising such cultures. Liberals cannot have it both ways.

This discussion has attempted to indicate the kind of limits to cultural and religious pluralism which a consistently applied liberalism would be able to tolerate. To the extent that conclusions drawn from the foregoing analysis can be generalised, it can be ventured that liberal political theory can find coherent grounds for tolerating only those cultural and religious communities which approximate to the characteristics of the liberal cultural community.

CONCLUSION

If liberalism is much less tolerant of pluralism than it purports to be, are there any other political theories which can do better? In the space remaining I can only hint at an appropriate answer to this question. Such an answer would need to begin by challenging the idea that there is any *independent* yardstick of toleration against which different theories could be ranked as more or less tolerant of cultural or religious pluralism. I noted at the beginning that all political theories, whether they admit it or not, imply limits to what can be legally and politically tolerated. Another way to put this in the light of the above is to say that all such theories offer a different package of acceptable pluralistic diversity (Marshall: 1989). We have seen what kind of diversity liberalism is likely to offer. A Christian political theory is likely to offer a somewhat different package, perhaps less tolerant of 'experimental' family structures or of the limited liability company, or both (depending on which strand of Christianity inspires it). A libertarian socialist theory will come up with a different package again, equally suspicious of capitalist industrial structures but implacably hostile to any restraints on sexual experimentation.

If these claims are valid, then the liberal project of devising a universally valid conception of justice which is endorsable by all irrespective of their particular conceptions of the good is unattainable (cf. Mendus: 1989, chapters 4 and 5, for a detailed and persuasive presentation of this argument). If it could be shown that all theories necessarily rest on 'perfectionist' assumptions of one kind or another, then the conclusion is that no theory will be able to succeed where liberalism fails. No conception of the acceptable limits of cultural and religious pluralism can be generated which is independent of particular (thick) conceptions of the good human life.

From a liberal standpoint this will of course appear as a distressingly pessimistic conclusion. But it does not mean that contending particular religious or cultural communities (including liberal communities) cannot succeed in living together in relative tranquillity within the same political society. Where their respective conceptions of the tolerable are deeply and diametrically opposed they may well not be able to, unless one cultural community becomes dominant and hence is able to enforce its own conception on minority communities (as has occurred in Canada and the USA with respect to aboriginal communities). We need to take some comfort here from history, which illustrates that political compromises can often be struck where a partial consensus emerges. These are likely to be unstable and in need of continual renegotiation, but the preservation of civil peace depends on the willingness of all communities to strike them.

I am indebted to Paul Marshall for his comments on an earlier version of this paper. It shortcomings are, of course, entirely my own.

BIBLIOGRAPHY

Jones, P. (1989) 'The Ideal of the Neutral State' in R.E. Goodin and A. Reeve (eds), *Liberal Neutrality* (London: Routledge).
Kymlicka, W. (1989) *Liberalism, Community, and Culture* (Oxford: Clarendon Press).
Lustgarten, L.S. (1983) 'Liberty in a Culturally Plural Society' in A. Phillips Griffiths (ed.), *Of Liberty* (Royal Institute of Philosophy Lecture Series: 15) (Cambridge: Cambridge University Press), 91–107.
MacIntyre, A. (1988) *Whose Justice? Which Rationality?* (London: Duckworth).
Marshall, P. (1989) 'Liberalism, Pluralism and Christianity: A Reconceptualization', *Fides et Historia*, vol. 21, no. 3, 4–17.
Mendus, S. (1989) *Toleration and the Limits of Liberalism* (London: Macmillan).
Nozick, R. (1974) *Anarchy, State, and Utopia* (Oxford: Blackwell).
Okin, S.M. (1991) Review of Kymlicka (1989), *Political Theory*, vol. 19, no. 1, 123–9.
Raz, J. (1986) *The Morality of Freedom* (Oxford: Clarendon Press).

4 Liberal Neutrality, Traditional Minorities and Education
Deborah Fitzmaurice

Liberalism has long been complacent about both its theoretical capacity to subsume and dominate traditional world views, and about the capacity of the liberal state harmoniously to contain plural, ethically divergent groups. The reassertion of religious fundamentalism reveals that such complacency is ill-founded.

Liberal self-satisfaction on both theoretical and political fronts is grounded in a certain conception of the relation between justice and the good life. Principles of justice are supposedly independent of conceptions of the good, providing mere boundary constraints within which such conceptions may be pursued. But in attempting to contain certain religious modes of life the liberal state has recently come to resemble the boa-constrictor in Saint-Exupéry's illustration, which has swallowed an elephant and is looking uncomfortably out of shape. To understand why religious fundamentalism is proving so indigestible for liberalism, we need to understand the pervasive modern tendency to see the liberal values of reason, freedom and neutrality as interconnected and mutually supporting.

In the modern liberal imagination, it seems, these values mesh as follows. Liberal principles of justice, that is, structuring principles for public institutions, are supposedly grounded in reason. As far as principles of 'private conduct' are concerned, for example, concerning personal and family relations, sexual orientation, religious practice and the like, liberalism does not pronounce. It is, famously, 'agnostic about the good for man'. This agnosticism of liberal theory is often assumed to lead directly to the ideal of neutrality of the liberal just state, in which state coercive power enforces principles of justice only, leaving questions of the good life, of the conduct of the private sphere, to individual choice. And according to liberal theory, a just political state is one which allocates to each individual as large a sphere of private freedom as is compatible with the egalitarian restraints of justice, as in the familiar slogan which calls for 'the most extensive liberty compatible with like liberty for all'.

There is therefore an influential strand in modern liberalism that does not conceive of itself as a rival to religious world views. For it claims to legislate only about what can be universally rationally justified, and has nothing to say about matters of religion. And it takes this to be a view which is shareable even by the religious. If principles for the conduct of the public sphere are grounded in universal human reason, then all rational beings can assent to them. Since, furthermore, these principles demand religious freedom, even the devoutly religious have no cause for dissent. How, then, are we to understand the present conflict between religious minorities–most strikingly, in the United Kingdom, Muslim minorities–and the larger liberal cultures within which they are located? There are at least two plausible construals of the problem.

The first is to see the conflict as a dispute about the consistency of actual liberal states with liberal principles of justice. If present laws and institutions are not in fact neutral, and what religious minorities are demanding is a better approximation to neutrality, then the debate can take place within liberal parameters. The political rhetoric of Islamic leaders, emphasising religious freedom and equality, suggests that this is how they see the issue. Even if this account is correct, solutions are unlikely to be obvious: liberal principles are famously abstract and indeterminate, and it is far from clear what state neutrality would actually amount to. Nevertheless, the debate can go forward within liberal parameters.

However, if it is the case that the Islamic minority have a case that we must answer, it is only in virtue of the fact that they are able to make it in the terms of a political morality alien to their tradition. For a traditional understanding of the proper relation between religion and the public sphere is quite other than that of the liberal. What liberal principles in fact demand is freedom of religious practice for the individual in the private sphere. However, according to the self-conception of many religions, religion is neither a matter to be left to individual choice, nor a private matter. Private religious observance, which is what liberalism permits, is a matter of worship either alone or with like-minded others, the celebration of religious festivals, and the observance of customs like the avoidance of proscribed food. But according to, say, Islam, the good life is not that of the citizen of the liberal state who goes home to halal meat. Rather, it is a life suffused in every aspect by religious observance, and can be lived only in a certain sort of community. The good state does not maximise equal freedom but fosters the virtuous community, which is a very different matter. Whereas liberalism takes it that principles of political right are prior to and independent of conceptions of the good or of virtue, traditional world views standardly take it the other way round.

Recognition of the deep foundational differences between secular liberal thought and traditional religious world views invites a different construal of the conflict between the religious minority and the larger community. Perhaps the actual laws and institutions of the United Kingdom as they stand do approximate to liberal requirements, and we are dealing with a minority making demands for a non-neutral state which run counter to those of justice, versus a majority upholding the requirements of justice. And if, furthermore, principles of liberal justice are grounded in principles of reason, independently of any conception of the good life, then the dissenting religious minority are making what are in some sense irrational or unreasonable demands.

Let me try to summarise these two possibilities in a way that ducks the big questions of moral epistemology and ontology. Either our institutions fail by our own standards, in which case we have reasons for self-reform, or they fail by a set of standards not binding upon us, in which case we have no such reasons. Unfortunately, this tidy-looking dichotomy does not exhaust the possibilities. For what I have characterised as the dominant values of liberalism – rational principles of justice, individual liberty and state neutrality – may turn out not to support one another, at any rate, not straightforwardly. The difficulties for liberal theory presented by the resurgence of religious fundamentalism demand a return to foundations, and those foundations may turn out to be other than have been supposed. That is the subject of this paper.

THE IDEAL OF LIBERAL NEUTRALITY

Over-expansive talk of neutrality is one of the bugbears of modern liberal and anti-liberal theory, and it is impossible to make argumentative progress without first clarifying what liberal neutrality amounts to. There are at least two quite distinct sorts of neutrality principle at work in liberalism. The first neutrality requirement falls on the fundamental principles on which political institutions are grounded – that is, on principles of justice. The requirement of neutrality here is a version of the requirement that principles of justice be universally rationally justifiable. Just what universal rational justifiability amounts to is a question to which different strands of the liberal tradition return rather different answers. But it is a dominant theme of liberalism that in order to be universally rationally justifiable, such principles must be derived without presupposing the objective superiority of any particular mode of life. I shall call this 'the principle of procedural neutrality'.

Political principles may be independent of presuppositions about the objective superiority of any conception(s) of the good. In that: (a) they are derived independently of any conception of the good whatsoever, from principles of reason alone; (b) the derivation makes use only of such goods as are constituents of any conception of the good whatsoever, plus principles of instrumental reason; or (c) everyone's complete conception of the good is counted equally in the derivation of the principles. Formulation (a) corresponds to the austere Kantian project, and (b) to Hobbesian contractualism. Formulation (c) corresponds to Utilitarianism, which will not be discussed in this paper.

This understanding of neutrality emphasises the historic connection between reason, justice and agnosticism about the good for man. Roughly, if questions about value or the good are understood to be rationally irresoluble, matters of merely local and contingent commitment, then principles of justice can only be universally rationally vindicable if they do not presuppose that some particular set of values are correct. Hence the aspiration to derive principles of justice from principles of reason (with or without supplementary assumptions about human nature) without reference to the good or value.

The second sense of neutrality is quite different, and a good deal of unclarity is generated by the use of 'neutral' to mean 'universally rationally justifiable' on the one hand, and substantively neutral on the other. In the second, substantive sense, the institutions in which fundamental principles are embodied are required to be concretely neutral between different modes of life, or conceptions of the good.

The traditional liberal interpretation of this second neutrality requirement is that it is fulfilled by leaving the question of what mode of life is to be adopted to be settled by individual preference or judgement. The more recent interpretation is that substantive neutrality between conceptions of the good demands that the liberal state ensure that all conceptions have roughly equal chances of survival – a sort of equal opportunity principle for forms of life. I shall refer to both of these as versions of 'the principle of substantive neutrality'.

It is abundantly clear that liberalism cannot and is not intended to be thoroughgoingly neutral in this second sense. Whatever principles a state embodies, whether based on a particular conception of the good or not, it is an inescapable feature of a set of political institutions that it constrain the modes of life lived within it. Even the minimal nightwatchman state proscribes lives of overt coercion and deception. Clearly, any version of the principle of substantive neutrality is dependent on an antecedent principle which rules out those modes towards which neutrality is not required.

If we take it that this antecedent principle is that of procedural neutrality, then the ideal liberal state is one in which certain modes of life are ruled out by neutrally justifiable principles – principles which are derived without assuming the superiority of any particular conception of the good – and the state is then neutral towards whatever it doesn't proscribe. According to the first sense of substantive neutrality – liberty of individual choice – a state is substantively neutral if it does not intentionally encourage or discourage permissible modes of life. It is substantively neutral in the second sense if it equalises the chances of survival of all permissible modes.

Clearly, though, more is claimed for the liberal state than that it ignores, or nurtures equally, whatever modes of life it doesn't forbid. A thoroughly repressive regime could be neutral in this sense. What is supposedly distinctive about liberal institutions is that they leave space for the exercise of individual choice over a large range of significant options. Neutrality in the second sense is not supposed to be a trivial neutrality between conceptions of the good of basically the same sort.

The connection between the first and second principles of neutrality is by no means obvious. Deriving the principles of political right without assuming the intrinsic superiority of any particular conception of the good does not guarantee either that the resulting principles will require that the individual is allocated a conspicuously large sphere of protected individual choice, or that a wide range of significantly different modes of life will be given equal chances of survival. All but a few modes of life might be prohibited for extrinsic reasons, because, that is, the derivational procedure plus natural facts combined to exclude them. Imagine that the neutrally justifiable state is Utilitarian, or a Hobbesian tyranny – neither makes use of assumptions about the objective good for man, and neither is remotely liberal in the popular sense which has more to do with the second than the first principle of neutrality.

This popular, and powerful, strand of liberal thinking ascribes to the principle of substantive neutrality a foundational role. It is *because* the liberal state leaves a large and significant range of life choices unregulated by the State, or because it secures equal chances of survival for plural and diverse modes of life, that it is universally rationally justifiable. But this cannot be so. The second principle only has application to those conceptions not winnowed out by an antecedent principle – that is, to permissible conceptions. This antecedent principle must be logically independent of the principle of substantive neutrality. It cannot be that the correct determination of that antecedent principle, which demarcates the boundary between permissible and impermissible, should be decided in the light of the requirement that the second principle is to have application to a wide range of modes of life. If prior principle A is to define the scope of application of secondary principle B, A cannot itself be determined on the basis of the proper scope of application of B. The principle of procedural neutrality is a proper candidate for a first or foundational principle. The principle of substantive neutrality is not.

It seems, therefore, that any attempt to understand what justice requires of us by taking as basic the principle of substantive neutrality is doomed to failure. We must first settle the question of whether it is possible to derive principles of justice without presupposing the objective superiority of some conception of the good, and if so, what those principles of justice might be.

Principles of justice derived without assuming the objective superiority of any conception of the good must be derived from a consistently Kantian or consistently Hobbesian framework. That is, the argument must either show that there is reason to conform one's actions to certain recognisably moral principles – for example, non-coercion, non-deception, or more generally, respect for all others' agency equally, in virtue of the formal features of practical reason itself. Or it must show that, given that humans have certain desires, there is some coercively backed institutional framework such that everyone has a self-interested reason to opt into it, as a means to the pursuit of private ends. To show conclusively that either Kantian or Hobbesian projects must fail is beyond the scope of any possible paper. But some of the characteristic difficulties of neutralism are apparent in the work of Rawls.

RAWLS AND NEUTRALITY

In *A Theory of Justice*, Rawls aims to derive principles of justice which do not assume the superiority of any particular conception of the good. He does so by excluding particular conceptions from the choice situation in the Original Position. The choosers in the Original Position choose on the basis of the primary goods of the 'thin theory', goods which it is supposedly rational to want whatever one wants, because they provide the instrumentally necessary conditions for the achievement of any determinate conception of the good whatsoever, and are equally useful in the pursuit of all. They are, in this sense, neutral goods: goods desirable by rational beings as such.

The contractors' eventual particular conceptions of the goods are shrouded by the Veil of Ignorance, along with their natural and social advantages. Knowledge of the latter is excluded in the name of fairness, in order to prevent the choice of principles which will privilege particular social groups. This is a substantive and contentious conception of fairness, which forms the predictable focus of critique from the libertarian right. But the exclusion of particular conceptions of the good is initially conceived as an uncontentious device to make unanimity possible. The fairness of this exclusion is secured by the supposed neutrality of the primary goods. If the primary goods are neutral between particular conceptions, then the contractors have no interest in knowing what their actual conception is to be, as whatever it is, it will be equally well served by the secure possession of these goods.

The neutrality of the primary goods has been disputed by various critics, amongst them Thomas Nagel. Nagel argues that reasonable persons would not agree to the exclusion of their determinate conceptions of the good from the Original Position in favour of the index of primary goods. For 'the primary goods are not equally valuable in pursuit of all conceptions of the good...they are less useful in implementing views that hold a good life to be readily available only in certain well-defined types of social structure, or in a society that works concertedly for the realisation of certain higher human capacities and the suppression of baser ones.'[1] Such visions of the good are exactly those held by members of traditional religiously-based cultures, for whom the good society is not neutral, but both presupposes, and is structured to inculcate and foster, certain virtues.

In almost all such traditional societies, a certain form of family life in an extended family structure, suffused by religious observance, is taken as an essential condition and constituent of goodness. These structures tend to wither when transplanted into a larger liberal culture. Not only is religious belief subject to criticism in a discursive public sphere, but the extended family is eroded when women have equal educational entitlements and opportunities in the economic realm, and all citizens inherit the full complement of civil liberties in early adulthood. Hence, a state which secures the primary goods for all is bound to be inhospitable to traditional social forms. If Nagel's argument is correct, this provides grounds for reasonable grievance on the part of those who adhere to such forms.

Part of Rawls's response is to assume that these forms of life are excluded by the just state on the same basis as lives of force and fraud, because, that is, they allow some persons to enjoy a benefit at others' expense. They are hence ruled out by considerations of fairness, and fairness secured by the exclusion of knowledge of natural and social advantages.[2] But the goods of the religious person, or of someone whose conception incorporates a certain form of family structure, are thought of by those whose conceptions they are as goods for all members of the social whole equally. As Nagel points out, as long as the chooser in the original position does not know who she is, her object in choosing principles in the light of her own conception of the good is not to secure her own interests but to 'advance the good of everyone as defined by that conception'.[3] If the chooser behind the Veil of Ignorance would prefer a certain kind of society *whatever* the role or position she will occupy within it, then in opting for such a social world, she is not demanding an unfair advantage in Rawls's sense.

There is nothing unintelligible about a preference for traditional over liberal societies, even if traditional societies bestow more limited freedoms. Liberal social forms are arguably the best protection against some forms of subordination, especially the subordination of those who are capable of independence. But the goods of traditional societies may appear more choiceworthy from the point of view of dependent and vulnerable persons. Suppose, for example, that traditional societies tend to subordinate the young but reliably provide the good of security, companionship and respect in old age. From the point of view of someone with a complete life in mind, the maximin principle of choice under uncertainty may commend the traditional society.

In the face of this and other criticisms of *A Theory of Justice*, Rawls has retreated from his earlier claim that the principles of justice are derived independently of a conception of the good. His theory no longer aspires to what I have called procedural neutrality. He now acknowledges that the goodness of the primary goods derives not from their constituting the universal means to desire fulfilment, but from the fact that they provide the conditions under which the individual may form a conception of the good independently; may, in pursuing it, enjoy legal protection from certain impediments; and may revise it freely. Hence, the primary goods are choiceworthy only by those who value the conditions of choosing and defining their conceptions of the good for themselves *more highly* than they value the most instrumentally useful conditions for achieving the substantive goals which make up their conception of the good once chosen. This is surely to hold a conception of the good, namely the good of autonomy.

The later Rawls makes no claims for the universal rational justifiability of liberal principles of justice. He merely takes it that the fundamental values presupposed by liberalism are 'our' constitutive values.[4] This is his communitarian turn, towards liberalism as *Sittlichkeit* rather than *Moralität*. However, it is quite clear that not all those who presently inhabit liberal societies share the value of autonomy. Members of religious sub-cultures, especially those which have undergone a fundamentalist revival, do not. They have some quite other conception of the good, in which what matters is the realisation of determinate values, not the realisation of lives in which the constituent determinate values have been independently and freely arrived at.

Rawls attempts to negotiate the problem of ethical and cultural pluralism by means of the distinction between 'political' and 'comprehensive' conceptions of the good. A comprehensive conception of the good, whether provided by 'religious, philosophical or moral doctrine' encompasses values and virtues for the whole of life. A political conception merely specifies the first virtue of social institutions. Rawls argues that, whereas complete conceptions of the good are various, a certain conception of the good political state is unanimous in Western constitutional democracies.[5]

Even if one defines membership of constitutional democratic society in terms which exclude religious minorities, such a claim is disputable. But any such definitional exclusion is question-begging. And any non-question-begging generalisation about the hegemony of liberal political values is false. Religious groups do not share the liberal conception of the political good in so far as they conceive of the good political state as one which institutionally protects religious values in preference to the liberal good of autonomy.

At least, though, we now have a perspicuous account of the grounds of the dispute between religious minorities and the larger liberal state. Liberalism presupposes a conception of the good life which is not shared by some religious world-views. Once liberalism's self-conception no longer incorporates the belief that liberal principles of justice derive from a neutral procedure, and hence that they are vindicable to all rational beings whatever their conceptions of the good, conflict with religious minorities, however politically recalcitrant, becomes theoretically transparent. The relationship between the boa-constrictor and the elephant is properly viewed, not as a partial failure of incorporation, but as a head-on collision between forces competing for the same terrain.

AUTONOMY AS A GOOD

The later Rawls's defence of the primary goods suggests affinities between his theory and that of Joseph Raz, who argues explicitly for the foundational role of autonomy in liberal theory. In *The Morality of Freedom*, Raz defines the ideal of autonomy as 'the vision of people controlling, to some degree, their own destiny, fashioning it through their own decisions throughout their lives', and the conditions of autonomy as 'appropriate mental capacities, an adequate range of options, and independence'.[6] Autonomy, on this account, has internal and external conditions. The internal condition is the capacity for reflectively determining one's conception of the good. The external conditions are those which provide both the conditions of the development of the capacity for reflection, and the scope for its exercise. What follows will mainly focus on the capacity for reflective self-determination, and the external conditions which promote this capacity, rather than on the external conditions which provide scope for leading an autonomous life. Notice, however, that the Rawlsian just institutions, securing to each a share of the primary goods, constitute the partial institutional embodiment of the external conditions of both the autonomy capacity and the autonomous life. The civil liberties secure freedom from certain modes of coercion and allow for the exercise of the critical capacities. The requirement that positions and offices be open to all ensures access for all to a range of professional and vocational options. A guaranteed income protects the agent from 'choices' imposed by sheer material necessity.

The idea that what makes liberal institutions valuable is that they provide the social conditions of autonomy is a familiar one. But it is quite unsatisfactory without a theoretically adequate description of autonomy itself. What does it mean to say of a person that she is autonomous – that she reflectively determines her own conception of the good? In what follows, I offer an account which incorporates certain non-empiricist assumptions. First, a person may, and standardly does, value most, and hence have most reason to pursue, ends and goals which she does not most want in the appetitive sense of want. To have a goal is not to feel the pull of a desire, but to aim at an end under a desirability description, or value-concept. That is, the description under which the goal is pursued names something objectively good, desirable or valuable about the object.[7] Secondly, an agent's standing goals need to be concretely determined before she can act to achieve them. For example, suppose one's goal is a satisfying and worthwhile career. One needs to locate a specification of the goal, say, becoming a teacher or doctor, before one can proceed to form a plan of action. This means that a large part of practical reasoning is not instrumental, but the determination of what would count as an instantiation of one's values. This is 'constitutive' reasoning.[8]

Theories of objective value are often taken to be incompatible with any conception of autonomy. For if what is good is good independent of any individual's wanting or preferring it, where exactly is the place for self-determination? The solution here is to see culture, tradition, and evaluative discourse as radically *under-determining* what may intelligibly be regarded as a good mode of life for oneself. This under-determination derives from the plurality of different ways of instantiating the basic human goods; goods such as intimate relations, the development of talents, the appreciation of beauty and sensual pleasures, and membership of a community. The different concrete embodiments of these goods are incommensurable and non-compossible: they cannot be cashed into a common metric and compared, nor can all be realised in a single life. The life of the doctor can be neither compared nor combined with that of the concert pianist, but both are good.[9]

Because there are plural ways of instantiating basic human goods which are all intelligibly good, basic value concepts are indeterminate in scope. All concepts are, strictly speaking, indeterminate in scope, for it is not true of all particulars that they either do or do not fall under the concept. But it is the definitive feature of modernity that basic value concepts are *highly* indeterminate. They are subject to a wide range of intelligible determinations, the adequacy of which *as* modes of instantiation of the basic value is the subject of fierce debate. What is to count as the good of, say, intimacy? Extended families, nuclear families, unmarried partners, homosexual partners, communes? The extreme indeterminacy of the scope of application of value concepts is a feature of modernity because modern culture is constituted by multiple moral traditions, each offering different accounts of how best to instantiate the good for man in concrete practices and institutions.

The person who is autonomous in the modern sense arrives at constitutive solutions – solutions to the question of what is to count as the most adequate instantiation of her fundamental values – by the use of reflective reasoning. She makes a conscious effort to avoid being moved semi-automatically, without question, by the unreflected-upon demands of habit, custom, peer group and traditional authorities. And in the course of reflecting upon how to realise her value commitments in action, the commitments themselves, and previously accepted instantiations of them, become the objects of critical thought, and may be critically re-appropriated or rejected. Such a person is a familiar, and highly regarded, citizen of modernity. The ideal of autonomy is indeed one of our dominant cultural ideals. But I want to make a stronger claim than this on behalf of the value of autonomy, and to argue that it is a condition of a life's being good that it could be reflectively affirmed by the person leading it. And this is to say that the capacity for autonomy, and hence the external social conditions of that capacity, are necessary conditions of the good life.

This is a strong claim, and despite the familiarity of autonomy as a cultural ideal, it is hard to defend. One familiar way of justifying autonomy is as an instrumental value, as a necessary condition of happiness, independently defined. Suppose no one else can know as well as I what will make me happy. By following authority and custom, I run a large risk of living a much less happy life than that of which I am capable.[10] However, this argument is clearly vulnerable to the counter-claim that in traditional cultures, people are arguably happier than in modern cultures. This paper therefore offers an alternative defence of autonomy, which does not accord it merely instrumental value.

This argument in favour of autonomy rests on the concept of the rational good. A person's life is rationally good only if there are good reasons for *her* to believe that it is a good life *for her*. That *there are* good reasons for her so to believe means that the reasons in favour of her mode of life are such that she could come to accept them by ordinary processes of deliberation and reflection from her actual starting point, where that starting point includes not only her existing factual beliefs and values but her background epistemic norms and norms of rationality – what she takes to be good evidence, a good argument and so on. The modal verb cashes, therefore, as a counterfactual: 'Could accept' means 'Would accept if she were rationally to reflect'. The second 'for her' simply registers that, given ethical pluralism, then the question about the good life is essentially indexical. If there are plural and incommensurable modes of acceptably good life, an argument to show that such and such is the best life for some particular person will not do so via the claim that it is the best life for anyone. Rather, the argument will show that it is both an objectively good mode of life and one especially suited to a person with her particular, individual goals, character traits, tastes and capacities. The standard of rational goodness is applicable only to self-conscious beings, that is, to those who have a conception of their good rather than merely living in a certain way. It may be inapplicable to the lives of wholly primitive peoples, who would then be properly judged by other standards of flourishing, such as absence of disease. But I shall assume without further discussion that a self-conscious being must espouse the axiom. It is unintelligible to claim that a certain mode of life is good without believing that there are good reasons for one's claim, even if one cannot immediately rehearse them.

The rationally good life for an agent is one which she *could* reflectively affirm. An agent is autonomous if she actually *does* choose or affirm her way of life reflectively, on the basis of having followed and grasped the chain of reasons which commend it as the best way of life (for her). It is therefore quite clear that a person may non-autonomously lead a life which closely resembles that which she would choose or affirm were she to reflect. She may have become settled quite fortuitously in a way of life which just suits her. I accept that this is a rationally good life. A person's life does not have to be autonomously led if it is to be rationally good. In which case, I have surely not shown that the autonomy-capacity and its external conditions are necessary conditions of the rationally good life, since such lives need not actually be autonomous.

However, it is the possession of the capacity, not the fact of its exercise, that is a necessary condition of a rationally good life. For if, as I have argued, a person's life is rationally good only if there are reasons for her to believe it good (for her), and if this cashes as a hypothetical claim about what she would choose or affirm, were she to reflect, then the life of a person who does not possess the autonomy-capacity cannot be rationally good. For if a person lacks the capacity to reflect, no hypothetical of the form 'She would affirm such-and-such a life, were she to reflect', can be true of her. The reflective affirmation of any particular mode of life is forever beyond her grasp.

The argument for the external conditions for the exercise of autonomy is weaker, for it does not strictly follow from the fact that a person lacks real options that she cannot be leading a rationally good life. There could be good reasons for her to believe that her life is better for her than any one of a number of alternatives that she never had the real option of espousing. For example, a member of an aboriginal culture, born and raised before it was realistically possible to leave her tribal homeland, may reasonably believe that staying there was and is a better way of life for her than the alternatives which would have been available had she belonged to a later generation. However, the argument against deliberately or coercively limiting others' range of options follows straightforwardly from the fact of pluralism. If a number of ways of life are good, hence reflectively choiceworthy, there can be no justification for denying any persons the opportunity to adopt any one of them.

However, to help oneself to ethical pluralism, and hence to a conception of rational reflection which involves the independent and critical comparison of different modes of life, with a view to coming to an independent judgement both about their claim to adequacy as modes of the good, and their suitability to oneself, is to assume a good deal. So far, the argument has failed to register the deep differences between the conceptions of adequate reasoning that prevail within modern and traditional world views. I have used the locution 'X is leading a rationally good life if there are good reasons for her to believe that her life is good', and have cashed this as 'She would affirm her life if she were to reflect'. But this claim must itself be made from the perspective of a discursive public. Standards for rational belief are hence being invoked both implicitly and explicitly. They are invoked explicitly in referring to the standards which govern the agent's hypothetical reflections. They are invoked implicitly in that the claim about what the agent would affirm, were she to reflect, presupposes standards for the rational assessment of others' deliberations, actual or hypothetical. The locution hence assumes a standpoint from which well-grounded assessments of the rationality of others' actual reflections on questions of the good life, or well-grounded beliefs about the outcome of their hypothetical reflections on such questions, can be made.

This creates complications when we come to consider assessments of rational goodness between diverse cultures, only some of which acknowledge ethical pluralism. In discussing this situation, I want to make use of ideal types. Imagine two cultures, careerist and family-centred, whose practices of marriage and childrearing are very different. The women of the careerist group integrate marriage and childrearing with extensive participation in economic and political life. The family-centred women lead lives entirely focused on marriage, the family and the home. And imagine that the careerists are ethical pluralists, but that members of the family-centred group are ethical monists, acknowledging only the goodness of family-centredness, and regard the careerists as simply misguided. In developing this argument, I shall treat as the focus of concern the autonomy of women in both groups. This is both a simplifying device and makes for realism.

In this idealised example, the family-centred group represent the members of a traditional society. Let us suppose that the careerists, as well as being pluralists, are also liberals. And suppose that both groups inhabit a single democratic state, but the careerists are greatly in the majority, and hence have the political power to secure some of the conditions of autonomy for all. Such conditions might be an education which promotes the critical consideration of both ways of life, and protects civil liberties, work opportunities, and access for all *qua* individuals, not *qua* members of family units, to welfare benefits. Would the careerists be justified in exercising that power on the grounds just cited: namely that neither they nor the family-centred women have grounds to believe that a family-centred life is good for any particular woman unless she could affirm it autonomously?

The trouble is that we now have a serious discontinuity between the perspectives of the careerists, who are pluralists, and the family-centred, who are ethical monists. And this discontinuity, if it is stable, is not merely between pluralism and monism, but between paradigms of rationality. The family-centred know that the careerists live in a certain way. They know that they do not do so because of overt coercion. But they do not believe that their lives are good. If the family-centred are rational, and hold the axiom that there is no reason to think a person's life good unless there are reasons to believe that, if she were adequately to reflect, she would consider it good, then they must believe that if the careerists were rationally to reflect, they too would conclude that family-centredness was the best mode of life. This belief is sustainable if there is radical discontinuity between the paradigms of rationality to which the two groups adhere: that is, if the practices of reason-giving within the culture of the family-centred women render supportable their belief that, if the careerists were to reason adequately, they too would conclude that family-centredness was the best way of life.

What this reveals is that autonomy, as I have so far defined it, is a merely formal value. For the autonomous life is the life consciously led on the basis of the agent's *reasoning* about the good life. And talk of rationality is never innocent. If we accept that universal standards of consistency are insufficient to constitute the whole standard for rational thought, and that reasoning follows standards provided by frameworks or paradigms which are to some extent historically and culturally variable, then any substantive conception of autonomy will presuppose culturally particular standards of reasoning. What I have been defending as the conditions of autonomy are in fact the conditions of modern autonomy, where what it is rationally to reflect on the best life for oneself is reflectively to compare a number of different ways of life, taking into account one's own particular tastes and talents, and treating custom and tradition as, to a considerable extent, just so much grist to the mill of the reflective individual's reasoning. But what counts as reasoning about the good life is culturally variable. What is or is not a rationally defensible view of the good depends on prevailing paradigms of rationality. In a homogeneous culture, where the goodness of certain social practices is never put into question, the fact that one could not easily provide further grounds for thinking these practices good does not give one reason to doubt their goodness. In a religious culture, even one marked by some level of debate and dispute, what counts as an intelligible defence of a mode of life will not so count by the standards of secular humanism. For a person might intelligibly think that what she, or anyone else, has most reason to do is to conform her conduct to the pronouncements of religious authorities.

If the perspectives of the family-centred (traditional) and the careerist (liberal pluralist) communities are based on different paradigms of what it is to reflect on the nature of the good life, the careerists are clearly in an awkward predicament. As liberals, they do not regard themselves as justified in imposing on the family-centred public institutions which they, the family-centred, cannot rationally accept. And the family-centred do not see any rational grounds for accepting institutions which are autonomy-supporting in the liberal sense. Since family-centredness is the only good mode of life, the best social institutions are those which nurture and support the family and hold in abeyance the forces of corruption: namely careerism. If this is the right description of what is going on, we have stalemate. Even if the liberal community has the political power to overrule the traditional community, they do not conceive of themselves as being justified in doing so. The liberal is paralysed by plural practices of reasoning, for how can public institutions be rationally justifiable to a plurality who do not share common standards of rationality?[11] It is this situation which many liberals believe themselves to face in confronting the question of how justly to accommodate traditional minorities within a larger liberal culture.

There are, I think, three interrelated solutions to the liberal predicament as described. These are the argument against coercion, the argument against the incommensurability of paradigms of reasoning, and the argument for the epistemic obsolescence of certain paradigms. The first argument is as follows. If there is overt coercion and violence in the family-centred community – if, for example, younger women are often forced into marriage and childbearing when they themselves have careerist goals – then the liberal has every reason to believe that at least some members of the family-centred community do not adhere to family-centredness on the basis of *their own* best efforts at practical reasoning in accordance with *their own* internalised paradigms, nor, by implication, would all the non-reflective members of the community embrace family-centredness were they to reflect. For force and the threat of force are necessary only to compel us to do what we do not consider ourselves to have most reason to do. Hence, the liberal is justified in acting to prevent the use of force and threats of force by the family-centred community to police its own members. For in doing so, she merely makes it possible for members of that community rationally to determine for themselves how they should live, and hence to aim at good lives. Doubtless, some members of the traditional community will categorise dissenters as mad or wicked. But since the renegades can presumably explain their determination to lead less family-centred lives in terms of reasons which the liberals can and do follow and endorse, there is no reason for the liberal to accept as correct the categorisation of the situation favoured by the most traditional members of the family-centred group.

The second and third arguments are continuous with this, as they articulate the grounds for believing that dissent within the traditional community does not depend on a violent gestalt switch out of the traditional paradigm of rationality and into some totally incommensurable modern paradigm. Recall the characterisation of the liberal predicament: that is, the description of the stand-off between ethical pluralists and ethical monists. The liberals are stymied because they believe that the members of the family-centred community, given *their* paradigms of reasons and reasoning, not only have reason to believe that anyone who reflected rationally on the question of how best to live would conclude in favour of family-centredness, but have reason to believe that the social conditions of good practical reasoning are not as the liberals themselves believe them to be. But this belief on the part of the liberals must itself be a rational belief. Only if the liberals are able to understand and follow the modes of reasoning of the family-centred community, and on the basis of that understanding see how questions of the good life and of rationality appear from the family-centred's point of view, can they themselves have any rational beliefs either about the goodness of the family-centred way of life for the family-centred themselves, or about the rationality of the family-centred's belief that the social conditions of excellence in reasoning, and hence of the possibility of well-grounded beliefs about what kind of life is good, are quite other than as supposed by the liberal.

The liberals are hence in a state of what one might call the paralysis of relativism with respect to the traditionals in so far as there is sufficient commensurability between their practices of reasoning for the former to have some sense of how the world, including the ethical world, appears to the latter. The very characterisation of their predicament gives the lie to the claim of full incommensurability between liberal and traditional paradigms of rationality. This lays the ground for the third argument: the argument for epistemic obsolescence. Once the difficulties created by the cultural differences between practices of reasoning are recognised, the traditional liberal aspiration to public institutions rationally vindicable to all who must live under them must be reformulated to take account of these differences. The aspiration to public institutions which all could rationally accept, which, that is, they would accept if they were rationally to reflect, must now incorporate the recognition that reflection is not merely the practice of reasoning according to fixed standards, but an activity which has the power to shift standards. If the liberal is to conceive of herself as justified in sustaining the institutional conditions of individual autonomy in the teeth of dissent from traditional minorities, she must believe that, if they were rationally to reflect, they would be rationally compelled to relinquish the aspects of their traditional practices of reasoning which allow them to categorise the condition of liberal autonomy as merely the conditions of moral degeneracy. Suppose the liberal can show that the paradigm of good reasoning on the basis of which the family-centred hold their beliefs is vulnerable to criticisms which their own is not, in ways which *the family-centred* can come to acknowledge. Such an argument would take the form of showing that, if the family-centred continue to adhere to the paradigms of rationality which are the source of the (partial) incommensurability between themselves and the liberals, they face, in MacIntyre's phrase, an epistemological crisis.[12] Such a crisis occurs when a set of theoretical beliefs can no longer make intelligible the experience of those who hold them.

The crisis which must be faced by the traditionalists is this. Monism about the good is not in itself a rationally indefensible position. The difficulty for the traditionalists is that their paradigm of reasoning is not even significantly procedural. That is, right reason is viewed Platonically, as the capacity to discern determinate moral truth, rather than, as I have characterised it, as the capacity independently to interpret an order of value which does not offer an antecedently determinate blueprint for the one truly good way of life. Hence, the counter-factual claim that A would endorse a certain way of life if she were to reflect simply amounts to the claim that it is the one good mode of life. The substance of a person's ethical judgement about how to live – not, even in part, her manner of making it – is what determines whether or not her life is good. Call this conception 'simple monism'. My claim is that, given cultural diversity, simple monism becomes unsustainable.

It is quite clear that the cultural circumstances most hospitable to simple monism are those in which everyone shares the same determinate conception of the good. In a homogeneous, cohesive culture, where determinate judgements invariably coincide, everyone is justified in thinking of their determinate moral judgements as straightforwardly true, of the goodness of traditional practices as self-evident, and of that goodness as providing good reason for participating in and sustaining them.[13] In such a society, custom and habit underpin the way of life and, depending on whether the culture has the equivalent of a priestly caste, so may the pronouncements of cultural authorities. But once there is contact with another, different culture, neither the self-evident goodness of customary practice nor the unquestioned legitimacy of traditional authority can remain unproblematic.

Let me revert to my ideal-type traditionalist, the member of the family-centred culture. How is she to answer the challenge to the goodness of certain norms of marriage and motherhood, incorporating the virtues of, say, chastity and obedience? She can engage with the question directly, and try to relate the goodness of these practices to concepts of honour, family loyalty, the internal rewards of wifedom and motherhood, and very probably to a conception of sexually differentiated human nature. This is to give reasons by showing how the constituents of her way *count* as instantiations of values which, on a more abstract level, she and her interlocutor share. Or she can cite the source of the claim that obedience and chastity are essential goods for women. She may say 'It is customary' or 'The canonical text, as interpreted by the priests, prescribes it'.

If she does the latter, then the rational untenability of her position derives simply from the existence of plural customs and competing authorities. Once she is actually facing an intelligible challenge to her way of life from a member of another culture, she already inhabits a world in which, if not all gods and demons, at least the minor deities and devils, are at war. If more than one mode of life is customary, and many authorities extant, then reference to 'custom' or 'authority' cannot justify a particular mode of life. One has to give reasons for treating *these* customs or *this* authority as binding, and this is necessarily to engage with the substance of what they commend or prescribe.

If then, the traditional monist acknowledges the need to defend the content of her conception of the good, she is already engaging in a practice which is bound to bring home to her the value of autonomy. In attempting to defend her mode of life as good, she tacitly recognises that the claims of alternative modes, if they are to be repudiated, must be discursively repudiated. She already recognises alternative modes of life as intelligibly thought good, if not truly good. And of course, in entering debate, she opens herself to the possibility of becoming convinced that at least some other modes of life are also good. Actual interaction between diverse cultures produces mutual recognition, hence the 'fact' of pluralism and the acknowledgement of the necessary indexicality of the question about the good life.

But even if the traditionalist successfully sustains her monism, the grounds on which she rationally does so must shift. In attempting to articulate the worth of her mode of life to adherents of another, she is already acknowledging the demand for a reflective defence if she is to sustain her belief in its goodness. If she remains monistic, it is what might be called complex monism: the discursively grounded belief that a certain way of life is best, and that all would acknowledge it were they to reflect on the question of the good life sufficiently openly, intensively and exhaustively. Through engaging in conversation, comparison and argument, she acknowledges that a life can reasonably be thought good only if it can be rationally endorsed *in the modern sense*: that is, critically and reflectively affirmed. Hence she must acknowledge that the capacity for modern autonomy is necessary for a good life and hence that the social conditions which nurture it are valuable.

The conclusion of this discussion is as follows. If pluralism is acknowledged, then the value of the conditions of autonomy and of its exercise cannot consistently be repudiated. Simple monism depends on an untenable paradigm of practical reasoning. And complex monism, the intelligent defence of monism in conditions of cultural diversity, must involve the exercise of the capacity for autonomy, hence the acknowledgement of the value of the external conditions for the development of that capacity. If these arguments are successful, then the strongest possible case has been made for the good of autonomy as a capacity. To demand more is to pursue a chimera of mathematical demonstration in ethics.

Autonomy, Education and Traditional Communities

These arguments for autonomy have very significant implications for questions of education. For the Rawlsian institutions which provide the social conditions of autonomy are noticeably incomplete. If the internal condition of autonomy is the capacity for reflecting thought about how lives should be led, then educational institutions of the right sort are clearly essential. What is more, in arguing for autonomy, it has been stressed that it is interaction between diverse cultures over time that makes traditional outlooks rationally untenable. If the dissolution of traditional frameworks takes place over a couple of generations, then the young of traditional communities embedded in larger liberal communities are awkwardly placed. They confront authoritative members of their primary culture who are simple monists, and a wider social world in the terms of which a life cannot be rationally thought good unless it has or could have been reflectively chosen under conditions of freedom. If the arguments offered above are correct, the responsibility of the wider liberal community in respect of this younger generation is clear. We must ensure that all enjoy the conditions of autonomy whether their families and the leaders of their primary traditional communities approve or not. As Raz points out, 'communities whose culture does not support autonomy ... immigrant communities, indigenous peoples, religious sects [in so far as] they insist on bringing up their children in their own way ... are harming them.'[14] The argument for autonomy is therefore a strong argument against unconditional parental rights and unlimited parental choice with respect to schooling. What, concretely, does this imply for educational practice? In particular, what does it suggest about the permissibility of schools with a distinctively religious, even doctrinal, foundation? Such questions are the stuff of practical politics in both the United Kingdom, where the locus of dispute has been the demand of Muslim communities for voluntary-aided Islamic schools, and in the United States, where it has been the claim of some Christian sects to decide permitted textbooks in literature and biology, and of others to withdraw their children from school before they reach the legal minimum age.[15]

Some forms of religious schooling deprive the individual of autonomy. To do so is to cause harm, and such schools are emphatically impermissible. But it is clear that not all do so. Many religious world-views do not require unquestioning obedience to religious authorities and do not treat their canonical texts as authoritative repositories of determinate answers to every moral question, but rather as starting points for moral reflection. Furthermore, they may accept some version of the liberal public/private distinction, although not on familiar liberal grounds. That is, they will think of the state as properly enforcing only a part of morality, not on the basis of individual rights, but on the grounds that true virtue is possible only if the individual embraces it freely, hence that a sphere of legally unregulated activity is a necessary condition of virtue. Such religious views are compatible with respect for individual autonomy and for the social institutions which secure it.

There are other positive claims to be made on behalf of an appropriate sort of religiously-based education. Individual autonomy has been defined as the reflective determination by the individual of how best to instantiate her fundamental goals and values. Autonomy, as the exercise of a *procedural* virtue, is by definition insufficient for a good life. The individual who critically reflects must start from a pre-reflective set of goals and values, and must be able, on reflection, to settle on a set of goals sufficient to make up a life with a continuous character. To be autonomous is not to be free-floating, but to be always engaged or potentially engaged in a kind of dialectic between reflectiveness and embeddedness. The inculcation of settled standards in early life is as much a prerequisite for this as the nurture of the critical faculties.

The practical proposal with which this paper ends was suggested by Bruce Ackermann's *Social Justice and the Liberal State*. Ackermann distinguishes a child's primary culture, the arena of socialisation and the inculcation of settled standards, from her secondary education, when the critical habits are fostered.[16] He does not intend this distinction to correspond neatly to the division between primary and secondary schools, since he regards all schools as the proper locus of secondary education only, but perhaps there is a case for treating the primary school as, at least in part, an extension of the primary culture of the home. We are increasingly aware of the dangers of deracination and that 'wrenching members [of traditional communities] out of their social forms may prevent them from having any life at all'. So, roughly, I am suggesting that the religious complexion of the primary school should be, within limits and where possible, a matter of parental choice, and that all secondary schooling should be, as on the French model, strictly secular. The dialectic between embeddedness and reflection is thereby recognised in a division of labour between different kinds of educational institutions.[17]

NOTES

1. Thomas Nagel, 'Rawls on Justice', in Norman Daniels , ed., *Reading Rawls* (Oxford: Basil Blackwell, 1978), p. 9.
2. John Rawls, 'The Priority of Right and Ideas of the Good', in *Philosophy and Public Affairs*, vol. 17, no. 4 (1988), pp. 251–76, at p. 265.
3. Thomas Nagel, op. cit., p. 8.
4. John Rawls, 'Justice as Fairness: Political not Metaphysical', *Philosophy and Public Affairs*, vol. 14, no. 3, (1985), pp. 223–51, at p. 225.
5. John Rawls, 'The Priority of Right and Ideas of the Good', pp. 252–60.
6. Joseph Raz, *The Morality of Freedom* (Oxford: Clarendon Press, 1986), pp. 370, 372.
7. See G.E.M. Anscombe, 'On Practical Reasoning', in Joseph Raz, ed. *Practical Reasoning* (Oxford: Oxford University Press, 1978), pp. 33–45.

8. Bernard Williams, 'Internal and External Reasons', in *Moral Luck* (Cambridge: Cambridge University Press, 1981), pp. 101–13, at p. 104, and David Wiggins, 'Deliberation and Practical Reason', in Raz, ed., *Practical Reasoning*, pp. 144–52, at p. 145.

9. I follow Raz, op. cit., pp. 321–57. Raz, however, talks about plural and incommensurable goods, rather than instantiations of basic goods. My formula emphasises that only modes of life which are recognisable instantiations of common values – not necessarily fully adequate instantiations – can appear as modes of the good.

10. J.S. Mill, *On Liberty*, ch. 3, 'Of Individuality'.

11. Common institutions may be acceptable to such a plurality if the various factions happen to overlap on them from different directions. In 'The Idea of an Overlapping Consensus', *Oxford Journal of Legal Studies*, vol. 7, no. 1, pp. 1–25, Rawls suggests that the stability of liberal institutions is due to this phenomenon. But it is clear that without a common framework for reasoning, the different groups do not have the resources rationally to reach agreement despite initial disagreement.

12. Alasdair MacIntyre, 'Epistemological Crises, Dramatic Narrative and the Philosophy of Science', *Monist 60* (1977) pp. 453–472.

13. See Bernard Williams, *Ethics and the Limits of Philosophy* (London: Fontana and Collins, 1985), pp. 146–52.

14. Raz, *op. cit.*, p. 423.

15. See *Wisconsin vs. Yoder*, discussed in *Children's Rights and Children's Lives*, ed. Onora O'Neill and William Ruddick (New York: Oxford University Press, 1979), pp. 279–305.

16. Bruce Ackermann, *Social Justice and the Liberal State* (London: Yale University Press, 1980), pp. 140–60.

17. For arguments very similar to those presented in this section see T.H. McLaughlin, 'Parental Rights and the Religious Upbringing of Children', *Journal of Philosophy of Education*, vol. 18, no. 1, 1984; and '"Education for All" and Religious Schools' in G. Haydon, ed., *Education for a Pluralist Society: Philosophical Perspectives on the Swann Report*, Bedford Way Paper no. 30 (London: University of London Institute of Education, 1987).

5 Trust and Toleration: Some Issues for Education in a Multicultural Democratic Society

Patricia White

Philosophical reflection (Baier, 1986; Bok, 1978; Luhmann, 1979) agrees with commonsense observation on the pervasiveness of trust in human life. In complex societies, whether or not they are pluralist, two forms of trust seem to be widespread. There is trust in institutions, for instance money, the political process, as well as personal trust between individuals, for instance friends and colleagues. And as well as trust there is also distrust. These facts raise a number of questions: what is trust? how is it, for instance, connected to seemingly related notions like expectation and hope? how, if at all, are trust in institutions and personal trust connected? is it possible to distinguish between rational and pathological forms of trust, of both institutions and persons? how might trust of institutions and persons be created and maintained in a pluralist, multicultural society? is distrust always to be seen negatively? is there, for instance, a positive role for distrust in relation to institutions? what is the role of education in promoting trust (and perhaps distrust?) in institutions? can education make people trustworthy and also able rationally to assess when they should trust others?

This is a formidable list of questions to discuss in one paper. Papers in this field tend to discuss trust in institutions from the point of view of economics or political theory *or* personal trust but not both and they certainly do not take on the issues raised for education as well. Why am I attempting the triathlon? Trust and distrust in institutions and people are learned. The school in a pluralist, multicultural society provides opportunities, whether or not its staff and students are aware of this, for learning attitudes of trust and distrust towards the institution of the school community and the wider political society. In addition members learn to trust (or distrust) one another on a personal level. Perhaps the school is even influential in shaping some of its students into basically trusting or basically distrustful, suspicious characters or people who see themselves as untrustworthy. These processes are all going on in the same institution, cutting across one another and perhaps cutting across attitudes that parents are encouraging or discouraging. It seems to me necessary to achieve some understanding of these processes.

WHAT IS TRUST?

As Annette Baier has noted, despite the pervasive nature of trust in human life, there have been relatively few discussions of it in either classical or contemporary philosophical texts. Plato presumably expected the citizens of *The Republic* to trust the philosopher kings, Aristotle implicitly recognised the importance of trust in his discussion of friendship, while John Locke gave a central role to trust in his discussion of legitimate government. This seems to be more or less the limit of classical treatments. Recently, however, social scientists and some political theorists have begun to consider trust, particularly in the context of cooperation. At the start of his monograph on trust Niklas Luhmann refers to trust 'in the broadest sense' as 'confidence in one's expectations' (Luhmann, 1979: 4). Diego Gambetta summarises the definition of trust shared by most of the papers in the book he edited on trust and cooperation as follows:

> trust (or, symmetrically, distrust) is a particular level of the subjective probability with which an agent assesses that another agent or group of agents will perform a particular action, both *before* he can monitor such action (or independently of his capacity ever to be able to monitor it) *and* in a context in which it affects *his own* action.... When we say we trust someone or that someone is trustworthy, we implicitly mean that the probability that he will perform an action that is beneficial or at least not detrimental to us is high enough for us to consider engaging in some form of cooperation with him. (Gambetta, 1988: 217)

These definitions highlight trust as a form of reliance on other people which involves beliefs about the likelihood of their behaving or not behaving in certain ways. As such they illuminate aspects of economic and political behaviour (particularly influenced perhaps by the Prisoner's Dilemma problem) involving formal voluntary relationships. They fail, however, to capture the kind of relationship between parents and children, friends and lovers which, before we open philosophy books, strike us as the obvious examples of trust relationships. Here trust seems to involve reliance on others' good will towards one (Baier, 1986: 234). What seems to be common to all the very different phenomena falling under the concept is that trust is a form of belief. It is a matter of believing that you can rely on X. What makes a case of trust more than a matter of simply believing that X will be the case (for example, the person will perform the beneficial action, will show good will towards you) is the element of risk involved. One believes despite the uncertainty. Related to the degree of uncertainty involved there is a continuum of consciousness of the trust relationship. The risk of one's belief that one can rely on someone (or something) proving to be illfounded may be so slight that it may not enter one's consciousness. For instance, when I get on the bus in the morning, *as a matter of fact* I trust in the driver's competence. I do not in the normal case get on the bus with my heart in my mouth willing it to be the case that we shall all arrive in one piece. My behaviour, as I settle down to read my newspaper, shows my trust in the driver. On the other hand, if I accept a lift in a car from a driver whom I know to be notoriously accident-prone, I shall be conscious of the fact that I am taking a risk and that, despite what I know, I have decided (on this occasion at least) to trust him. My behaviour shows this in that I do accept the lift and it shows the degree of my trust as I nervously grip the seat, take furtive glances at the wing mirrors and so on. If I have no choice but to take the lift I may just hope for the best rather than trust.

There is also another continuum in trust relationships, a continuum of feeling or commitment. At the extreme end of the continuum in trusting someone or some group I will, for instance, rely absolutely on their good will. This will be for me a deep commitment. This will typically be the case with lovers and in longstanding relationships between friends but it may also be the attitude of some people to their political leaders or members of the royal family. Our reactions will be different in the event of a breakdown in relationships at different ends of what might be called the commitment continuum. If our expectations are not met in those cases where our commitment is slight, we shall be disappointed, but if our absolute reliance on another's good will is met with ill will or indifference we shall feel let down or betrayed.

Trust, then, involves the belief that you can rely on someone (specifically, their beliefs, dispositions, motives, good will) or something (for example, the efficiency of a piece of equipment) where there is a greater or lesser element of risk. One may or may not be conscious of the trust relationship and it will involve varying degrees of personal commitment. In this paper I shall be mainly concerned with those cases of trust in which there is reliance on beliefs about others' good will towards one, although I shall also make reference to other sorts of trust.

PERSONAL TRUST

Let me now try to give a more detailed picture of a trust relationship. This is, in the first instance, an account of personal trust. In the next section we shall see how far trust in institutions is similar.

Trust in the sense of a reliance on the good will of another person is an attitude which typically has no definite beginning but grows slowly and may not be verbally acknowledged. More than that, it may be that one is not aware of one's reliance on the good will of another and even if one is aware of it the other person may not acknowledge this reliance. In other words there can be implicit trust, unwanted trust and trust of which the trusted is unaware.

Trust relationships can be easily destroyed and are not easily repaired, as was Sam's in Singer's 'A Peephole in the Gate' when, having seen the woman he was to marry kissing another man, he knocked out three of her teeth and left Warsaw for America. Or, again, as Luhmann says:

> one falsehood can entirely upset trust and, by their symbolic value, quite small mistakes and misrepresentations can unmask the 'true character' of somebody or something, often with unrelenting rigour. (Luhmann, 1979: 28)

Those who have been lied to are likely to be resentful, disappointed and suspicious. They look back on their past beliefs and actions in the light of the lies they have been told and realise that they were manipulated. As a result they were, for instance, unable to make choices for themselves according to the most adequate information they could have had. They feel wronged and are wary of new overtures (see Bok, 1978: 20). Both Baier (1986: 238–9) and Luhmann (1979: 74–5) have sensitive treatments of the supporting attitudes which are needed to maintain and repair trust relationships. Between them they stress, for instance, self-confidence, tact, delicacy of discrimination in appreciating what one is trusted with, good judgement as to whom to trust with what and a willingness to admit and forgive fault. All of which will be more easily learned and appropriately exercised in a social climate which is supportive of trust.

Can one be too trusting? Are there perhaps pathological versions of the trust relationship? In one sense the answer seems to be that there clearly are. Those who trust blindly, in the face of evidence which suggests that the trusted person is indifferent to their good or even ill-disposed towards it, are frequently criticised for leaving themselves open to manipulation. The wife who continues to believe her husband's stories about working late at the office to get important export orders off on time, or sudden summonses to weekend meetings with his boss to discuss export policy, after the director has told her at the staff dinner about the closure of the export department, may be regarded as culpably gullible by her friends. Such trust will be seen as moral weakness which should be replaced by a more carefully monitored trust. Trust, if it is to be rational, it will be argued, should be based on good grounds for confidence in another's good will or at least the absence of good grounds for expecting their ill will or indifference. Yet from the wife's point of view it may seem wrong even to *think* that her husband is untrustworthy. Being circumspect in the relationship to which she has committed herself would be destructive of that relationship.

Certainly vigilance in monitoring personal relationships can go too far. Luhmann (1979: 71–5) paints a horrifyingly convincing picture of a way of life in which distrust has become a habit, a routine. The distrustful person regards members of his family and colleagues as potential enemies against whom he must muster an array of defences to protect himself. He needs more information all the time and at the same time he narrows down the information he feels confident he can rely on. Like Sam in 'A Peephole in the Gate' again, who having been deceived by a number of women (and deceiving more himself), concludes, 'All my thoughts led in one direction: there is no love, there is no loyalty. Those with whom you are close will betray you even faster than total strangers' (Singer, 1990: 114).

At the same time the distrustful person can hardly avoid his distrust being perceived and someone who sees himself as the object of distrust will hardly be disposed to see the cause of this in himself. Rather he will react negatively to the distrustful person. In this way distrust feeds on itself and the dispositionally distrustful person is likely to be a very lonely person. As George Eliot noted, 'What loneliness is more lonely than distrust?' Both personal relationships and communities need to be protected from the damaging effects of distrust. As I have indicated above, both Baier and Luhmann are extremely sensitive to the issues raised by the repair of trust relationships. Drawing on their work I shall consider some strategies for the repair of trust in communities in the next section and I shall take up these issues again more generally in the section on the role of education.

TRUST IN INSTITUTIONS

No pluralist democracy could survive simply on the basis of personal trust relationships between individuals; it will require a basis of social trust. What I have in mind as social trust in the democratic context is the widespread belief among citizens that the whole system is functioning to promote the well-being of all its members. By analogy with personal trust, citizens in a democracy need to believe that the institutions within which they are living are informed by good will towards all members of the society. This is most obviously where one link with the cluster of values in the toleration family comes in. In pluralist multicultural societies, whatever precise form toleration takes, trust is needed. For instance, whether a stand-off, live and let live relationship between individuals and groups in a society who are committed to values different from one's own prevails, or whether a more positive attitude of concern to promote their flourishing holds, widespread trust in the supporting institutional framework is needed. It seems to be, for instance, a necessary condition for social trust that citizens do not regard their society as structurally unfair (Dunn, 1988: 77). Concretely they need to believe that the society's legal, economic and political rules and procedures are fair and are being fairly applied. As a corollary they need to believe that where the system breaks down for any reason there will be procedures and the political will for swift redress of any wrong. This is not to say that they have to believe that each and every official has the public good and the good of individuals at heart, although it is to be hoped that most will. They simply have to believe that the system as a whole works in such a way as to promote the good of its members. It is in fact a plus if this can be achieved despite the fact that some of its officials are motivated, for instance, by the thought of the pay packet at the end of the week rather than the public good.

More broadly, as well as a belief in fairness and other democratic values, citizens need to have a more general attitude if trust is to be widespread. This is what I have elsewhere, following Bernard Williams (1985: 170–1), called social confidence. For a society to have social confidence is for its members to be conscious of its major values (though not necessarily self-conscious about them), to think them important (though not necessarily to think *about* them all the time) and to mutually reinforce them implicitly and sometimes explicitly (White, 1991). Social confidence and social trust are mutually supportive social values.

Social trust is at its best and strongest when nobody notices it. If it becomes a matter for public debate it is because it is in need of repair. Widespread social trust has an invigorating effect on social and institutional life. Within institutions, for instance, it makes all kinds of initiatives possible. In a climate of trust people will be prepared to try new patterns of working, make suggestions for changes and so on because they know that, even if things do not turn out as anticipated, their colleagues will appreciate that they were acting in a spirit of good will.

How then is such social trust achieved? Certainly not by demands for it. The politician in a democracy who says 'Trust me!' ought to be regarded with deep suspicion. In the late twentieth century we should be only too aware of the dangers of investing a quasi-personal trust in political leaders, even elected representatives. A childlike trust in powerful political leaders and the systems over which they preside has too often proved disastrous.

How, then, to achieve an appropriate level, and kind, of social trust in democratic institutions? Luhmann reminds us of an illuminating answer in the light of the best practice in democratic systems. As he puts it, 'The trust in systems as a whole can ... depend decisively on trust being curtailed at critical points and distrust being switched in' (Luhmann, 1979: 92).

As others besides Luhmann have noted (Dunn, 1988: 85; Shklar, 1984; 185, 190), a political system which wants to promote the well-being of all its citizens must have well-designed institutions into which distrust as a protective device has been built. An established democracy, for instance, will have a legal opposition, an independent judiciary, independent commissions of inquiry into matters of public concern, a free press and, it is to be hoped, a vigilant public who will judge the government by what it does rather than by its rhetoric. These different bodies and devices will question how far government policies really do promote the well-being of individuals, groups and/or the general public. They will do this by operating with two sorts of distrust which can be directed at persons or systems. First, what might be termed fundamental distrust which questions the good will of the person or, in the case of a system, the fundamental aims or ends of the system. Second, procedural distrust directed, not at the person's good will, but at her competence or personal qualities or, in the case of a system, not at its aims but at its means or procedures. In this need for a fine balance between trust and distrust institutional trust differs sharply from personal trust. In personal trust relationships trust feeds on trust and when even hints of distrust creep in they tend to be destructive. A friendship is not enhanced by slight elements of distrust!

The place of distrust in institutions, however, is not altogether unproblematic, for distrust, particularly fundamental distrust, is a powerful destructive force. A system may be able to tolerate large amounts of procedural distrust as long as there is little fundamental distrust. As Luhmann (1979: 75) points out, those social systems which require, or cannot avoid, distrusting behaviour among their members, must also have ways of preventing distrust from gaining the upper hand. For unless distrust is strictly controlled it may become dangerously rampant and come into conflict with other important institutional values. A common way of 'neutralising' actions which indicate distrust is by explaining that they do not stem from a *true* distrust of the person at whom they are directed but are rather required by the role. This allows for distrustful action while at the same time preserving the general ethos of trust between participants in the enterprise. An assistant in a local shop serving a regular customer who demands identification before accepting a cheque will explain apologetically that, although she knows it's all right, the system demands this. The assistant is making it plain that there is no question of fundamental distrust nor even procedural distrust of this customer. Attempts to safeguard institutional trust in this and similar ways may, of course, not work. The disclaimer may not be accepted. Indeed it may not be a gracious disclaimer. Women, members of some ethnic groups, adolescents and elderly people in our society may so regularly meet with distrust-disclaimers of various sorts ('Yes, we *always* ask for the spouse's occupation for credit for men or women'; 'We always ask for a deposit'; 'We always ask for driver identification') that they correctly see that they are regarded as belonging to a group to be treated with procedural distrust and perhaps even with fundamental distrust. In this way the relationship between trust and distrust in institutions and the control of distrust itself relies on trust. The mechanisms of distrust – the supervision and the monitoring of government and other institutions – and the ways of controlling them themselves have to be trusted.

Trust, then, is the foundation of our most intimate personal relationships as well as our social life. It is often called a device for dealing with the freedom of others (Luhmann, 1979; Dunn, 1984) in the absence of which we are simply left with hope. Trust, though, is no easy option. It is, in Luhmann's words, always 'a gamble, a risky investment' (Luhmann, 1979: 24). Perhaps, however, it is a gamble always worth taking – for societies and individuals. Alternatively we have to contemplate a society in which treachery, betrayal and dishonesty are rife and a suspicious distrustful stance to the world is an individual's most rational attitude. As Diego Gambetta puts it, 'if we are not prepared to bank on trust, then the alternatives in many cases will be so drastic, painful and possibly immoral that they can never be lightly entertained' (Gambetta, 1988: 235).

Even if we are persuaded, though, that we should take a gamble on trust, how do we go about laying our bets? How can institutional and personal trust be promoted? In the following section I shall attempt to provide a few tentative answers to that question which start from the assumption that trust has to be learned.

TRUST: THE ROLE OF THE SCHOOL

Children will have been in trust relationships with those who are caring for them (Spiecker, 1990), in a society in which there is *some* degree of social trust, before they ever enter a formal educational institution. The tasks of the school, crucially important ones in a pluralist multicultural society, are to (a) instantiate social trust in its own ethos; (b) attempt to give its students an understanding of social trust and distrust in a democratic society; (c) encourage students to apply that understanding not only to their society but to the school as an institution; and (d) foster and maintain conditions for the development of personal trust between its members, as well as giving them an understanding of trust in personal relationships. All educational institutions, whether nursery schools or sixth form colleges, will be concerned to create conditions for personal and social trust, while the understanding of trust and the application of that understanding to the wider society and in the school situation will assume increasing importance in the later stages of education. This is no easy programme for a school, which will have to be extremely careful that distrust does not get destructively out of hand.

Social trust and the ethos of the school

Let us look first at social trust in the context of the ethos of the school. The school's contribution here is unique in the early years as the institution where the child first encounters social trust (and distrust) as a participant in an institution. The first task of the school will be to *show* trust, sometimes, but not as a general rule, making this explicit. Its procedures, as far as possible, will be framed in such a way that, in and of themselves, they say: we trust you, i.e. we confidently rely on your good will towards this community. British primary schools are often particularly good at this, giving individual children and groups of children responsibility for the conduct of many aspects of their school life. So much so that when they go on to the secondary school where they are treated as 'the babies' who need considerable supervision, children often feel resentful, since it seems to them that in this new institution they are not trusted.

In the nature of the case much of the attention that the school pays to the fostering and maintenance of social trust will be focused on the avoidance of negative messages. The school will want to avoid unwittingly conveying the impression to its students: we don't trust you, or, even worse, some of you. The issues that arise here will present teachers with some dilemmas. On the one hand, as we have seen, in order to be trustworthy, any institution has to build into its procedures mechanisms of distrust, in the school case for instance, procedures for checking on students' attendance. The significance of these may be misperceived by school students. On the other hand, the school is concerned with other educational aims besides the creation and maintenance of trust, for instance the promotion of knowledge and understanding, and the means it may employ in the realisation of these aims may suggest that it does not trust its students. Teachers may judge, for instance, that the promotion of knowledge and understanding requires, *inter alia*, the monitoring and supervision of young students' learning, and may ask parents to countersign homework. As a consequence students may feel they are not trusted. This must present teachers with a problem, particularly if the countersigning of homework seems to be raising standards in academic work in the school.

It may be the case that the school's demonstration of lack of trust is not unwitting. School staff may believe they have good grounds for not trusting some of their students. It is important, though, to say at this point that these will be *individuals* whom school staff believe bear the school ill-will. Staff could not have good grounds for a blanket distrust of whole groups of students, say those from a minority group. (How could they know that each individual bears the school ill-will? If they do know this, then this would be to distrust them as individuals.) Students who feel themselves to be distrusted *as members of a group* can rightly object that they are victims of prejudice.

It is perhaps helpful to categorise the students whom a school staff will typically distrust as 'criminals', 'terrorists' and 'outsiders'. The criminals are those students who by and large accept the school's values and rules but who nevertheless persistently infringe them. These are the children who are always suffering the school's standard punishments. The terrorists are those students, few in most schools, who accept neither many of the school's values nor those of the wider society and will frequently attack the fabric of the school as well as other members of it. Finally there are the outsiders: students, who may come from minority groups, who do not accept the school's major values and ethos. The extent of their commitment to the school, for instance, may be as a place to get necessary examination qualifications. They cause no problems but to a large extent they live by values and have attitudes quite other than those which the school exemplifies in its ethos. Teachers must distrust the terrorists and show that they do since this is part of what it is to behave with social confidence in the school's ethos. In certain circumstances teachers will have good grounds for having (what will usually be a procedural) distrust of the criminals, although it is important that there are routes by which they (and indeed the terrorists too, if that is possible) can regain trust, as I shall indicate in a moment. It is not clear, though, that school staff should regard the outsiders with suspicion, as they sometimes do. Here it seems that intolerance leads to a damaging attitude of fundamental distrust, which can only feed on itself. More appropriate here would be an attempt at dialogue to achieve some understanding of the values of the outsiders so that their flourishing can be a genuine aim of the school in a pluralistic democracy.

As far as distrusted individuals are concerned however, ways have to be found for them to become trusted again. Circumstances may indicate different possibilities. It may be important to stress to the child and her peers that one or two lapses do not make someone an untrustworthy individual. Part of becoming a trustworthy person is seeing oneself as a person who can be trusted and not as some inherently leaky vessel. If Luhmann is right on the significance of punishment, penance and pardon (Luhmann, 1979: 75) it may be important for schools, particularly in the case of young children, to consider semi-formal ways in which students might rehabilitate themselves in the eyes of other members of the community. These can have the function of indicating that the affair is closed and there is no further legitimate occasion for distrust.

This paper cannot provide substantive solutions to these problems. What I hope it suggests is that teachers need to have some understanding of the issues raised by the notion of social trust in an educational institution if they are to approach the practical problems confronting them daily with insight and sensitivity. Understanding of these issues by individual teachers, however, is not sufficient. It must be complemented, as in the related case of social confidence (White, 1991), by the school's use of its resources as *an institution* to promote trust (and keep distrust within bounds). The school staff as a whole, not only teachers but support staff as well, need to discuss and frame together whole school policies which instantiate democratic values and create and foster, rather than violate, social trust. At some point school governors, parents and, where appropriate, school students need to be involved in this process. The point of the deliberations will be the framing of policies which are supportive of a social ethos in which trust can for the most part be taken for granted and in which the conflicts and tensions highlighted above can be as far as possible resolved or at least recognised for what they are.

Students' understanding of social trust and distrust

In a pluralist society where trust may be under threat, teachers and other members of the school's staff need to have an understanding of social trust, if they are to create, maintain and perhaps repair an ethos of trust in the school. What about school students? For them, coming to understand social trust and the role of distrust is part of their political education into a democratic system. Building on the basis of their years of first-hand experience as members of the school as an institution, their political education can give them, probably at some quite late stage in their school education, a reflective understanding of the role of trust and distrust in a democratic system. Let me indicate some possible themes in it. A principal focus will be the grounds for trust in a political system. Why trust democracy? According to what criteria does the citizen decide to trust this party or this politician? Are they different from those she might use in personal relationships or face to face encounters? What is the nature of trust in an unequal power relationship? Relevant here will be some discussion of the role of distrust in democratic systems (see pp. 75–6 above) and one problem will be that of encouraging a healthy scepticism of politicians and their claims without tipping one's students over into an apathetic cynicism. What is probably important here is the encouragement of realistic expectations. Luhmann (1979: 79) refers to psychological research which indicates that if the possibility of some disappointment of an expectation is built into it, if we meet with a particular case of disappointment then the expectation is felt to be confirmed overall ('Yes, there are some bent coppers but most of the police are doing a good job'). It will be important, too, to encourage an appreciation of the different objects of trust and distrust and how they are interrelated in the political area. As well as judgements about a politician's good will there are judgements to be made about his competence and in some cases about his motives. This is not the place to work out where, and in what precise form, in the schema of a political education a treatment of the roles of trust and distrust should occur. My intention has been only to indicate that there is a need for some understanding of these notions.

Applications of trust and distrust in the school and society

An important, but delicate, area in education for social trust and distrust is that of the application of these notions to society and the school itself. Dangers abound here. Generally speaking, it is important for teachers to try to guard against the blinkers that hamper us all. For in encouraging distrust of *our* bogeymen it is all too easy to nurture an implicit trust in things which need to be questioned. A friend of mine said that his parents and teachers effectively got him to distrust strange men who might offer him rides in cars but never so much as suggested that he might extend the same wariness to the government. Is the counsel of perfection perhaps to try to encourage students at least to entertain a distrust of one's idols? If so, this has to be managed in a way which does not take a nihilistic turn, leaving students feeling that there is nothing worth valuing.

More particularly, in a democratic society it will be right for school students to entertain and, where appropriate, express distrust of the school as an institution. For, as I have argued above, such distrust is democracy's chief protective device and there is no reason to exempt the school from its searchlight. If, however, there is not only massive procedural but also fundamental distrust, this will be totally destructive of the school's efforts in all areas of its life. As a model of a responsive democratic institution, therefore, the school should be quick to pick up on the first signs of distrust. Concretely this will mean having an openness to students' views in both formal and informal ways and being prepared seriously to consider those views. This will be possible in a school with a strong ethos of social trust, as outlined in my examination of social trust and the ethos of the school, above.

Trust and personal relationships

What can the school do about fostering personal trust relationships between its students? Even more so than in the case of social trust, the role of the school cannot be an aggressively positive one – it cannot demand that its students trust each other – but it can provide invaluable support for such relationships. It can create space for them and sensitive teachers can nurture them and help their students when they are faced with the downside of trust relationships – distrust, suspicion and betrayal. In this respect the school should play the same supporting role in relation to trust relationships as it should do in the closely related, (indeed overlapping, since trust is centrally involved in friendship) matter of friendships between students (White, 1990).

Perhaps most importantly in a pluralist multicultural society like our own the common school provides a meeting ground in which people from different groups can form personal relationships in an environment relatively protected from the extremes of prejudice. (This, in my view, is one powerful argument against separate schools for different ethnic or religious groups, an issue discussed in Deborah Fitzmaurice's paper.) For the growth of trust in personal relationships is a slow, tentative business where each party cautiously tests the ground. It is likely to be most successful where both parties to it are relatively self-confident so that they are not daunted by small setbacks and can both acknowledge and forgive faults. A sensitive teacher can be immensely helpful in this process in being aware of the pitfalls in forming and maintaining trust relationships and unobtrusively encouraging a student to have more realistic expectations, to make a more tactful approach, to appreciate what she is being trusted with and to be prepared to see a betrayal, now bitterly regretted, for the single mistake that it was. Teachers, especially teachers of young children, often spend a great deal of time helping children to form relationships with other children, supporting them when the relationships are foundering or helping them to repair and re-establish them. Some have told me that they feel guilty about the time they spend in this way but they surely should not do so in the light of the fundamental importance of these relationships.

Unlike the understanding of social trust, the promotion of students' understanding of trust in personal relationships is likely to be most helpfully pursued in an informal way. Could there be any point in formal talks on aspects of the nature of trust, except perhaps for budding philosophy students? It will occur *pari passu* in coming to understand and appreciate many books and films – *Othello* is only one obvious example – and on those occasions when the teacher is attempting to help students with, for instance, problems of conflicts of loyalties and betrayal. For these latter occasions are not to be seen simply as a matter of the teacher appearing like a helpful AA man who fixes things, but as occasions when students sometimes achieve acute insights into personal relationships of lasting significance for them.

The *word* 'toleration' has not occurred very frequently in this paper but the *notion* of toleration has been present at many points as a counterpoint to the notion of trust. It would certainly take another paper to explore in any more depth the relationship between the these two notions. Which depends on which? Do they stand in a dialectical relationship to each other? Do they come into being simultaneously? This paper has perhaps at least prepared the way for such further explorations.[1]

NOTE

1. I would like to thank John White for his support during the work on this paper and for his perceptive comments in our discussions of the main issues. I would also like to thank Ray Elliott for the many insights into this topic which his comments on a first draft of the paper gave me.

BIBLIOGRAPHY

Baier, A. (1986) 'Trust and Antitrust', *Ethics*, vol. 96, 231– 60.

Bok, S. (1978) *Lying: Moral Choice in Public and Private Life* (Hassocks, Harvester Press).

Dunn, J. (1988) 'Trust and Political Agency', in D.Gambetta (ed.) *Trust: Making and Breaking Cooperative Relations* (Oxford, Blackwell).

Luhmann, N. (1979) *Trust and Power* (Chichester, Wiley).

Gambetta, D. (ed.) (1988) *Trust: Making and Breaking Cooperative Relations* (Oxford, Blackwell).

Shklar, J. (1984) *Ordinary Vices* (London, Harvard University Press).

Singer, Isaac Bashevis (1990) 'A Peephole in the Gate', in *The Death of Methuselah* (Harmondsworth, Penguin).

Spiecker, B. (1990) 'Forms of Trust in Education and Development', *Studies in Philosophy and Education*, vol. 10, 2.

White, P. (1990) 'Friendship and Education', *Journal of Philosophy of Education*, vol. 24, no. 1.

White, P. (1991) 'Hope, Confidence and Democracy', *Journal of Philosophy of Education*, vol. 25, no. 2.

Williams, B. (1985) *Ethics and the Limits of Philosophy* (London, Fontana).

6 Tolerance and Education
Peter Gardner

To some parents and teachers the idea that they should encourage their children and pupils to be tolerant may seem as obvious as the idea that they should encourage kindness and considerateness. Indeed, amongst parents and teachers of a liberal persuasion a concern to promote tolerance is likely to occupy a central place in their vision of moral education, for whatever else liberalism embraces, tolerance along with liberty are its central ideals.[1] It may seem hardly worth adding that in a multicultural and multifaith society, tolerance takes on extra importance and becomes what has been called 'a major aim in education'.[2] In fact the Swann Report maintains: 'There is now an acute need for a new dimension of tolerance',[3] the acute need no doubt arising from diversity and variety and the regrettable accompaniment of prejudice. After all, there is little call for tolerance in a society where differences in hues, backgrounds, attitudes and customs are at a minimum or where people share one set of values and pursue one vision of the good life. In this respect it may be worth recalling Sir Isaiah Berlin's observation:

> The history of ideas ... has its surprises ... Among them is the discovery that some of the most familiar values of our own culture are more recent than might at first be supposed ... The notion of toleration, not as a utilitarian expedient to avoid destructive strife, but as an intrinsic value; the concepts of liberty and human rights as they are discussed today ... all these are elements in a great mutation in western thought and feeling that took place in the eighteenth century ...[4]

That century spawned a diverse range of ideas and values, and with their coming questions about the value of tolerance came to the fore. As Susan Mendus observes: 'the problem of toleration arises in circumstances of diversity'.[5]

Yet even if questions about the value of tolerance (and I will use 'tolerance' and 'toleration' interchangeably) arise out of diversity, it might be argued that it is intolerance that most frequently confronts diversity: 'oases in a desert of human uniformity, intolerance, and oppression'[6] is how Berlin describes those former periods and societies in which variety was tolerated. Perhaps the existence of variety tells us more about people's determination to hold on to and live by what they believe in than it does about societies' commitment to tolerance. Perhaps, too, a certain generosity leads Berlin to look to the past when talking of a lack of tolerance; in truth it may often be difficult to see our own times and our own society as legacies of Milton, Locke or Mill. We may pay lip service to tolerance, but this can be as far as we go.[7]

But some might say we are right not to go far in this area. Mendus, they may claim, is correct to talk of the 'problem of toleration', for the fact is that the case for tolerance, the case for its encouragement and development, is not as clear cut as some parents and teachers may assume. Those who voice these misgivings may well agree that a general argument for tolerance as some kind of 'utilitarian expedient' is always available to those who support Voltaire's view that 'candour and toleration have never excited civil commotions; while intolerance has covered the earth with carnage'.[8] Yet, by employing A.L. Goodhart's claim that 'Tolerance not infrequently leads to more tolerance',[9] those with reservations about tolerance might mount a utilitarian case of their own, and argue that tolerance not infrequently leads to indifference and moral apathy.

Further reflection may raise further doubts about the desirability of developing tolerance. Would we say, for example, that it should be encouraged amongst those groups and sections of our society which, for various reasons, lack power and influence? Is such encouragement not at best as pointless as giving contraceptive advice to the sterile and at worst, as supporters of Herbert Marcuse may insist,[10] a thinly disguised attempt to ensure subservience? There again, in any debate about the desirability of encouraging tolerance, we need to consider the feelings and attitudes of those being treated tolerantly. For will they not feel, not acceptance or fraternalism, but a sense of being *permitted* or *allowed*, and, hence, of being the object of someone's forbearance? Being treated tolerantly may seem to carry all the implied guilt of forgiveness without even the benefit of a clean slate. Tolerance, it is tempting to suggest, is best kept secret.

And what of those we encourage to be tolerant? It might be argued: if we try to encourage children to be tolerant, even if this does not involve supporting their prejudices and intolerant inclinations, nevertheless it treats these as a kind of given, and seeks to promote inactivity; it aims, therefore, to stop certain effects, not the problem itself, for the problem consists of the very prejudices and intolerant inclinations that tolerance seeks to bottle up. To this some might add: it's not tolerance we need develop, it's respect.

So, the case for tolerance as a major educational aim does not appear as obvious as some suppose. But clearly in order to make more progress in examining that case we need first to establish some clear idea of what tolerance is.

ON BEING TOLERANT: POWER, NON-REJECTION AND ATTITUDES

In the literature on tolerance there is much support for the view that amongst the various necessary conditions of tolerance there are what, following Peter Nicholson's lead, we may call the power condition and the non-rejection condition.[11] Typically one satisfies the power condition by being able to stop or prevent something; hence, cultivating tolerance amongst the powerless looks pointless. However, to restrict the power condition to the ability to stop or prevent is, as Joseph Raz observes, to be guilty, as many political theorists are, of seeing the use of coercion 'as the only possible manifestation of intolerance'.[12] Nicholson also seems opposed to the kind of restriction Raz attacks,[13] and I, too, would support Raz on this matter. Not condemning something as disgusting and corrupting, despite one's inclination to do so, may be a matter of being tolerant, even though one may have the power to condemn that thing, but not the power to stop it.

As for the non-rejection condition, one is said to satisfy this by not exercising the power one has. But with this condition we could also encounter a dispute, for followers of Lord Scarman may favour the view that tolerance requires not non-rejection, but something more positive, something like helping and encouraging.[14] Now not only does this approach require a radical transformation of the non-rejection condition, it also requires a transformation of the power condition as well, for the mere fact that I have, say, the power to stop a person doing something does not mean that I am in a position to help him do that thing more easily or more frequently. There again, some might object that unless we place strict moral limits on what we may help others to do, the case for tolerance, under this positive guise, being a virtue becomes impossible to defend. But here we may note that a somewhat similar point can be made when tolerance is seen as essentially a matter of omission rather than commission. After all, it is wrong to tolerate the intolerable. Still, the fact is that even when circumscribed by suitable moral proscriptions, tolerance under Scarman's preferred positive guise becomes transformed into something else. Something that may have elements of positive discrimination, helpfulness and political activism. This is not to criticise it, but it is to say it is not tolerance.

Yet the power and non-rejection conditions do not provide a sufficient condition for tolerance. A teacher who is unaware that her pupils are passing notes to one another is not being tolerant towards their behaviour even if it is within her power to stop it and she does not do so. Tolerance involves awareness; one cannot be tolerant of what one is ignorant of. That some kind of awareness condition is not mentioned in much of the literature on tolerance may seem surprising until it is realised that it is covered by other conditions. The non-rejection condition, for instance, is seen as not being something one can satisfy unknowingly or unintentionally. More importantly, the awareness condition is an implicit part of what I propose to call the attitudinal condition, for the person who is tolerant is said to have a certain attitude towards what he tolerates.[15] There is, however, some disagreement as to what this attitude involves. Some writers favour a restricted view according to which the tolerator has to disapprove of what he tolerates. The majority of those who support this view would agree with Peter Johnson's claim: 'A necessary condition of toleration is that it is exercised towards conduct which is sincerely regarded as wrong',[16] where by 'sincerely regarded as' Johnson can be taken as meaning 'believed to be' or 'sincerely believed to be'. But, in so far as sincere belief can fall short of certainty, some supporters of a restricted attitudinal condition would insist that Johnson's position is not sufficiently demanding. Etienne Gilson, for instance, claims:

> It is only when we are certain that what somebody says or does is wrong, that we can judge it advisable to tolerate it. In short, where there is no dogmatism, there can be no tolerance, because there is nothing to tolerate ... the very definition of tolerance implies ... intellectual dogmatism.[17]

Faced with a choice between Gilson's and the commoner restricted view as advanced by Johnson, I would favour the latter. Tolerance, though not as common as we might wish, is not as rare as Gilson's account would have us believe. It is also interesting to note that writers from Fitzjames Stephen to Sir Richard Livingstone have endorsed the idea that 'if we are not certain, it is wise and right to be tolerant'.[18] Now whatever one may think of the ethics of the idea that uncertainty justifies tolerance, such an idea is at least coherent. But it is this very point that Gilson rejects, which is another reason for opposing his claim.

Since, as already noted, a belief that something is wrong is compatible with a lack of certainty, the preceding argument need not oppose the kind of restricted view that Johnson and others favour. Nevertheless, such a view does face considerable opposition from those who support a more inclusive account of the attitudinal condition.[19] According to supporters of this inclusive account, while we can be tolerant of what we disapprove of, we can also be tolerant of what we dislike, even when what we dislike is not something we judge to be, or to stem from, something bad.[20]

Faced with a choice between these two accounts, we may feel inclined to support Mendus's conclusion that in terms of capturing everyday meaning, the inclusive account is nearer the mark.[21] To take a mundane example, we may talk about someone being tolerant about the smells of her flatmate's cooking, although in this kind of case the tolerator may not think that her flatmate is doing something wrong or, particularly if the tolerator is good at hiding her feelings, even that her flatmate is being insensitive; it may just be that the person who is being tolerant dislikes the smells in question. However, there are writers, such as Nicholson and D.D. Raphael, who while they might not contest that there is an inclusive kind of tolerance, would argue that if we are concerned with defining the moral ideal of tolerance, we 'must exclude "dislike"' and concentrate on disapproval.[22]

By way of examining the restricted account further as well as the stand taken by Nicholson and Raphael, let us consider some more cases. Suppose I claim the Dutch are tolerant about many things. Given the restricted account, I am, by implication, saying the Dutch disapprove of many things, but this might not be what I mean at all. Indeed, I might think that one of the reasons for the Dutch being so tolerant is that they disapprove of so little. I might also claim that a resident tutor in my university is too tolerant by far, and offer as an explanation of his tolerance the fact that he disapproves of hardly anything the students in his hall get up to. Nicholson and Raphael could insist, of course, that I cannot be praising or commending those I mention in these claims, but why can't I be praising the Dutch even when I am prepared to explain their laudable tolerance in terms of their not disapproving? And why, as Nicholson and Raphael also seem to be suggesting, cannot refraining from interfering with what one dislikes be worthy of moral commendation? Is forbearance only praiseworthy when accompanied by disapproval?

One argument that might be advanced to support the stand taken by Nicholson and Raphael is that where we disapprove of something, more forbearance is needed if we are to be tolerant than if we merely dislike something. In reply we could point out that it might take greater effort for someone not to complain about the smells of her flatmate's cooking, which she dislikes, than for her not to complain about something she disapproves of, such as her flatmate's flirting with their landlady's husband. This suggests that the factual premise of this argument is false. But even if this premise were true and, in addition, even if it is forbearance that makes tolerance commendable, this line of reasoning would not show that dislike-grounded tolerance is not commendable, but that disapproval-based tolerance is the more so.

Turning to inclusive accounts of the attitudinal condition, a similar objection to that which we levelled against the restricted account earlier can also be levelled against the inclusive account. For example, I could repeat my claim that a certain tutor is far too tolerant while agreeing that he dislikes or disapproves of very little that his students do. All of which leads me to conclude that the attitudinal condition, even the inclusive version, is too restrictive. People can be tolerant where they dislike or disapprove, but they can also be tolerant where others, but not they themselves, do, would or would be likely to, dislike or disapprove. In fact people may be tolerant about what they, but not others, like or approve. Raz has claimed: 'one is tolerant only if one inclines or is tempted not to be'[23]. I am saying: one can also be tolerant when others, but not oneself, would not be tolerant or would be likely to be inclined or tempted not to be tolerant. I would also contend that a person might be tolerant without appreciating that what he is tolerant about is what other people disapprove of or dislike or are likely to disapprove of or dislike. This means people can be tolerant without realising it. In some cases when they realise they are tolerant, they may stop being so for the reason, say, that they don't want to allow what other people may find disgusting.

By way of supporting the stretched attitudinal condition sketched out above, consider the following consequentialist defence of tolerance presented by Albert Weale. It concerns the brilliant researcher into computing, Alan Turing:

[Turing] was a ... homosexual, at a time when homosexuality was a legal offence in the United Kingdom. When ... his homosexual activities came to the notice of the Manchester police, he was prosecuted and convicted. For his sentence he was given the choice of a term in prison or hormone treatment. Having chosen the hormone treatment, he spent three years in despair before finally committing suicide in 1954. His premature death, not to mention the anxiety and desperation of his last years, were a direct consequence for Turing of intolerant laws regarding sexual practice. In a more liberal climate he would have lived out his life In a productive and personally satisfying way. The general practice of toleration in sexual matters, it is asserted, will prevent the misery and personal suffering to which people like Turing would otherwise be liable.[24]

Many similar cases might be presented where intolerance has led to misery, even to carnage. But what point are those who might use such cases making? It may seem clear that Weale is saying that beneficial consequences would have followed if the law and, presumably, if we had been more tolerant about certain sexual practices, the import of his argument being that we were right to become more tolerant about such things. But what did our becoming more tolerant involve? Given the restricted account of the attitudinal condition, it involved our continuing to disapprove of, but doing less about, certain practices. Now possibly Weale is insisting we were right to change in this way, but there is another interpretation that can be put on his argument which, I believe, is the correct one.[25] It is to see Weale as arguing that we were right to become more tolerant about certain sexual practices, and our becoming more tolerant was a matter of our or of many people ceasing to believe that those practices are wrong. No doubt many other consequentialist cases *for* tolerance can be seen in a similar vein, as arguments for tolerance which are designed to change people's beliefs that certain things are wrong.[26] In other words, we can be more tolerant by disapproving of fewer things. We can be tolerant without disapproving.

Those who favour including dislike in the attitudinal condition might respond that even if Weale is implying that there can be tolerance without disapproval, this does not threaten their stance. However, under the interpretation I am putting forward, what Weale is in effect saying is that we were right to become more tolerant about homosexuality; we were right to change whatever inclined us to be intolerant towards homosexual practices. And this might be seen as a threat even to the inclusive account of the attitudinal condition.

So, one way of trying to make people more tolerant is to get them to *change* their attitudes, possibly through the use of consequentialist arguments, and, thereby, to get them to disapprove of or dislike fewer things. Yet, given the accounts of the attitudinal condition that we have been considering, the reverse seems to be the case; providing you have the power to be intolerant, one way of becoming more tolerant is to disapprove of or dislike *more* things than you do now but not to exercise that power! This is surely very odd, partly, I suspect, because we normally assume that people become more tolerant by changing their attitudes or by not changing their attitudes but interfering or protesting less than they did.

But there is another matter involved here which warrants attention, although it often seems to be overlooked. It concerns the strength and extent of a person's negative attitudes. Suppose someone is disgusted by many of the things people do, and only with great effort does he manage to stop himself from telling people just what he thinks of them. Such a person clearly satisfies both the restricted and the inclusive accounts of the attitudinal condition, though even if he has the power to stop or hinder the deeds of many who upset him and decides not to exercise that power, we would be reluctant, irrespective of his motives, to call him a tolerant person.

What is significant here is the matter of equanimity. A somewhat similar point is raised by David Carr about patience. Carr suggests: 'if a person who regularly appeared patient had always to suppress powerful feelings of anger or irritation, it would be better to describe him as a person trying to be patient than as a patient person'.[27] Tolerance follows a similar path; the tolerant person is not fighting against powerful moral imperatives or strong feelings of disgust or aversion. The tolerant person is not someone who frequently has to keep counting to twenty or biting his lip. Those accounts which concentrate on power, non-rejection and attitude but fail to consider the equanimity of tolerance may appear unsatisfactory for precisely this reason. This, too, may partly explain why we find it difficult to accept the idea of becoming more tolerant as the result of disapproving of or disliking more things. Borrowing from Aristotle we might say the person who is tolerant has a settled disposition.

It would be wrong of me to end this section without dealing with the main objection to my attack on popular accounts of the attitudinal condition. Mendus no doubt speaks for many writers in this area when she says that it is only when we have 'disapproval, dislike or disgust ... [that] we may properly speak of toleration as opposed to liberty, licence or indifference',[28] by which is meant: to be tolerant towards something, a person has to disapprove of, dislike or be disgusted by that thing; if there is no such negative attitude, there is something other than tolerance, for example, indifference. But if I were to be accused of talking of indifference rather than tolerance, I would draw attention to the fact that one can be indifferent towards something without satisfying the power condition that I have described, for one can be indifferent towards some practice, say, without having the power to change or stop it or without being in a position to be intolerant towards it. I would also argue that one can be indifferent towards something without satisfying the stretched attitudinal condition that I have described. It seems at least possible for there to be something which we are all indifferent towards and which never has attracted and is unlikely ever to attract a negative attitude. One cannot say this of being tolerant under my account. However, if it should be argued that talk of anyone's indifference presupposes an attitude or likely attitude held by others, I could point out that that attitude might be positive rather than negative, which means that even given this presupposition, a distinction can be drawn between tolerance, as I have defined it, and indifference. Consequently, I do not see myself as talking about indifference.

I would, therefore, amend Mendus's claim: we cannot properly speak of tolerance unless there was, is or is likely to be disapproval, dislike or disgust, but, while those who are tolerant often have such negative attitudes themselves, this is not a necessary condition for the use of the concept of tolerance; it is good enough for the proper use of the term if others have had, have or are likely to have such attitudes. Religious tolerance, for example, presupposes some kind of hostility or antipathy, but those who are tolerant on religious matters need not have these attitudes themselves.

DISPOSITIONAL AND DELIBERATIVE TOLERANCE

In many of the writings on tolerance the impression is given that the person who satisfies the power, non-rejection and attitudinal conditions is, *ipso facto*, tolerant or being tolerant. Yet, as our brief remarks about equanimity show, this is false. It is also false because it fails to take into account an agent's motives. Raz seems to be one of the few authors to be mindful of this point: 'Whether a person is tolerant or not depends on his reasons for action'.[29]

Some examples may help illuminate this neglected feature of tolerance. Suppose I do not stop a person from doing something I regard as wicked precisely because I believe far harsher treatment than I could ever mete out, awaits that person if he carries on with what he is doing. Or suppose I do not stop someone doing something that I regard as wrong precisely because I recognise that it would be disadvantageous to me to do so. Such cases might satisfy many analyses of 'tolerance', but it is surely questionable that these are examples of tolerance. Acting tolerantly excludes certain motives, which is why we may doubt whether repressive tolerance, if intentional, is tolerance at all.[30]

Still, there may be people who are uneasy about too great a stress on reasons for being tolerant; they may feel that the more our inactivity is preceded by ratiocination, the less it becomes a matter of tolerance. In this connection consider the following example. As a resident tutor in a university hall of residence, one of my responsibilities is to ensure that the students do not make so much noise that they disturb other students. Now suppose I hear loud music coming from the room of one of the students in my hall. This is the kind of thing I would normally put a stop to and, more than likely, give a warning about 'doing it again'. But suppose I know that the student who lives in the room, whom we may call James, has lots of troubles: his girl-friend has just left him; he has just heard his parents are getting divorced; and his third-year project is going badly. Taking these things into account as well as the effect my complaining about the noise might have on him in his present state, I decide, after much deliberation, not to get James to turn his music down. I may well hope that in a day or two he will be more considerate of those around him. I might even tell the other students on his corridor that it might be best if no one complained about the music for a day or two.

Here I satisfy most of the standard conditions for being tolerant, but in discussion several people have expressed doubts as to whether I am being tolerant. They have said I am being considerate and thoughtful, but not tolerant. What lies behind their reservations is the matter of my weighing things up, considering the circumstances, etc. If I were tolerant, they say, I wouldn't have to do so much pondering, because tolerance doesn't require deliberation.

By way of pursuing this, consider Kirk F. Koerner's attack on Marcuse's recommendation that tolerance as we have it should be abandoned:

> Do away with tolerance and it becomes necessary to decide which ideas are permitted and which are not, to decide what is admissible and what is not, and to designate someone or some group as having an infallible grasp on the true and the good.[31]

What interests me here is the start of Koerner's criticism, where he reasons that if tolerance is done away with, it will be necessary to take decisions about what is and is not permissible, the presupposition being that where there is tolerance, there may be no need to take such decisions. Like those with doubts about my tolerance in the case of James, Koerner is also accepting that tolerance does not require or, at least, does not require much in the way of deliberation about what is to be tolerated.

✦ What these considerations help illuminate is the difference between being disposed to be tolerant towards certain things, which is a characteristic of a tolerant person, and acting tolerantly after some deliberation. In the case of James, I would contend that I decided to and did *act* tolerantly, but this does not mean that I am a tolerant person or a tolerant tutor or that I am disposed to be tolerant about noisy students in my hall. If I were thus disposed, then, borrowing from Aristotle again, perhaps my response to James's loud music would have been second nature or, at least, more a matter of responding to the situation than was the case. Koerner would probably say that if I were a tolerant tutor, I would not have needed to deliberate all that much, if at all. But this, of course, does not mean that a person who is tolerant and is disposed to be tolerant towards certain things does not act tolerantly. What I want to suggest is, first, that one can act tolerantly though one may not be disposed to be tolerant, and, second, and more controversially, that in acting tolerantly, one may not act as the tolerant person does.

The first point seems unproblematic. Faced with a particular situation, a person may decide for certain reasons to act tolerantly towards something, but in general that person might not be disposed to tolerate that type of thing. I may tolerate James's loud music, but I am not disposed to tolerate students' loud music in every case. The second seems to oppose the Aristotelian idea that acting virtuously involves acting as the virtuous person does,[32] where this is understood as acting in the way one does because one has the virtue in question. Such an idea, some claim, leads to a problem, for it may seem that in order to start acting virtuously, we already have to be virtuous. So how can we learn to be virtuous?[33] What I would say is that in the case of tolerance, one may act tolerantly without acting as the tolerant person would, as when, after weighing things up, I decide to allow James to carry on playing his music loudly. The reason why I am not acting as the tolerant person or tutor would act is because, borrowing from Aristotle once more, I am not acting from a settled disposition. Even if in the future I come across what seem to be similar cases to James's, I might still not act from a settled disposition; even though I consider my decision with regard to James to have been correct, I might still assess each new case in detail and consider the extent to which it was relevantly similar to James's case.

Now I believe that some people doubt whether I am being tolerant with regard to James because they associate being tolerant with acting from a settled disposition, with being disposed to act in a certain way, such as being inclined to let students play their music loudly if they want to or when things are not going too well for them. In fact it may well be a condition of having a disposition that a generality of deeds or responses could follow from that disposition.[34]

So, when we consider tolerance we need to be clear whether or not we are concerned with dispositions, for someone may act tolerantly after deliberating about a particular case, and not because he is generally disposed to being tolerant or is disposed to being tolerant towards the kind of thing of which the particular case is an instance. If he had either of these dispositions, deliberation, if needed at all, would be kept to a minimum. This why I believe we should distinguish between what we may call dispositional tolerance, which is what we attribute to the Dutch when we describe them as tolerant people, and deliberative tolerance, which is where, after some kind of pondering or deliberation, someone acts tolerantly. Dispositional tolerance need not involve disapproval or dislike by the person who is dispositionally tolerant, though its objects are what attract, or are likely to attract, dislike or disapproval from some quarters. Deliberative tolerance, however, always seems to involve disapproval or dislike by the person who is deliberatively tolerant, at least initially, for then there is the temptation not to be tolerant and deliberation about whether he should or should not be tolerant. In the case of James, I would say I was being deliberatively tolerant. As a resident tutor, I doubt if I have much in the way of dispositional tolerance.

Given this distinction, it is interesting to consider some of the accounts of tolerance we have touched upon. The frequent lack of concern for people's deliberations may encourage us to conclude that most of those accounts are about tolerance as a disposition, though the insistence on the necessity of a negative attitude and the lack of concern for equanimity reveal a deficiences in those accounts. Raz, on the other hand, unlike most writers in this area, focuses on the tolerant agent's reasons and motives, which suggests that Raz is mainly concerned with deliberative tolerance.

Yet our distinction clearly needs further amplification lest the impression is given that dispositional tolerance involves no consideration or reasons. The point I would make is that where there is no dislike or disapproval, there will be no need to look for reasons for being tolerant, and that even when there is dislike and disapproval, what will be appealed to by the person who is dispositionally tolerant will involve some broad or general principle. Thus you will hear people say, 'If it doesn't frighten the horses, so what?'; 'As long as children aren't involved, let them carry on'; 'It's a free country'; 'They're adults'; 'It's a private matter'; or, following Mill, 'As long as they harm no one but themselves'; or, more parochially, 'An Englishman's house is his castle'.[35] The broad principles appealed to or implied here suggest that people are operating at what R.M. Hare calls the intuitive level, the level of general *prima facie* principles.[36] In addition, just as Hare would argue that there is another level of moral thought to which those who operate at the intuitive level may have access,[37] so I would argue that on occasions someone who is dispositionally tolerant towards certain things may come across a particular case which, though it may fall under one of his general principles, may have certain features which prompt him to engage in detailed deliberation, and this may result in that person being deliberatively tolerant towards something.[38]

Moreover, deliberative tolerance, though it results in people acting tolerantly, can involve various routes to that end. For a start, deliberation may lead to a change in attitude. Reading and thinking about Turing's suffering may lead some people to change their views about the 'evils' of homosexuality, though, possibly, finding out that their son or daughter is homosexual may be more likely to bring about a change in attitude. And while changes in judgement need not necessarily lead to changes in our emotional responses, it can happen that as a result of more information or thought, we may cease to dislike or loathe or feel disgusted by various pursuits, practices and people. Coming to appreciate that homosexual acts can be just as expressive of love as heterosexual ones may lead someone to cease regarding those acts with any kind of negative feeling. Perhaps, too, getting the racist child to try articulating the reasons behind his dislike of 'them' or blacks and to assess the soundness of those reasons may lead to a change in attitude. In this way deliberative tolerance can involve changes in attitude and give rise to dispositional tolerance. The main objection to all this is to insist that if there is such a change, people can no longer be tolerant, but this is something I hope I dealt with earlier.

What also deserves mention is that deliberative tolerance may involve considerations which lead to a lack of certainty which, in turn, may lead someone to follow Livingstone's advice and act tolerantly. But again there is an objection. It is to claim, as Gilson does, that tolerance necessitates certainty, but this, too, I hope I dealt with earlier.

What I have described are not, of course, the only kinds of deliberative tolerance. In the case of James, I neither changed my attitude about students disturbing others nor became any less certain about my position on this matter. What I decided was that in James's case there were special and overriding considerations, though the particular nature of those considerations need not have led me into being any more tolerant about any other student in my hall who plays loud music. James's case could well have been a one-off; no disposition need have ensued from it.

EDUCATION AND TOLERANCE

If I were to ask whether we should concentrate on one or both aspects of tolerance in schools and in moral education, my question might prompt various replies, some of which could be seen as hostile. Opposition to developing dispositional tolerance might come from those who would see it leading to moral indifferentism. They might pursue the argument sketched out earlier, that while Goodhart is right in claiming that tolerance leads to more tolerance, this is only part of the story, for with this degenerative process, forbearance becomes indifference and critical appraisal atrophies. Another objection to developing dispositional tolerance is what some may see as its presumptiveness, though talk of an assault on autonomy and indoctrination might also figure in this criticism. For it could be argued that developing dispositional tolerance in a child is, in effect, *fixing* a child's personality.

The idea that dispositional tolerance frequently leads to more tolerance is, I think, explicable without having to accept that dispositional tolerance leads to moral indifferentism or apathy. If we are concerned about consistency, then, as we go through life, we may find that further cases are relevantly similar to those towards which we have been inclined to be tolerant. (The same thing, incidentally, can happen with deliberative tolerance.) As for the claim that dispositional tolerance paves the way for indifferentism and indolence, this seems to have little evidential support. What needs stressing is that dispositional tolerance can be restricted to certain areas of life or certain activities, and need not spawn some wide-ranging lack of concern for other issues.[39] People, for example, may be dispositionally tolerant about religious matters and practices or about adults' sexual activities,[40] but so far as I am aware there is no evidence to suggest that this leads such people to care or do less about those who are starving, or racism, or torture. What may happen here is that those who object that tolerance leads to moral indifferentism take tolerance, especially dispositional tolerance, about some things as being in itself evidence of moral decline or indolence.[41]

In reply to the objection that cultivating dispositional tolerance involves an unacceptable predetermination of character, we could point out that all education can be seen in this light; to say we should not attempt to influence children's values is to propose abandoning education. Equally, I can think of no reason for concluding that developing dispositional tolerance constitutes any greater assault, if 'assault' be the right term, on a child's future autonomy than the development of other moral dispositions.[42] Possibly some who raise this objection are not actually objecting to predetermination as such, but to what we encourage children to be tolerant towards. So what we might be faced with here could be a variation of the previous objection. In which case the debate is not about the unacceptability of predetermination, but about whether some things should be tolerated.

Concerning deliberative tolerance, it may be objected that where teachers concern themselves with this, even if they are not encouraging children to dislike and disapprove, they are not attempting to change children's attitudes and prejudices. Consequently, or so the argument goes, fostering this kind of tolerance, as was mentioned earlier, is only tackling the effects of a problem, not the problem itself, which is disliking and disapproving in the first place. But, it will be insisted, we should tackle the racist child not only at the level of his deeds, but also at the level of his judgements, feelings and opinions.

In response we could draw attention to what has already been argued about deliberative tolerance and change of attitude or becoming less certain. Where a teacher is trying to get children to be deliberatively tolerant, there will be a situation or range of situations in which, because of dislike or disapproval, those children are either not being tolerant or are likely not to be tolerant. What the teacher could then do is to get the children to deliberate about the situation or situations in question in an attempt to change the children's attitudes or in an attempt to get them to be less sure or certain about where they stand. In such cases, the teacher is not agreeing with or condoning the children's attitudes or treating those attitudes as some acceptable given. Admittedly where a teacher finds nothing wrong in a pupil's general attitude, but still tries to get the pupil to be tolerant or more tolerant, there is acceptance, but we must not think that there is such acceptance in all cases where teachers endeavour to promote deliberative tolerance. As for claims about simply dealing with effects, there are times when this may be the only remaining strategy, but we should not abandon other strategies without a full exploration.

As well as defending the promotion of dispositional and deliberative tolerance, we also need to emphasise that there need be no conflict between attempts to promote these kinds of tolerance. No doubt there will be occasions when the need to promote deliberative tolerance may indicate a failure to develop dispositional tolerance in a certain area, but the point to stress is that there is no incompatibility here. Moreover, in encountering new situations, people are often confronted by cases and problems to which their dispositions are not geared. This is why deliberative tolerance can play an important role even in the lives of people who are dispositionally tolerant in various areas. In brief, then, in cultivating tolerance, teachers must not concentrate all their efforts into developing dispositions.

What of the objection raised at the outset that in considering the desirability of developing tolerance we should consider those who are treated tolerantly, for won't they feel not only that they are being thought badly of, but also that they are being permitted to do or be what they want only as the result of someone's forbearance? If this is so, then tolerance can hardly pave the way for fraternalism or for being accepted for what one is. In reply I would argue, as I did in the first section, that there can be tolerance – what I would call dispositional tolerance – without those who are tolerant disapproving or having a negative attitude towards those they treat tolerantly. Those Roman Catholics, for instance, who find greater tolerance in England than they knew in parts of Northern Ireland may well be encountering tolerance *without* disapproval or dislike. There can in fact be tolerance with acceptance and fraternalism. Even deliberative tolerance need not end up involving disapproval or dislike, for deliberation can lead to a change of attitude.

All of which leads to the conclusion that there can be tolerance without its upsetting those to whom that tolerance extends. This is why tolerance does not have to be kept secret – it can speak its name – though it may carry an element of self-congratulation which is why we may feel it is better practised than talked about. Being told 'We're very tolerant here' may well mean that you can carry on doing whatever prompted the remark; and it need not imply that the 'we' in question disapprove of or dislike whatever prompted the remark. Therefore, it need not be or sound patronising, but it can sound self-congratulatory.

At this juncture it might be insisted, first, that even under my analysis, to talk of tolerance carries the implication that some people had, have or are likely to have a negative attitude with regard to something, which means that talk of tolerance implies unacceptance or the likelihood of such from some quarter. Second, even under my analysis, there can be dispositional tolerance which does involve a negative attitude, but which is overruled by some general principle, and deliberative tolerance where there is dislike or disapproval but where other considerations win the day.

In reply, we could accept both points but wonder what hinges on them. Concerning the first, if it is being suggested that we should drop a concern with tolerance because it implies actual or likely opposition from some quarter, then isn't this being oversensitive? In fact it is often salutary to keep reminding ourselves just how intolerantly some groups have been treated. As for the second matter, while agreeing there can be cases of tolerance involving negative attitudes, this does not mean that teachers who are concerned with trying to get children to be tolerant need condone or approve of their children's attitudes. However, if attention is being drawn to this matter because it is thought we should have no educational aims which might accommodate negative attitudes, then this is an extraordinary one-sided view of education. Education is not just a process in which we learn to judge and assess what is right and good and worthy of approval, but also what is bad and wrong.

Turning to another of the objections raised at the outset, that cultivating tolerance amongst the powerless is at best pointless, at worst a thinly disguised attempt to ensure subservience, we might start our response by drawing attention to our account of the power condition. Intolerance, we can stress, is not the preserve of those with the power to coerce; those with the power to insult and besmirch can also be intolerant. Consequently, the cultivation of tolerance amongst the seemingly powerless is not as pointless as it may at first appear. As for subservience, this very much depends on what people are tolerant about, and I can see no reason for accepting that many of the things we may encourage children to be tolerant about will lead to their becoming meek or readily oppressable adults; and if someone thought that by encouraging, say, religious tolerance, people would cease to be concerned about inflation, the cost of living or health provision, one might seriously wonder about the quality of his armchair sociology or the sample for his market research. If we encouraged girls to tolerate boys' boorish behaviour, we could be on the way to developing humble women who 'know their place', but what this supports is the point we have been making; what matters here is what you encourage people to be tolerant about. No doubt some Marcusians will insist that whatever kind of tolerance is encouraged, this reflects well on the political system in which there is such encouragement, which makes people more humble and gives the system more power to oppress.[43] But surely freedoms and allowances in some areas may well fail to placate those who are dissatisfied with their systems of government for other reasons. And if Marcusians were to accept their own ideas, would they cease advancing them, lest their being able to do so testified to the tolerance of the systems they opposed?[44]

The final objection we mentioned at the outset was that we need to develop respect rather than tolerance, the implication being that we should set our sights higher than tolerance. But what is meant by 'respect' in this context? The principle of respect for persons, as discussed by philosophers, seems to involve certain minimal rights, such as the right not to have one's autonomy violated by, say, indoctrination or brainwashing, and the right to have one's views considered and not dismissed out of hand.[45] This principle, however, does not confer immunity from criticism or render one free from having one's views thought of as silly, and those who subscribe to this principle are certainly not committed to liking or not disapproving what people think and do and are. This is why, when we are urged to respect other people, what seems involved is some stronger principle than that of respect for persons, and something more demanding than tolerance. By extension, when we are asked to respect other people's views or cultures, it seems that we are being asked to be more than tolerant towards those views and their expression and those cultures and their practices. With this in mind, consider Berlin's account of where Mill stood regarding tolerance and respect:

[Mill] asked us not necessarily to respect the views of others – very far from it – only to try to understand and tolerate them; only tolerate; disapprove, think ill of, if need be mock or despise, but tolerate ... [For] without tolerance the conditions for rational criticism, rational condemnation, are destroyed. He therefore pleads for reason and toleration at all costs. To understand is not necessarily to forgive. We may argue, attack, reject, condemn with passion and hatred. But we may not suppress or stifle ...[46]

Here, too, respect is not being viewed in a minimal way, which is why accounts like this may help us see why some people, teachers involved in multicultural education for example, may claim tolerance is not enough. They want a variety of ideas and cultures to be respected, not just treated tolerantly.

In response I would first repeat the point that we can be tolerant without our disapproving or despising or hating or feeling moved to condemn. I would also suggest that some of the attitudes mentioned by Berlin seem to threaten the requirement of equanimity we discussed earlier, which casts into doubt the extent to which this passage deals with dispositional tolerance. There again, we can surely question the consistency of insisting that we should not 'suppress or stifle' while allowing for hateful condemnations, mockery and making public the fact that we despise something. For at some stage outbursts and condemnations become intolerant. Tolerance allows for our thinking something is wrong or foolish and it allows for criticism and for argument, but isn't Mill, under this account, prepared to go beyond what tolerance allows?

Still, those who say we should encourage respect rather than tolerance will have their worst fears aroused by this account and my response will hardly allay their anxieties, precisely because my response allows for tolerance to be compatible with those attitudes and deeds that are incompatible with their view of respect. But what are those who favour such respect recommending? The law of the excluded middle means that if we hold a belief, we are thereby committed to holding that whatever beliefs are inconsistent with what we believe are false and that those who hold those beliefs are mistaken.[47] If a commitment to respect in the enriched sense we are dealing with here eschews thinking of people as holding or cultures as involving mistaken ideas, then such a commitment seems to threaten the very business of holding beliefs. Furthermore, if the position we are examining embodies the claim that no person's or culture's beliefs should be thought of as silly or worthy of criticism, then what we have here is a proposal to abandon much of what anti-racist and anti-sexist education aims to achieve, for to be committed to anti-racism and anti-sexism is to accept that some positions are wrong and are worthy of criticism. In addition, the position we are examining seems to threaten what many will see as a central feature of a liberal society, for such a society, it will be claimed, is not just one where diversity may flourish, but one which will be host to debate an argument. The position we are exploring also threatens one of the central features of a healthy academic life and a primary route towards seeing if ideas are worth retaining. And if some people are silly enough to eschew criticism, presumably, they must accept that my rejection of their stance is above criticism. In short, tolerance may fall short of some people's preferred view of respect, but this is no reason for having reservations about the insufficiencies of tolerance.

Finally in this section let us consider how tolerance might be promoted in and through education. In this connection it might be argued that tolerance is something which is caught rather than taught and because of this schools are unlikely settings for its acquisition. Now whatever one makes of the last part of this argument, what needs stressing is that even if, say, dispositional tolerance is something which we 'catch' from others, it is surely only 'caught' in so far as it is perceived. This means that if a teacher wants his pupils to appreciate that he is being tolerant, he needs to ensure that they can perceive his deeds as those of a tolerant person, not, say, those of a person who is forgetful or unaware of what is happening. As for the claim that tolerance is best caught, some might argue against this and point out that teachers might encourage dispositional tolerance, for instance, by discussing general principles, such as Mill's 'harm' principle, with their pupils, and also by considering whether certain areas of life, such as the religious domain, are ones where the state should not interfere. As for deliberative tolerance, this, as already mentioned, can be encouraged as particular situations arise or look likely to arise, though what may deserve stressing is that where teachers are successful in encouraging deliberative tolerance, this may well be because they have helped develop the disposition of being prepared to consider whether there are good reasons for not interfering with certain things.

Talk of trying to promote tolerance in schools, however, might prompt the idea that its promotion is essentially a secondary goal, the primary goal being to cultivate certain other values and attitudes. According to this line of reasoning it is only when these other values and attitudes are in place that one can proceed to try to develop tolerance. Thus, it may be insisted that it is only when we have pupils who have come to appreciate the importance of punctuality or tidiness that we can proceed to encourage them to be tolerant towards their peers who may be late or untidy. But this line of reasoning is based on the view that those who are tolerant need have negative attitudes. If we reject this view, tolerance, more especially dispositional tolerance, does not have to be seen as a secondary goal, and those concerned with its development do not have to play a waiting game.

CONCLUSION

I began this essay by noting that while tolerance might be seen as occupying an important place in a liberal conception of moral education and in an education for a multicultural society, several objections might be raised against the encouragement and development of tolerance. In order to consider the case for tolerance in more detail I proceeded to examine the nature of tolerance and I was eventually able to indicate ways in which we might respond to those earlier objections. As a result I hope that the case for tolerance, if not free from criticism, can be shown to withstand those criticisms that we have examined.

Yet this paper should not just be seen as a defence of that case. In fact there are two particularly important issues to emerge from this inquiry which can be viewed independently of an argument for tolerance, even though one of them has played a significant role in the development of our argument. The first of these is that, contrary to the accepted stances in this area, tolerance can be separated from negative attitudes in the sense that the tolerant person need not dislike, disapprove of or feel disgusted by what he is tolerant towards. This is why my inquiries should encourage people to look at tolerance afresh. With regard to education, this means that those concerned with encouraging children to be tolerant need not feel that they are in effect leaving prejudice or bigotry untouched and merely trying to stop children from acting intolerantly. Those concerned with anti-racism, for instance, need not feel that tolerance will leave in place the very attitudes that they want to change or that it need result in patronising forbearance. Equally, those concerned to develop tolerance need not always feel that they have to wait for other values and attitudes to be acquired before they can make their move.

The second important issue has been the difference between what I have called dispositional tolerance and deliberative tolerance. Since we will no doubt encounter particular situations in life where, though a tolerant response may be in order, we may lack the appropriate inclination or disposition, both kinds of tolerance warrant encouragement. What one often finds is that some people seem to be dispositionally tolerant whereas others, who may often act in similar ways, or maybe we should say often are inactive in similar situations, are deliberatively tolerant. It is tempting to suggest that this depends on the personalities of the people in question, on the kind of people they are, but of course what we are talking about here are constituents of personalities.[48]

NOTES

1. For a consideration of liberal values see K.F. Koerner, *Liberalism and Its Critics* (London: Croom Helm, 1985), ch. 6.
2. E. Hulmes, *Education and Cultural Diversity* (London: Longman, 1989), p. 18.
3. *Education for All: A Brief Guide to the Main Issues of the Report* (London: HMSO, 1985), p. 10.
4. I. Berlin, 'Nationalism: past neglect and present power', in H. Hardy (ed.), *Isaiah Berlin: Against the Current* (Oxford: Oxford University Press, 1989), p. 333.
5. S. Mendus, *Toleration and the Limits of Liberalism* (London: Macmillan, 1989), p. 8.
6. I. Berlin, 'John Stuart Mill and the meaning of life', in I. Berlin, *Four Essays on Liberty* (Oxford: Oxford University Press, 1969), p. 173.

7.   See M. Billig et al., *Ideological Dilemmas* (London: Sage, 1988), ch. 7.

8.   Voltaire, *Treatise on Toleration*, quoted in D.J. Manning, *Liberalism* (London: Dent, 1976), p. 47.

9.   A.L. Goodhart, 'Tolerance and the Law', *Robert Waley Cohen Memorial Lecture, 1955* (London: Council of Christians and Jews, 1955), p. 11.

10. See H. Marcuse, 'Repressive tolerance', in R.P. Wolff, B. Moore, and H. Marcuse, (eds), *A Critique of Pure Tolerance* (Boston: Beacon Press, 1969).

11. See P.P. Nicholson, 'Toleration as a moral ideal', in J. Horton and S. Mendus (eds), *Aspects of Toleration* (London: Methuen, 1985), p. 160.

12. J. Raz, *The Morality of Freedom* (Oxford: Oxford University Press, 1986) p. 403.

13. Nicholson (1985), p. 161.

14. See Lord Scarman, 'Toleration and the law', in: S. Mendus and D. Edwards (eds), *On Toleration* (Oxford: Oxford University Press, 1987).

15. Since this part of my paper marks the beginning of an inquiry into whether tolerance involves disapproval or whether it might also involve dislike without disapproval, my talk of attitudes might be thought to contain an element of prejudgement. After all, some emotivists stress that moral disapproval (and approval) are *attitudinal*, though I do not think they talk of likes and dislikes in this way. Furthermore, to disapprove is to hold a belief, and beliefs, unlike our dislikes, are propositional *attitudes*. However, as will become clear presently, there is no hidden preference in my talk of attitudes or about the attitudinal condition. I have merely tried to find a brief way of talking about a condition which some say is a matter of disapproval and others, who favour a more inclusive account (see below), say is a matter of either disapproval or dislike.

16. P. Johnson, 'As long as he needs me? toleration and moral character', in J. Horton and P. Nicholson (eds), *Toleration: Philosophy and Practice* (Aldershot: Avebury Press, 1992). See also Berlin (1969), p. 184.

17. E. Gilson, 'Dogmatism and tolerance', an address to the students and faculty of Rutgers University (New Brunswick: Rutgers University Press, 1952), pp. 7–8.

18. R. Livingstone, 'Tolerance in theory and practice', *First Robert Waley Cohen Memorial Lecture* (London: Council for Christians and Jews, 1954) p. 6. See also J.F. Stephen, *Liberty, Equality, Fraternity* (Cambridge: Cambridge University Press, 1967), p. 108.

19. See M. Warnock, 'The limits of toleration', in S. Mendus and D. Edwards (eds), *On Toleration*, op. cit., p. 125; and Mendus (1989), pp. 9–18.

20. See M. Warnock (1987), p. 125.

21. See Mendus (1989), p. 17.

22. Nicholson (1985), p. 160. See also D.D. Raphael, 'Toleration, choice and liberty', *Government and Opposition*, 6, 1971; and D.D. Raphael, 'The intolerable,' in S. Mendus (ed.), *Justifying Toleration: Conceptual and Historical Perspectives* (Cambridge: Cambridge University Press, 1988), p. 139.

23. Raz (1986), p. 403.

24. A. Weale, 'Toleration, individual differences and respect for persons', in J. Horton and S. Mendus (eds), *Aspects of Toleration*, op. cit., p. 19.

25. If Weale is to be seen as arguing for 'a more liberal climate' where there is the 'general practice of toleration in sexual matters', isn't he to be seen as arguing for a climate of *acceptance* rather than one of antipathy where this antipathy does not manifest itself in intolerant condemnations, behaviour and laws?

26. These considerations draw our attention to the relationship between tolerance and consequentialism. Where it is argued that we should treat something tolerantly, as when it is claimed that a practice *causes no harm*, though trying to stop it would cause much suffering, then, from a consequentialist point of view, is it not also

being argued, not just that we should not try to stop it, but also that we were mistaken in judging the practice in question to be wrong in the first place?

27.   D. Carr, *Educating the Virtues* (London: Routledge, 1991), p. 200. Carr also observes: 'having to put a lot of effort into being charitable or sympathetic may well be a clear sign that the virtues in question are not wholly present', op. cit., p. 208.

28.   Mendus (1989), p. 8.

29.   Raz (1986), p. 402.

30.   See Marcuse (1969). Raz insists: 'to claim to act out of toleration is to claim that one's action is justified, though in fact it may not be' (Raz (1989), p. 402). But we need more than this to identify the kinds of reason which do not exclude tolerance. Where I hold back in the expectation that someone will receive greater retribution than I could inflict, I might be sincere in my claim that my action is justified, but I am not being tolerant.

31.   Koerner (1985), p. 158.

32.   See Aristotle, *The Nicomachean Ethics*, Bk. II, 4.

33.   See A. Schwartz (1979) 'Aristotle on education and choice', *Educational Theory* 29, 1979, 101–4. Perhaps the problem we find in Aristotle, of how we can learn to act as the virtuous person does, has become lost in what is now regarded as 'the paradox of moral education', for this 'paradox' involves a conflict between psychoanalytic perceptions of childhood and moral agency. See R.S. Peters, 'Reason and habit: the paradox of moral education,' in W.R. Niblett (ed.) *Moral Education in a Changing Society* (London: Faber, 1963). See also P. Gardner, 'The paradox of moral education: a reassessment', *Journal of Philosophy of Education*, 19, 1985.

34.   We may talk of someone being disposed to look on the bright side of life because there are many opportunities for his doing so, including, possibly, his crucifixion, but we cannot talk of someone being disposed to look on the bright side of just one particular event, such as his crucifixion.

35.   See Livingstone (1954), p. 7.

36.   See R.M. Hare, *Moral Thinking: Its Levels, Method and Point* (Oxford: Oxford University Press, 1981), chs. 2 and 3. See note 38 below.

37.   See Hare (1981), pp. 49–53. See note 38 below.

38.   I should point out that I neither agree with Hare's claim that the nature of moral reasoning requires us to be preference utilitarians nor do I favour preference utilitarianism as an acceptable normative theory. Consequently, I am in no way suggesting that in justifying our general principles, resolving conflicts between them or in deciding what to do about difficult cases that fall under our general principles, we either *must* or *should* engage in preference utilitarian calculations.

39.   Yet clearly some people are too tolerant by far. One such person, as Steve Johnson has pointed out to me, is described in Thorne Smith's book *The Jovial Ghosts*: 'Steven's mind was so tolerant that he could have attended a lynching every day without becoming critical'. One of the interesting points about this remark, which is why I am very grateful for having it brought to my attention, is just how difficult it is to reconcile this view of Steven with restricted accounts of the attitudinal condition. Moreover, I take it that what underlies this remark is not that Steven disliked but did not disapprove, rather that one can have a tolerant mind towards certain things *without* having a negative attitude towards those things. But notice also that what Steven is tolerant towards is what others would or would be likely to be critical of.

40.   Just as people can be tolerant towards some things without being or becoming tolerant about many, so people can be intolerant about some things without being

intolerant about many. On this point Steve Johnson has drawn my attention to an observation in John Mortimer's *Two Stars for Comfort*, Act I, Scene II: 'Eddy was a tremendously tolerant person, but he wouldn't put up with the Welsh'.

41. Do those with an *idée fixe* about the evil of pornography see tolerance in this area as itself evidence of moral atrophy? And, despite lack of evidence, don't they insist that such tolerance leads to further evils? See B. Williams (ed.), *Obscenity and Film Censorship: An Abridgement of the Williams Report* (Cambridge: Cambridge University Press, 1979, 1981), esp. ch. 6.

42. On the relationship between influence and autonomy, see K. Strike 'Autonomy and control: toward a theory of legitimate influence', in D. Nyberg (ed.), *The Philosophy of Open Education*, (London: Routledge & Kegan Paul, 1975), pp. 182–8.

43. See Marcuse (1969).

44. For further difficulties within the Marcusian position on repressive tolerance, see N.E. Bowie and R.L. Simon, *The Individual and the Political Order: An Introduction to Social and Political Philosophy* (Englewood Cliffs: Prentice-Hall, 1977), pp. 178–181.

45. But it has to be admitted, as Weale observes, 'The concept of respect for persons is of itself somewhat vague', (1985), p. 28. See also ibid, pp. 28–34; and S. Lukes, *Individualism* (Oxford: Blackwell, 1973), pp. 125–7, 131–3 and 148–9.

46. Berlin (1969), p. 184.

47. See P. Gardner, 'Religious upbringing and the liberal ideal of religious autonomy', *Journal of Philosophy of Education* 22, 1988, 93–4. See also P. Gardner 'Propositional attitudes and multicultural education, or believing others are mistaken', in J. Horton and P. Nicholson (eds), *Toleration: Philosophy and Practice* (Aldershot: Avebury Press, 1992).

48. I would like to thank Geraldine Herrick, Terry McLaughlin, Sean Neill, A. Phillips Griffiths and Paul Standish for their comments on several of the ideas touched upon in this paper. I am particularly indebted to Steve Johnson and Derek Pope for their detailed and perceptive comments on many of the matters I raised in earlier drafts of this paper.

7 The *Satanic Verses* Controversy: A Brief Introduction

John Horton

On 26 September 1988 Viking/Penguin published in the United Kingdom *The Satanic Verses*, a new novel by Salman Rushdie.[1] The novel was keenly awaited in the literary world where Rushdie was regarded as among the most inventive and ambitious novelists of his generation. He had already won the Booker Prize, probably the most prestigious literary award in Britain, for his second published novel *Midnight's Children*, in 1981.[2] His subsequent novel, *Shame*, was also short-listed for the prize, though to Rushdie's undisguised dismay it did not win, and he was internationally recognised as a novelist of the first importance.[3] However, Rushdie was also a controversial writer – both his novels and his essays and critical writings had generated heated debate – and even before it was published it was known that the new novel would create more than a literary stir, though the extent of the controversy it eventually provoked could not have been anticipated by anyone.

Rushdie's background is an interesting and unusual one, and far from irrelevant to the controversy that was to envelop *The Satanic Verses*.[4] He was born in Bombay on 19 June 1947, only two months prior to Indian independence from Britain. His parents were prosperous and devout Muslims, who remained in Bombay after the partition of India and Pakistan. His father was a successful businessman who had been educated in Law at Cambridge University. Rushdie was the only son though he had three sisters. His experience of Bombay clearly had an enormous influence on Rushdie. He was one of the privileged in a city where millions were destitute, but also a member of the Muslim minority in a city dominated by Hindus and where religious violence was an intermittent reality and a constant threat. As a boy he was brought up to speak both Urdu and English; he went to an English mission school; and in his own words 'was brought up in a very Anglophile and Anglocentric way'. It was expected, therefore, that he would complete his education in England, which he did first at Rugby, the exclusive public school, and then in 1965, he went, as his father had done to Cambridge, having won an Exhibition.

Rushdie's early experience of England was traumatic. He was totally unprepared for the ingrained and routine racism with which he was received and continued to be treated by his fellows at Rugby. In consequence, after completing his schooling, Rushdie had not wanted to return to England and it was only under protest and his father's assertion of parental pressure that he went to Cambridge at all. Moreover, while he was at Rugby his parents had moved to Karachi in Pakistan, separating him further from his childhood in Bombay. In fact Cambridge proved to be a much less disagreeable experience than he had expected. He read History at King's College and was active in the Footlights Club, the University's drama society. Though Cambridge too had its snobbery and exclusiveness, Rushdie responded much more positively to both the variety of university life and the relative diversity of the student population. In addition his time as an undergraduate coincided with the emergence of the counter-culture, of hippies, drugs and flower-power; and anti-Establishment feeling, increasingly focused around opposition to the expanding war in Vietnam, became fashionable.

It seems that Rushdie experienced his time at Cambridge as largely liberating but it also created some problems for him. While at Cambridge he had undertaken a historical investigation of Islam and it afforded him the opportunity to read many books which would not have been available to him in India or Pakistan. (It was at this time that he first read of the so-called 'Satanic Verses' which were to be so important later.) Partly as a consequence of this study of it, and no doubt under other influences too, Rushdie became highly sceptical of his Islamic faith. This produced some strain in relations with his family, and on his return to Pakistan he found its Islamic codes increasingly alien and restrictive. He came to feel ill at ease there and his discomfort clearly showed. He was viewed with some suspicion, even by many of his friends, as one who had been corrupted by Western atheism and materialism. In consequence Rushdie moved to London and opted for British citizenship. He initially adopted a fairly bohemian lifestyle, later marrying an Englishwoman, Clarissa Luard, with whom he had a son. At first he supported himself mostly by acting in the fringe theatre, later by working as a part-time copy-editor for Ogilvy and Mather; and he also began to write.

Rushdie's first published novel was *Grimus* in 1975, though it was not the first novel he had attempted to write; he had earlier abandoned *The Book of the Fir*, a novel about a successful Muslim holy man. *Grimus* was not a success on its first appearance. It failed to win the Victor Gollancz science fiction competition for which it had been entered and the reviews in the English literary press were almost universally poor. However, when, four years later, the book was published in the US the reviews were much more positive. In the interim he had written another novel, *Madam Rama*, about the movie industry – as befits a man from Bombay, Rushdie is a great film enthusiast – which he decided not to try to publish. He then began work on a novel about India which was to become in its final form *Midnight's Children*. The title referred to those Indians born in the first hour after Indian independence and the novel itself was an enormously ambitious undertaking. It is also in part a coming to terms by Rushdie with his complex cultural heritage, a critical but affectionate portrait of his Bombay and an exploration of his own identity; though of course it cannot be reduced to these biographical concerns. It mixes realism with fantasy, real characters such as Mrs Gandhi and some of his own family with entirely fictional creations, and historical events with imaginary ones. The narrator is partly himself and partly not; but with hindsight the closing words of the novel seem uncannily prescient of his own situation after the *fatwa*: 'it is the privilege and the curse of midnight's children to be both masters and victims of their times, to forsake privacy and be sucked into the annihilating whirlpool of the multitudes, and to be unable to live or die in peace.'

It is almost impossible not to be impressed by *Midnight's Children* with its exuberant narratives and constant inventiveness, even if at times it is a bit too absorbed by its own cleverness, and its reception was in marked contrast to that of *Grimus*. It was instantly hailed as 'brilliant', 'marvellous', 'magnificent', 'a *tour de force*' and in the *New York Review of Books* as 'one of the most important novels to come out of the English-speaking world in this generation'. Moreover, not only was the novel a great critical success it was also a great commercial one too. In a very short space of time, in almost fairy-tale fashion, Rushdie had been transformed from a struggling aspirant novelist to one of the leading figures not merely of literary London but the international cultural scene. However, Rushdie's penchant for provoking political controversy was evident even at this time. *Midnight's Children* was also an intensely political novel and Rushdie's treatment in it of Mrs Gandhi, the then Prime Minister of India, was extremely hostile and disparaging. In fact Mrs Gandhi sued Rushdie and his publisher, Jonathan Cape, about one passage which suggested that her son Sanjay had accused her of ill-treating her late husband. Mrs Gandhi won, securing a public apology and the withdrawal of the libellous passage from all future editions, in addition to Rushdie and Jonathan Cape having to pay all the costs.

Several events, some personal and some public, seemed to stimulate Rushdie's next novel *Shame* which, perhaps not surprisingly, focused on Pakistan, his second home on the Indian sub-continent. However, to describe it as his second home may be to suggest an affection for Pakistan which Rushdie had never possessed. As was mentioned earlier his time in Pakistan had not been particularly happy and this was to be reflected in the new novel which was consistently more bitter and savage than *Midnight's Children*. Both Presidents Bhutto and Zia, thinly disguised in the novel, and the most important of Pakistan's recent political leaders, were subjected to Rushdie's biting satire and the novel was notably more harshly critical of the country it recreated. (Though *Shame* was never formally banned in Pakistan its publication there was known to be risky and it was principally available only in a pirated edition.) However, this darkening of tone seemed to have little effect on the reception of the novel which received similarly glowing reviews to *Midnight's Children*. It was also another resounding commercial success, despite its failure to win the Booker Prize. Moreover Rushdie, who had always been deeply interested in politics, became an increasingly prominent political figure. For example, he spent three weeks in

Nicaragua as a guest of the Sandinista Association of Cultural Workers, and his subsequent reflections in *The Jaguar Smile: A Nicaraguan Journey*[5] contained a fierce attack on American foreign policy in that country. He was an enthusiastic supporter of Charter 88, and he was frequently and volubly critical of Mrs Thatcher – herself an object of his literary satire – and her Conservative governments in Britain.

Rushdie was also a trenchant opponent of the ever-increasing political power of Islam and its leaders, and Islam was to be very important to his next novel, *The Satanic Verses*, though in no sense is it simply a novel about Islam. While literary interpretation is always difficult and often controversial there is widespread agreement that the novel is centrally concerned with questions of identity and modernity. The book links the experience of the migrant with the loss of certainty and moral absolutism characteristic of the modern age in a narrative which champions doubt against certainty, and particularly the certainties of the Qur'an. Rushdie himself has described it as 'a love-song to our mongrel selves' though his own pronouncements about the book, his intentions in writing it and what it is about, have been various and sometimes conflicting, and therefore need to be treated with some scepticism. However, it would be wrong to make much of that since even at the best of times authors are often unreliable commentators on their own work, and many of Rushdie's utterances have been made at anything but the best of times. There seems little doubt though that he expected the novel to be controversial and that he was well aware that it would be received with widespread hostility in the Muslim world. The publishers had been warned by their reader of likely trouble even before publication. But there is similarly little doubt that Rushdie was taken aback by the extent of the controversy it generated even prior to the *fatwa* (which he most certainly did not anticipate).

It is tempting, and might be thought appropriate here, to reproduce some of the passages in *The Satanic Verses* which have been found most offensive by Muslims. However, this is a temptation which ought properly to be resisted. The offending passages cannot simply be taken from their context since that context is not merely essential to Rushdie's defence of his novel but to the meaning of the passages. For example, most of the passages which have given greatest offence relate to the dreams of Gibreel, one of the central characters, and to ignore that they are dreams would be to misrepresent what is being depicted in the novel. Of course this is not to claim that because the book is a novel it cannot be blasphemous or offensive: it is to accept that some passages will certainly be so if detached from the novel and simply presented as straightforward assertions or insults. Nor does it settle what difference context will make. It should be noted that Rushdie has himself explicitly repudiated any defence along the lines of 'after all, it's only a novel', and analogously it would not be enough to say of the offending passages that, 'after all, they are only dreams'. Any evaluation of the meaning or merits of the novel must presuppose a reading of it, though as is evidenced by the different responses of Muslim and liberal Western readers there is unlikely to be any agreement about either its meaning or its merits.

Some Muslims see *The Satanic Verses* simply as a piece of hate literature – a gratuitous vilification of the Prophet and a deliberate insult to all Muslims. Rushdie and his defenders have emphatically and consistently denied what he calls 'the "insults and abuse" accusation'. Yet there have also been more sophisticated critiques of *The Satanic Verses*. One of the best-documented of these is by Ziauddin Sardar and Merryl Wyn Davies in their *Distorted Imagination: Lessons from the Rushdie Affair*.[6] They argue in some detail that *The Satanic Verses* 'fits neatly into, indeed is a logical culmination of the well-known tradition of Orientalism'. The term 'Orientalism' was coined by Edward Said to characterise the process by which the Western scholarly tradition has systematically distorted the understanding of the Orient and Islam to emphasise both its 'otherness' and its inferiority as a means of buttressing Western domination. According to Sardar and Davies *The Satanic Verses* – 'the colonial picture postcard of modernist fiction' – reinforces and perpetuates Western ignorance and prejudice about Islam, which for Muslims 'reveals the abject poverty of an historical legacy that insists on demeaning their collective history, themselves and all that they hold sacred'.[7] From this perspective, that the novel should be so lauded by Western literary critics – it was again nominated for the Booker Prize and won the Whitbread Prize for Fiction in addition to the many enthusiastic reviews – only added to the insult and confirmed Muslims in their view of Western hostility towards them.

It is more than a little ironic that Rushdie, himself of Muslim origin and a virulent critic of Western neo-colonialism, should be accused of furthering the distortions of Orientalism. However, whatever the merits of that charge, there is no doubt that the fact that Rushdie was a Muslim has itself been an important aspect of the controversy over *The Satanic Verses*. It is most unlikely that if the book had been written by a Westerner it would have generated the same level of hostility among Muslims or led to the *fatwa*. Of course they would not have liked it any more but the subsequent reaction would not have had about it the sense of betrayal that has marked much of the Muslim response to Rushdie. Indeed in an attempt to try to convey the nature of their feelings to bemused Westerners some Muslims have likened Rushdie's action in publishing the novel to an act of treachery, not unlike that of a national traitor in time of war. Yet it is difficult to know quite how to respond to this kind of claim. On the one hand it does help to convey an understanding of the intensity of the Muslim response, perhaps especially to a secular audience.[8] On the other hand it seems to imply a relationship between a religious community and its members which is no longer acceptable in the West: a church may expel or excommunicate a member but only from that church. Moreover, it is a familiar feature of Western experience, and has been for some time, that it is often former believers who are the fiercest and most implacable opponents of a religion, and their right to oppose is widely thought to be worth protecting. Some of the essays in this volume attach considerable importance to the good of cultural membership and its relationship to self-respect but the Rushdie affair brings out just how cautiously such considerations need to be treated.

It is impossible to catalogue all of even the most important events which followed from the publication of *The Satanic Verses*. In Britain some Muslim leaders almost immediately called for a ban on the book and for Rushdie to be prosecuted for libelling Islam. Prime Minister Margaret Thatcher replied that there was no legal basis for action against the book or Rushdie. The first significant Muslim demonstration against the book appears to have taken place in Bolton in early December 1988 when a copy of *The Satanic Verses* was publicly burnt. However, this event did not receive any national publicity and it was not until a similar but larger demonstration took place in Bradford on 14 January 1989 that the issue really began to receive any prominence in the British media. (Predictably when the press did begin to take an interest in the issue its contribution was, with a few honourable exceptions, mostly ill-informed and provocatively tendentious.) Later in the month there was a major demonstration in Hyde Park to petition Viking/Penguin, the publishers, to withdraw the novel, but without success. On the whole it must be said that the response of the publishers and especially Rushdie himself to Muslim protests was uncompromising.[9] The book also had an immediate international impact, being effectively banned in India within a few days of its publication in England. In the following weeks the novel was additionally banned in South Africa, Pakistan, Saudi Arabia, Egypt, Somalia, Bangladesh, Sudan, Malaysia, Indonesia and Qatar, and there were numerous protests by Muslim groups around the world.

The crucial month in many ways, however, was February 1989. It began with the British Home Secretary, Douglas Hurd, announcing that there were no plans to reform the blasphemy laws to take account of Muslim objections to the unfairness of the existing law. On the 12th six people were killed in Islamabad in rioting provoked by the novel and the following day there was another death and many were injured in a riot in Kashmir. But the event which was to dramatically change Rushdie's life and radically transform the whole situation took place on 14 February. On that day the Ayatollah Khomeini of Iran proclaimed a *fatwa* against Salman Rushdie informing 'all the fearless Muslims in the world that the author of the book entitled *The Satanic Verses*, which has been compiled, printed and published in opposition to Islam, the Prophet and the Qur'an, as well as the publishers, who are aware of the contents, have been sentenced to death. I call on all zealous Muslims to execute them quickly, whenever they find them, so that no one will dare to insult Islamic sanctity. Whoever is killed on this path will be regarded as a martyr'. The following day was declared a national day of mourning in Iran for those Muslims who had died in the disturbances surrounding Rushdie's book and there was a massive demonstration outside the British Embassy. All Viking/Penguin books were banned from Iran and Hojatalislam

Hassan Sanai, head of a religious foundation in Iran, offered a reward of over two and a half million dollars to any Iranian, and one million dollars to any non-Iranian, who succeeded in assassinating Rushdie. Reportedly these sums were soon doubled.

There followed considerable support for Khomeini's *fatwa* among Muslim leaders across the world, though significantly the Saudi-dominated Islamic Conference Organisation did not endorse it, and demonstrations against the book continued. In Bombay ten people were killed and about fifty seriously injured in anti-Rushdie riots ten days after the *fatwa*. A brief attempt to defuse the situation through Rushdie's issuing a (qualified) apology to Muslims came to nothing when the apology was rejected as insufficient and the *fatwa* confirmed. The whole affair had become an international political event and Rushdie's ability to influence it was now very slight. It seems indisputable that the *fatwa* and subsequent happenings were increasingly determined by larger political priorities.

The precise status of a *fatwa* within Islam is controversial among Muslims. It is unclear, for example, whether once issued a *fatwa* can be withdrawn or set aside. It has further been claimed that Khomeini was acting exclusively as a religious leader and that the *fatwa* has no political standing. Whatever the merits of this latter claim, and it seems to run contrary to many Muslims' insistence on the necessary interconnectedness of the political and the religious within Islam, there can be no doubt as to the *fatwa's* gravity. While the exact status of the *fatwa* must be a very important issue for Muslims there seems no reason to doubt that it effectively made Rushdie a target for assassination, whether officially sponsored by the Iranian government or through an isolated act of an aggrieved Muslim. It was no paranoid fantasy of Rushdie's or politically motivated exaggeration by the British government to believe that his life was under serious threat. As a result Rushdie went into hiding with police protection, a situation which still pertains at the time of writing, over three years after the *fatwa* was issued and after the death of Khomeini himself. Indeed, without being too pessimistic, it is quite hard to see how Rushdie is ever likely to be free of fear of possible assassination by Muslim extremists whatever the position of the Iranian government.

The impact of the *fatwa*, though, was not limited to its dramatic consequences for Rushdie personally. As mentioned earlier, it also transformed the nature of the affair into an international incident. Diplomatic relations between Britain and Iran were broken off and both the European Community and the USA provided extensive support for Britain. The affair became part of a political struggle between Iran and the West and of the power struggle within Islam between Iran and Saudi-Arabia. However, subsequent international developments though obviously very important have less relevance to the issues with which this book is concerned. In so far as a range of additional issues about non-interference in the domestic affairs of another state and state-sponsored terrorism are raised, they are not the focus of discussion here.

Another, more relevant, effect of the *fatwa* was, not surprisingly, to significantly alter the terms in which *The Satanic Verses* affair was discussed. Most obviously in Britain and the West it shifted sympathy much more in Rushdie's direction. While Rushdie had not lacked supporters prior to the *fatwa*, especially amongst liberal opinion and the literati, many had felt that while Rushdie was entitled to publish what he did, he was not deserving of much sympathy for the animosity he had provoked. At its simplest this took the form of, 'if you insult people you cannot be surprised if they do not respond kindly to it', while from a broader perspective it was thought that Rushdie's book could only have an adverse effect on race relations in Britain (and perhaps jeopardise the safety of British hostages then held in the Lebanon under Iranian control). However, after the *fatwa* it undoubtedly became more difficult to criticise Rushdie or the book without being interpreted as providing support for the *fatwa*.[10] In short the *fatwa* polarised discussion about *The Satanic Verses*, for not only did it shift non-Muslim opinion behind Rushdie, it made it extremely difficult for moderate Muslims to dissociate themselves from the more militant representatives of Islam. Indeed it took extraordinary courage for Muslims to speak out against the *fatwa*, especially after two moderate *imams* were shot in Brussels, and though many Muslims have voiced criticism, it is difficult to assess how far Muslims opposed to the *fatwa* have been understandably cowed into submission by fear of the consequences of not being seen to support it.

The subsequent history of the Rushdie affair is not without its interest but there would be little point in trying to chart it in the context of the concerns of this book. Most of the immediate tensions, both international and within Britain, have lessened: diplomatic relations between Britain and Iran have been restored; the hostages have been released; and public protests against *The Satanic Verses* are fairly rare. Yet Rushdie himself remains in hiding, though making a few more 'public' appearances, and the *fatwa* remains in force. The book has not been banned in Britain or most of the Western world, and though Viking/Penguin did not publish one, a paperback version has appeared in Britain and America, published by a syndicate of anonymous US publishers in 1992. Rushdie has written and published a fairy-tale, *Haroun and the Sea of Stories*, which has proved utterly uncontroversial though well reviewed.[11] He has also published *Imaginary Homelands*, a collection of his occasional non-fiction writings, which includes 'In Good Faith' and 'Is Nothing Sacred?' his two principal defences of *The Satanic Verses* and the role of the creative writer.[12] Those readers interested in Rushdie's self-justification should consult those two essays in particular. More surprisingly perhaps, Rushdie appears to have effected a very partial and uncertain *rapprochement* with Islam and his Muslim heritage though not of course with its more militant leaders or the 'Actually Existing Islam' of Muslim states such as Iran. However, the predominant feeling is that there is at best a weary if uneasy truce rather than any very deep meeting of minds over *The Satanic Verses*.

The long-term effects of the Rushdie affair on relations between Muslims and the dominant community in Britain cannot yet be established. It seems to have helped Muslims find a voice in British politics, though also made more manifest differences within the Muslim community.[13] Whether this will be a prelude to a series of future confrontations, for example over education and family law, is as yet uncertain. However, the affair has exacerbated racial tensions; and that the very name 'Rushdie' should have been used to taunt the supporters of Pakistan at recent Test cricket matches is a depressing irony, which will not be lost on Rushdie himself.

However, these later events are largely irrelevant to an understanding of the various dimensions of the Rushdie affair which were essentially delineated by the middle of 1989. Little that has happened since has introduced new issues or contributed much to the clarification (or indeed resolution) of the old ones. What are these issues?[14] Even this is a matter of controversy but *inter alia* the Rushdie affair is in part about the grounds and limits of free expression; the place of religion in a secular society; the nature of Islamic fundamentalism; the foundations and limits of liberalism; the preservation of cultural identity in a multicultural society; the proper basis of legislation; the social, political and cultural consequences of racism and the colonial heritage; the meaning of novels; and much else besides. Perhaps at the most pressing level it is primarily about the terms on which we are prepared to live together, one with another, whatever our differences of faith, culture and value. Certainly this concern lies at the heart of most of the succeeding essays, which engage more substantively with some of the above issues, and with questions of moral principle for which this chapter has done no more than set the scene.[15]

NOTES

1. Salman Rushdie, *The Satanic Verses* (London: Viking/Penguin, 1988).
2. Salman Rushdie, *Midnight's Children* (London: Jonathan Cape, 1981).
3. Salman Rushdie, *Shame* (London, Jonathan Cape, 1983).
4. The principal sources for the following account of Rushdie's life and the dispute about *The Satanic Verses* are W.J. Weatherby, *Salman Rushdie: Sentenced to Death* (New York: Carroll & Graf, 1990); Lisa Appignanesi and Sara Maitland (eds) *The Rushdie File* (London: Fourth estate, 1989); Malise Ruthven, *A Satanic Affair: Salman Rushdie and the Wrath of Islam*, revised and updated edition (London: Hogarth Press, 1991); Shabbir Akhtar, *Be Careful With Muhammad! The Salman Rushdie Affair* (London, Belleur, 1989); Salman Rushdie, *Imaginary Homelands* (London: Granta, 1991); and various interviews and reports in the *Guardian*, *Independent*, *The Times*, *Observer* and *Independent on Sunday*. It has not seemed appropriate to cite a specific source for every assertion or quotation.
5. Salman Rushdie, *The Jaguar Smile: A Nicaraguan Journey* (London: Picador, 1987).

6. Ziauddin Sardar and Merryl Wyn Davies, *Distorted Imagination: Lessons from the Rushdie Affair* (London: Grey Seal Books, 1990).
7. Edward Said, *Orientalism* (London: Routledge & Kegan Paul, 1978).
8. Probably the fullest account of the Rushdie affair from a robust Muslim perspective can be found in Shabbir Akhtar, op. cit.
9. Rushdie's response to the banning of *The Satanic Verses* in India was especially myopic. Even many of his supporters recognised that to straightforwardly permit publication there would have been irresponsible, given the certainty of violent public disturbances.
10. It is perhaps appropriate to note here, therefore, that none of the contributors to this volume, whatever their views of the Rushdie affair, support or endorse the *fatwa*.
11. Salman Rushdie, *Haroun and the Sea of Stories* (London: Granta Books, 1990).
12. Salman Rushdie, *Imaginary Homelands: Essays and Criticism 1981–1991* (London: Granta Books, 1991).
13. I have in mind groups such as 'Women Against Fundamentalism' which largely consists of Muslim women opposed to the 'authoritative' interpretation of Islam offered by (male) community leaders.
14. For an interesting account of some of the issues and their implications for political philosophy see Bhikhu Parekh, 'The Rushdie Affair: Research Agenda for Political Philosophy', *Political Studies* 38, 1990. It should perhaps be noted that this book is not concerned with issues such as state-sponsored terrorism, which are also important and clearly relevant to some aspects of the *Satanic Verses* controversy.
15. I am very grateful to Susan Mendus for her most helpful comments on an earlier draft of this chapter.

8 Respecting Beliefs and Rebuking Rushdie[1]

Peter Jones

Freedom of expression and freedom of religion are two freedoms which have seemed securely embedded in the culture of modern Western societies. Their conjunction in the right of people to express themselves freely on religious matters has seemed a particularly secure and widely-held conviction. So true has this been that, for decades and with few exceptions, that freedom has passed virtually unchallenged both in the politics of Western societies and in Western political thought. The publication of Salman Rushdie's *The Satanic Verses* and its aftermath put an end to that comfortable consensus and compelled people to re-examine the basis and implications of principles and commitments that they have long taken for granted.[2]

In this chapter, I want to consider some of the general issues raised by the Rushdie affair for a plural society. By a 'plural society' I mean one characterised by a diversity of fundamental beliefs and, more especially, one characterised by a diversity of religious beliefs. I shall assume that all parties to the argument accept the legitimacy of a plural society. The issue therefore, as I shall examine it, is not one of which of a number of competing religions, if any, should be adopted by a society as 'correct' to the exclusion of all other (false) beliefs. It is not about whether a society should be committed to Christianity or to Islam or, indeed, to atheism. Rather all parties to the argument are assumed to accept that members of the society should be able to hold and to live according to their own beliefs; so the issue amongst them is simply about the way in which the society should accommodate the diversity of beliefs that they hold. In examining this issue I shall make use of the arguments and claims thrown up by the Rushdie affair, but my ultimate concern will not be to deliver a verdict on the rights and wrongs of the affair in its every detail. Rather my interest will be in the general question of what should be required of the members of a plural society by way of deference to beliefs that they themselves do not share. In particular I shall consider the plausibility and the implications of the claim that we should show 'respect' for the beliefs of others.

In examining the principle of 'respect for beliefs' I shall argue that, although it has some affinity with the idea of not offending people's sensibilities, it is actually a distinct idea with a different moral foundation and some different practical implications. I shall examine the principle both in its strong form, in which it would limit substantive criticism of people's beliefs, and in its weaker form, in which it would constrain only the 'manner' in which others' beliefs are treated. Finally, I shall consider whether the difficulties that we confront, when we invoke the offence principle or the principle of respect for beliefs, can be bypassed by focusing instead upon the requirements of public order.

COPING WITH CONFLICT

Now it should not be taken for granted that there *must be* some set of rules that is acceptable to all members of a plural society in spite of their different beliefs. Different groups of believers may all accept the legitimacy of a plural society but may disagree about the rules that should govern that society. For example, if Christians, Muslims, Buddhists and humanists each draw upon their own bodies of belief in deciding what the common rules should be, there is no guarantee that they will come up with identical sets of proposals. If no such 'overlapping consensus'[3] is forthcoming, we may be stuck with a virtual 'state of war' between different bodies of believers. There are certainly elements of the Rushdie affair which fit that description, the most notorious of which was Ayatollah Khomeini's *fatwa* sentencing Rushdie to death and calling upon 'all zealous Muslims' to ensure that the sentence was carried out. Recently the Japanese translator of *The Satanic Verses* was stabbed to death and the Italian translator of the novel was also attacked. Rushdie's own life is likely to be under threat for the rest of his days. Khomeini was not interested in providing for a plural society and he did not command the allegiance of all Muslims. But many Muslims in Britain and in other Western societies accepted Khomeini's *fatwa* and affirmed their willingness either to carry out the death sentence or to collude in its being carried out by others. In addition bookshops have been bombed and a campaign of civil disobedience has been threatened. Other Muslims have rejected Khomeini's *fatwa* and are unwilling to resort to illegal tactics to achieve their aims but, even amongst those, there seems to be a general conviction that they can never give up their protests and simply accept that others have a right to subject their religion to the sort of treatment it has received at the hands of Rushdie.[4]

How might we get beyond this state of conflict? One possibility is peace based upon mere compromise. For example, Muslims might come to endure attacks upon Muhammad and the Koran, not because they believe that they are obliged to do so by some principle that supersedes their religion (what principle could that possibly be?), but only because, in practice, that is all they can do short of leaving the society. Alternatively, the non-Muslim section of the population might agree to the prohibition of severe attacks upon Muslim beliefs, not because it believes that there is really anything wrong with those attacks, but only to assuage those who would be outraged by them and who might react violently. I describe each of these as 'mere compromise' because neither is an arrangement that both sides regard as truly right or fair. Each is no more than a *modus vivendi*, a truce, in which force of circumstances has induced one side to concede something that, it believes, it should not have to concede. That may be preferable to open conflict but it is still an unhappy state of affairs for it does not represent a genuine consensus on what the rules of the society should be. Is there no more principled basis upon which people might defer to one another's beliefs?

What has become the standard liberal position may be regarded as a minimum starting point. All would at least agree that each should be free to hold and live according to his own beliefs, subject to the usual qualification that that does not involve his harming or infringing the rights of others. People can, of course, believe that this sort of liberal position is wrong in principle and that they are duty-bound to attempt to make everyone conform to their own uniquely right beliefs. However, I am contemplating a population whose members accept the legitimacy of a plural society and it is hard to see how, if they accept that, they cannot also accept, as a minimum, that each should be allowed to hold and to pursue his own beliefs.

The question is whether more than that minimum can be required. My right to hold and to pursue my own beliefs does not, of itself, impose any limit upon what others may say about, or do with, the beliefs that I hold. Rushdie's *Satanic Verses* cannot be said to interfere with Muslims' right to conduct their lives as Muslims, nor can Scorsese's *The Last Temptation of Christ* be said to impede the freedom of Christians to live as Christians. Yet there is a widely shared sentiment that some limit should be placed upon the treatment that may be meted out to other people's most cherished beliefs, particularly if they are religious beliefs. What can justify that sentiment? What reason can there be for a society's throwing a protective cordon around people's beliefs? If I am a Christian, I have reason to object to the vilification of Christ because, as far as I am concerned, he is the Son of God. But what reason can I give a non-Christian, which will count as a reason for a non-Christian, for refraining from what I regard as a sin? And why should I myself refrain from vilifying Muhammad since, as far as I am concerned, he is a figure who has no divine status and who was indeed a false prophet? Clearly, whatever reason there might be for limiting freedom of expression out of concern for people's beliefs, it cannot be a reason that presupposes the truth of those beliefs, for that would disqualify it as a reason for all except those who already hold those beliefs.

OFFENDING SENSIBILITIES

That goes some way towards explaining why 'offensiveness' has become such a prominent concern both in relation to the general question of whether people's religious beliefs should receive legal protection and in relation to the specific controversy over Rushdie's book. People can acknowledge the offence caused by attacks upon others' beliefs even though they themselves do not share those beliefs. The non-believer, because he is a non-believer, cannot share the Christian's or the Muslim's conception of the essential wrongness of blasphemy. However, he can recognise that blasphemies cause distress and offence to the devout, which distress and offence is undesirable and provides a (prima facie) case for prohibiting blasphemies. He must still regard these offended reactions as, in a sense, 'mistaken' for they depend upon beliefs which are (for him) false; but he may regard that as a matter of no consequence since the reality of offended sensibilities is unaffected by the truth or falsity of the beliefs upon which they depend. Nor is this reasoning relevant only for atheists. In so far as different religions do not have overlapping beliefs, they will have different conceptions of what is blasphemous. As far as the Christian is concerned, an attack upon Muhammad cannot be truly blasphemous; in relation to Islam, the Christian too is a non-believer. Thus he too must find reason for not attacking the Muslim's beliefs in something which does not imply his own acceptance of the beliefs at issue – such as the avoidance of offence.[5]

As for believers themselves, the offence caused by blasphemy is not likely to be their major preoccupation. For the Christian, impugning the character of Christ, and for the Muslim, impugning the character of Muhammad, is wrong as such. Each may be offended by the blasphemy but that offence is merely a by-product of the wrongful act; it is not the offensiveness of the act that explains its wrongness but the wrongness of the act that explains its offensiveness. If the Christian or the Muslim characterises the blasphemy as a wrong *to* anyone, he will regard it as principally a wrong to Christ (and to God) or to Muhammad (and to Allah) rather than to himself. It would be a derogation from his faith to do otherwise.[6] Even so, he has to recognise that he is in a society many of whose members do not share these beliefs and for whom these cannot provide reason for refraining from blasphemy. But he can present the distress and the offence caused to him by blasphemy as a concern that others ought to recognise whatever their own beliefs and, in so far as blasphemy is wrong because it is offensive, he can present himself as the person who is wronged by it.

Although being offended is a disagreeable experience, it is often a fairly slight one which does not bear comparison with harms such as physical injury. Consequently, when it is weighed against values such as freedom of expression, it is often found wanting. However, the potential for offence related to religious belief is very great. The conception of certain figures and symbols as 'sacred' in Christianity and in Islam makes them special objects of reverence, and acts which treat those figures and symbols irreverently are therefore especially offensive. That is why, of all belief-related offence, that occasioned by religious belief seems the most intense.

The current English law of blasphemy has developed in a way which is very much related to the prevention of offence. At one time the purpose of the common law of blasphemy was to uphold the truth of Christianity, for it was upon that truth that the social and political institutions of England were said to be founded. Blasphemy, either against Christianity in general or against the Church of England in particular, was viewed as a form of sedition. However, during the nineteenth century, the character of the law was gradually modified so that its prime purpose became that of protecting Christians from offensive treatment of their beliefs rather than that of asserting and upholding the truth of Christianity itself. Provided they observed the 'decencies of controversy', people could attack the very foundations of Christian belief without being guilty of the legal offence of blasphemy.[7]

Given that the modern law does not presuppose the truth of Christianity, its protection could be extended to other religions without anomaly for, as we have seen, preventing belief-dependent offence does not presuppose the truth of the beliefs at issue. Indeed, it now seems anomalous that its protection should be confined to Christians. If its purpose is to protect people from what they find offensive, why should that protection be extended to some citizens but not to others? That seems plainly inequitable. Thus the very character of the existing English law of blasphemy might be said to intimate its own reform. That reform would bring certain complications in its train, such as what exactly is to count as a religion for purposes of law, and these difficulties have evidently played some part in persuading the current British Government not to extend the scope of the law (even though they have also decided not to abolish it).[8] But, although 'no change' might seem an attractive political option in present circumstances, there is little to recommend it in either logic or equity.

I have examined how far a case can be made for the prohibition of blasphemy on grounds of offence on a previous occasion;[9] I shall not repeat that examination here. My earlier study was prompted by the *Gay News* case which was pursued in the English courts from 1977 to 1979. My conclusion then was that, while the offence caused by blasphemy deserved to be taken seriously, it was insufficient, when weighed against rival concerns, to justify blasphemy's remaining a crime. The Rushdie affair has not induced me to revise my earlier argument or its conclusion. Moreover, even if the law of blasphemy in its present form were extended to include Islam, it should not be taken for granted that a court would judge *The Satanic Verses* to have contravened it.

RESPECTING BELIEFS

However, offensiveness is not the only ground upon which different religious groups in a multifaith society may call for legal protection for their beliefs. The Rushdie case has served to highlight a distinct, if related, form of argument. That argument appeals to what I shall call the principle of 'respect for beliefs'. This principle holds that people should behave in a way which is consistent with their respecting the beliefs of others. As with the offence principle, 'respect for beliefs' is a principle that is especially relevant to a plural society in which different groups of people hold fundamentally different beliefs. It holds that, in such a society, not only should people be allowed to conduct their lives in accordance with their most deeply held beliefs, they should also not have to endure attacks upon those beliefs. An attack upon the beliefs of others is a violation of one of the understandings that should underpin a society in which people are expected to live together in spite of their fundamentally different beliefs.

Like the argument from offence, the appeal to respect for beliefs does not presuppose the truth of the beliefs at issue. For example, it would require people to refrain from vilifying Christ or Muhammad not because it presumes that Christ really was the Son of God or that Muhammad really was God's Prophet, but out of respect for those who hold Christian or Muslim beliefs. As with the offence principle therefore, the ultimate objects of concern in the principle of respect for beliefs are not beliefs as such but the people who hold them. The obligation of respect is an obligation owed to believers rather than to beliefs understood merely as propositions to which people may or may not subscribe.

The demand that we respect the beliefs of others is, as I shall argue in a moment, fraught with difficulties, particularly for liberal political philosophy. Even so, it is a principle that liberals should at least find intelligible. The idea of individuals as objects of respect has figured prominently in recent liberal thinking. The arrangements required for a liberal society have been worked out as those appropriate to persons capable of forming and acting upon their own views of the ends to which they should devote their lives.[10] A liberal society is one whose members are allowed to form and to pursue their own beliefs. It stands opposed to a society in which people are compelled to live in accordance with beliefs that they themselves do not share or which, in other ways, pays no heed to the conscientious convictions of those who make up its citizens. The principle of respect for beliefs, as I have described it, can be seen as an extension of this way of thinking. It holds that the mutual respect which is required of citizens who form a plural society should be taken to include their not acting in ways which affront one another's beliefs. That, it asserts, is one of the minimum guarantees that people should be able to demand as a condition of their accepting the obligations of citizenship.[11]

Before seeing how well this principle stands up to scrutiny, let me say a little about how it differs from an injunction not to offend people's sensibilities. These two will often be closely allied for it is likely that people will be offended when they find their beliefs being treated disrespectfully.[12] We should not therefore expect to find the distinction between these two sorts of complaint being closely observed when people register their protests. Yet, despite their close association, neither is reducible to the other. My person or my beliefs may be treated disrespectfully even though I experience little or no offence and, equally, my offended reaction does not, of itself, establish that either I or my beliefs are being treated without due respect.

The ethical substructures, from which each of these notions derives its appeal, are also quite different. The notion of 'being offended' encompasses a variety of mental states which share little in common except that they are unpleasant, perhaps sometimes painful, mental responses.[13] It is the disagreeable character of the experience that makes offence a ground for complaint and that, in turn, indicates that, underlying objections which appeal to offence, are considerations of an essentially utilitarian character. By contrast the principle of 'respect for beliefs' is an altogether more rights-based notion.[14] Its appeal derives not from the disutility that people suffer when their beliefs are attacked, but from the premise that people are 'self-originating sources of claims'[15] who are entitled to a certain minimum of respect from their fellows. To subject beliefs to attack, ridicule or contempt is simultaneously to subject the people who hold those beliefs to attack, ridicule or contempt, and that is to accord them less than the respect to which they are entitled.

As I have already indicated, the language of offence and the language of respect will not always indicate clearly which form of concern someone is intending to avow. Each thought might find expression in the language of the other. Thus, someone who asserts that we should treat the beliefs of others 'with respect', may turn out to believe, not that that respect is of intrinsic value, but only that it is of instrumental importance. He may believe, for example, that disrespect will cause offence or social conflict and that that is the main or the only reason why it should be avoided. Similarly, people may be offended by something, and may declare that they are offended, without intending to suggest that their offence is their reason for objecting to what they find offensive. People are offended and upset by the existence of genocidal concentration camps, but it would be a very odd person who cited their upset and offence as their reason for objecting to genocidal concentration camps. Analogously, people may find attacks upon their religious beliefs offensive but may hold that those attacks are wrong, not because they cause offence, but because they are intrinsically 'sinful' or because they do not accord to others the respect to which they are entitled. However, despite these 'semiotic confusions', the distinction between these two ways of condemning attacks upon beliefs remains and, in what follows, I shall give the terms 'offence' and 'respect' the specific interpretations that I have described.

Once this notion of respect for beliefs is brought to bear upon the Rushdie controversy, certain of its features become more intelligible. One reply frequently given to protesting Muslims has been that, if they believe they will find *The Satanic Verses* offensive, they need not read it. Indeed, that is a reply that has been given by Rushdie himself.[16] Yet Muslims seem to have been singularly unimpressed by this riposte. What is more, their own protests and demonstrations would seem to have been oddly counter-productive if their primary concern was with the offensiveness of Rushdie's writings, for by these actions they have greatly increased the number of people who have become aware of the alleged blasphemies and who have therefore been offended by them. Mosques have displayed samples of Rushdie's blasphemies and organisers are reported to have handed out photocopies of the offending passages during demonstrations. This would indeed be strange behaviour if the ground of their complaint was the offence, the 'mental pain', caused to the Muslim population. If, however, the essence of their complaint is not the offensive character of Rushdie's words but the disrespect that they manifest for the beliefs of Muslims, their conduct is altogether more intelligible and condonable. Spreading the word about Rushdie does not then amount to compounding the evil.

Another reason that Muslims have given for their being unimpressed by the invitation not to read the book, is that they do not need to read Rushdie's actual words in order to be aware of what he said and to be offended by it.[17] Mere knowledge of Rushdie's themes is enough to cause them anguish. Yet this too creates a puzzle. If Muslims are offended by their mere awareness of what Rushdie said, what would be the point of banning *The Satanic Verses*? By now virtually all Muslims in Britain and other Western societies must know about it and banning the book would not erase Rushdie's remarks from their consciousness. It is difficult therefore to see how a case can be made, merely on grounds of preventing offence, for banning the book. (It is, of course, easy to see how a case might be made for banning *future* books of this sort on grounds of offence.) However, more sense can be made of the call for the book to be suppressed if we introduce the idea of respect for beliefs. The suppression of the book might be demanded by Muslims as a gesture of respect for them and their faith and an acknowledgement of the respect that should be shown to their beliefs by members of the majority society who do not share them.

There is one further way in which respecting beliefs might be held to score over preventing offence. Offence can be a highly idiosyncratic reaction. What offends some people does not offend others and some people seem generally more easily offended than others. Should the freedom enjoyed by members of a society be at the mercy of such a subjective and erratic phenomenon?[18] Might not the fault sometimes lie with those who take offence rather than with those who purportedly give it? The dangers of idiosyncratic or unreasonable reactions may seem to disappear when we are concerned with large groups of people, as in the case of offence felt by the adherents of a religious faith, yet groups may also be very uneven in their propensity to feel offence. Imagine a society characterised by two religions. One of these has roots deep in the society's past but, with the development of secularity, its adherents have had to become accustomed to attacks upon their fundamental beliefs and have, in consequence, developed a degree of 'mental resistance' to them. The other religion is relatively new to the society. Its adherents are not similarly used to secular assaults upon their beliefs and consequently react with much greater hurt and indignation when their beliefs are questioned or attacked. Should the law give greater protection to the new than to the old religion? If our only concern is to prevent offence, it should. Yet it seems unjust that the adherents of the old religion should have to put up with a greater amount of ridicule and contumely merely because they have become more resigned to it. If people's most cherished beliefs are to receive legal protection, should not that protection be extended to all believers equally – as would be required by the principle of respect for beliefs – rather than be dependent upon the contingencies of their mental states?[19]

One final point about the different implications of preventing offence and respecting beliefs. If our purpose is to prevent offence, that provides some justification for singling out religious beliefs as of special concern. As I explained earlier, the sacral element in religious beliefs makes people particularly susceptible to offence in relation to them. That is why there seems something disingenuous about the atheist's riposte that he is just as liable to be offended as the theist and therefore should receive the same protection. However, if our guiding concern is securing respect for beliefs rather than preventing offence *per se*, it is not at all clear that religious beliefs can claim a unique status. If the rules are to remain neutral between the different contents of people's beliefs, should non-religious or irreligious beliefs receive any less respect than religious beliefs? Might not identical claims to respect be made for moral or political beliefs? Clearly, we do not think that all of a person's beliefs are equal candidates for respect. We would not ordinarily suppose that my beliefs about whether it will rain tomorrow, or about the likelihood of a team's winning a football match, impose strong obligations of respect upon others. It is not easy to specify what it is that makes some of a person's beliefs more demanding of respect than other beyond the general observation that it has something to do with the centrality of a belief to a person's life and being. But, however one makes the distinction, it is quite implausible to suppose that the principle of respecting beliefs should issue in an injunction to respect only religious beliefs. Thus I shall continue to focus on religious beliefs for the remainder of this chapter, not because I suppose that they have a unique claim to respect, but only because they are central to the Rushdie affair and because conflicts of religious belief have proved particularly difficult for plural societies to handle.

How strong a case is there, then, for embracing the principle of respect for beliefs? One thing I have not done so far is to specify the precise scope of the principle and that might seem to be an essential preliminary to subjecting it to examination. Just how demanding is it? What precisely does it forbid? Rather than simply stipulate an answer to these questions in a more or less arbitrary fashion, I would prefer to let one emerge from an examination of the general idea of the principle. However, I shall begin by assuming that the principle takes a fairly strong form – strong enough to forbid challenges and criticisms designed to undermine the beliefs of others. Is that a principle we should accept?

Little progress can be made in answering this question by invoking distributive values such as justice or equality, even though it is those values that have dominated recent liberal political philosophy. Justice and equality are concerned with how freedom and protection should be distributed amongst people rather than with what freedoms and protections there should be and, *prima facie*, a system of laws which extends the kind of protection at issue here to *everyone's* beliefs seems neither more nor less just than one which gives that protection to *no one's* beliefs. Where then are we to look for an answer?

Firstly there is the entire phalanx of arguments that may be invoked in defence of freedom of expression. I cannot review all of those here, so I shall confine myself to a few brief comments.[20] Much has been made of the rights of Rushdie as an author in a way which implies that creators of literature, because they are creators of literature, have some special claim to freedom. That is not perhaps the most persuasive of defences since it has the appearance of a mere prejudice which elevates the interests of a small group of literati above those of many millions of Muslims. Much has also been made of the requirements of a democratic society. Now the phrase 'democratic society' can be variously interpreted but, if it refers to the prerequisites of a democratic political process, it is not immediately obvious that restrictions upon blasphemy will seriously impede the operation of that process. However, I concede that it is difficult and perhaps impossible to state, *a priori*, which opinions will be relevant to a political process and which will not, so that some headway may be made in defending Rushdie by reference to democracy.

For my money, the most persuasive defence of freedom of expression in religious matters is the kind of argument developed by Mill in the second chapter of *On Liberty*.[21] If we are serious about wanting to possess true beliefs, and presumably anyone who professes a 'belief' must be concerned that it is a true belief, we must be willing to live in the kind of society that allows the truth of beliefs to be examined. That is a society in which all beliefs are open to question and none is immune from scrutiny. It is unnecessary for me to restate the arguments for freedom of expression and discussion so ably marshalled by Mill. His is the kind of non-distributive concern for liberty that has been unduly neglected in recent liberal thinking and which is of first importance for the Rushdie affair. It serves to show how we each have an interest, not only in our own freedom of expression, but also in one another's freedom of expression. Of course the concern here is not quite the same as Mill's. He feared the imposition of a uniformity of belief either by governments or by the pressure of social opinion; we are contemplating a society of diverse beliefs in which each body of belief is insulated from criticism and challenge by the rivals that exist alongside it. But the ideal of a society in which 'mutual respect' requires rival bodies of belief not to speak to one another is as vulnerable to Mill's criticisms as a society in which only one body of belief is respected.

I concede that Mill's argument about the need to test beliefs may not persuade someone whose beliefs depend entirely upon claims of revelation.[22] Such a person may hold both that the truth of his beliefs is utterly beyond question and that ordinary standards of argument and evidence are entirely irrelevant in matters of religious belief. However, that some people take that view does not entail that they *rightly* take that view. In fact belief in revealed truths is rarely based upon what has been directly revealed to the believer himself. Nor should we overlook the central places occupied by argument and scholarship in both the Islamic and the Christian traditions. Some of those who have spoken up on behalf of Muslims in the Rushdie affair have done so by suggesting that truth is not really at issue in religious beliefs and that it is misplaced to allow our response to the diversity of religious beliefs to be guided by a concern for the pursuit of truth. But that sort of argument is unlikely to be welcomed by Muslims themselves who would regard their own beliefs (rightly) as beliefs about what is supremely true. Rather than rushing to sever any connection between religious belief and truth, Muslims are more likely to regard the sceptical relativism implicit in that proposal as itself part of the unfortunate fallout of secular liberalism.

However a strong version of the principle of respect for beliefs is open to a second objection that is even more decisive than the strictures set out by Mill. In its strong form the principle would seem to require us to treat an individual's beliefs as a well-defined territory over which he has a sovereign right. Just as he may be said to possess an inviolable right over his person and over his property so too he may be said to possess an inviolable right over his beliefs. Indeed, on this view, his beliefs are virtually a part of his 'property' and that is why it is incumbent upon a society to ensure that they are protected.

There are two reasons why this way of viewing and valuing people's beliefs must collapse into incoherence. The first is that the content of people's beliefs overlap and conflict. That observation is as important as it is pedestrian and it is especially important in relation to religious beliefs. The very existence of different religious faiths, and of differences within religious faiths, must mean the existence of conflicting bodies of belief. Christianity impugns the truth of Islam and Islam impugns the truth of Christianity. Likewise Protestantism and Catholicism stand in contradiction to one another (although not of course in every detail). How are we to decide whose beliefs are to be privileged and therefore protected? Who should we regard as the victim and who as the assailant in this conflict of beliefs? Clearly those questions are incapable of receiving neutral answers. The only way of honouring the principle that no one's beliefs should be subjected to attack, either explicitly or implicitly, would be to require, absurdly, that no one should ever give voice to a belief.

This strong version of respect for beliefs is also at odds with itself in a second way. It may have some intuitive appeal as long as a person's beliefs are purely self-directed, that is, as long as they are beliefs only about the believer himself and how he ought to live. But as soon as those beliefs become beliefs about others as well, it becomes nonsensical for him to insist that the content of those beliefs is properly of concern to no one but himself. Yet it would be a very odd set of fundamental beliefs that had relevance to no one but the believer. Typically, fundamental beliefs are about what is true of the world or humanity at large and about the right or the good way for people generally to conduct their lives. Christianity and Islam, for example, are comprehensive bodies of belief about the nature of existence, about man's place in it and about the proper conduct of human life. It would therefore be singularly perverse for those who hold Christian or Muslim beliefs to insist that what their beliefs are beliefs *in* is a matter which is somehow private to Christians or Muslims and properly of concern to no one but them. On the contrary, they must, and do, insist that the content of their beliefs is of importance to everyone.

The distinction that is in danger of being overlooked in respect for beliefs is that between (i) a belief's being mine in the trivial sense that it is what *I believe* and (ii) a belief's being mine such that *what I believe in* comes to belong exclusively to me. My beliefs are obviously 'mine' in the first sense, but that does not make them 'mine' in the second sense. Propositions, ideas, theories, theologies, and the like cannot be appropriated and removed from the public domain simply by some individuals' coming to believe that they are true. 'The market-place of ideas' is a happy metaphor but it should not mislead us into supposing that adopting ideas, like buying goods, amounts to acquiring a right of private ownership over their content.

Finally, although what constitutes treating another's beliefs 'with respect' is a contestable matter, it is not infinitely malleable. On almost any view of what constitutes respecting a person, it is hard to take seriously the complaint that conducting a sober examination of the truth of another's beliefs amounts to not treating him, or his beliefs, with respect. Arguably, it is more insulting to have one's beliefs treated as though their truth or falsity were of no consequence; for that is to have one's beliefs not taken seriously as *beliefs*. That is a trap into which some varieties of multiculturalism seem to fall. There are many reasons for both tolerating and promoting cultural diversity and there is nothing illogical about supporting and encouraging diverse forms of music, dance, literature and lifestyle each of which has its roots in a particular culture. Now cultures are often caught up with beliefs, particularly with religious beliefs. Again there are many reasons for tolerating all of those beliefs. However, it would be odd to find amongst them the claim that a world characterised by different religious beliefs is the best of all possible worlds and that nothing should be allowed to diminish that diversity. 'Beliefs aim at truth' as Bernard Williams puts it,[23] and therefore different religious beliefs are rival beliefs. They constitute rival claims to the truth. For that very reason, to treat the truth of someone's beliefs as a matter of no consequence is already to have ceased to take them seriously as beliefs. But to seek to immure people's beliefs so that they will never be threatened or changed is effectively to do just that. It is to treat the continuance of those beliefs as of greater moment than their truth. It is to hold that it matters less that people should live lives grounded in falsehoods than that their existing beliefs, and the ways of life grounded in them, should remain undisturbed. At least those who challenge beliefs signal in so doing that they take them seriously as claims to truth. By contrast, those who seek to 'protect' beliefs so that they become, in effect, exhibits frozen in a social museum run the risk of reducing them to mere objects of curiosity which make no demands for serious consideration upon those who do not already hold them. No doubt those who wish to extend this protection to others' beliefs are generously motivated but their efforts may ultimately be more patronising than the attempts of others to refute them in the ordinary rough and tumble of argument.

Earlier I connected respect for beliefs with the liberal idea of respect for persons. If a strong version of respect for beliefs is untenable, and if indeed some of the reasons for rejecting it are reasons traditionally associated with liberalism, what is amiss in making that connection? After all, liberalism's propensity to treat beliefs, particularly religious beliefs, as essentially 'private' matters may itself have encouraged people to embrace the principle of respect for beliefs. The logic that I previously suggested ran from (1) respecting persons to (2) the right of individuals to form and to pursue their own beliefs and then to (3) their having the right not to have those beliefs attacked. The step from the first to the second notion – that is from respect for persons to the right to form and pursue one's own beliefs – is not without complications, but I shall not examine those here.[24] More to the point is the step from the second to the third – from the right to form and pursue one's own beliefs to the right not to have those beliefs criticised. Of course, in strict logic one does not entail the other – my being free to form and pursue my own beliefs does not require that others abstain from questioning and criticising those beliefs. Even so, there might still seem to be some affinity between these two notions. If my beliefs are reckoned to be of sufficient moment to be the subjects of guaranteed freedom, does that not imply that they constitute a territory which others should 'keep off'? Lord Scarman, for example, has argued, in the context of the English law of blasphemy, that article 9 of the European Convention on Human Rights, which provides for freedom of religion, also 'by necessary implication ... imposes a duty on all of us to refrain from insulting or outraging the religious feelings of others'.[25]

However, the apparent affinity between these two notions is, I believe, misleading. Why should people be free to form and pursue their own beliefs? That question can be answered in man ways, but the answer which seems fundamental to the deontological liberalism at issue here is that individuals' lives are their *own*; they should therefore be free to conduct *their* lives as they see fit. Thus the reason why I should be free to live in accordance with my beliefs is not that those beliefs come to acquire a peculiar sanctity merely because I adopt them. Rather I should be entitled to shape my life according to my beliefs because it is *my life*. In other words, in so far as there is something like a notion of ownership at work here, it is ownership over my life rather than ownership over certain propositions that I have come to believe in. That is why my right to live according to my beliefs entails that others are duty-bound not to prevent my so living but does not entail that they are duty-bound not to challenge the beliefs to which I devote my life.[26]

RESPECT, DECENCY AND MANNER

Are we then to conclude that the principle of respect for beliefs is entirely without merit? Are people to be free to speak, write and behave without having regard for the beliefs of others? My previous arguments have shown that a strong version of the principle of respect for beliefs is untenable. Can the principle receive a less demanding, and therefore more plausible, interpretation? Both sides in the Rushdie affair are to be heard espousing the value of freedom of expression, and both are also to be heard exhorting us to treat the beliefs of others with respect, albeit with varying degrees of enthusiasm.[27] That implies an interpretation of 'respect' which is not seriously at odds with, or which is at least in some way reconcilable with, freedom of expression. What might that interpretation be?

Some of Rushdie's defenders may mean by 'respecting another's beliefs' no more than the liberal idea of allowing people to live according to their own beliefs. If that is all that respect for beliefs requires, it provides no reason for limiting free expression. Indeed, it is sometimes suggested that exceeding that minimal liberal position would entail 'imposing' others' beliefs upon people.[28] However, others who have spoken in defence of Rushdie clearly do intend their injunction to respect others' beliefs to imply something more than the minimal liberal position, even though that 'something more' would leave substantial room for freedom of expression. Likewise, many of Rushdie's critics declare their acceptance of the right of freedom of expression and complain only that Rushdie has abused, or exceeded the limits of, that right.[29]

How then might we set a limit to the demands of respect for beliefs so that these fall short of prohibiting all serious challenges to people's beliefs? There are a number of possibilities.

Some of the antagonists in the Rushdie affair seem to want to place some subjects 'off-limits' altogether. Some matters, which religious believers regard with special reverence, should simply not be open to challenge. There are two difficulties with that view.

Even though it is only some aspects of a person's beliefs, rather than all of a person's beliefs, that are placed beyond the pale of criticism, that would still run into the objections that I have already outlined. Should any matter be placed beyond challenge and inquiry? If some aspects of a person's beliefs are of especial importance to him, is it not also especially important that the truth of those aspects be open to scrutiny? And can it really be an act of disrespect merely to question what another asserts however tenaciously that belief is held?

Secondly, how are we to decide which matters are off–limits and which are not? It is not easy to see how there could be a single criterion that could be applied across all religions, and it would clearly be unacceptable to let each religion, or each sect of each religion, determine for itself the schedule of subjects which should be excluded from public discussion. Moreover, even the faithful may regard this approach as unnecessarily severe. Their own understanding of the demands of 'respect' is often less one of what should, and what should not, be open to challenge and criticism and more one of *how* that challenge and criticism should be conducted.

That takes us on to a second possibility. Every subject, it might be said, should be open to challenge and critical scrutiny, provided that that challenge and criticism respects the 'decencies of controversy'. It is not criticism or questioning that is objectionable; it is the conduct of criticism and challenge in a way which exceeds the bounds of 'decent' or 'civilised' or 'respectful' discussion.[30] A standard of that sort has long been a part of the English law of blasphemy.[31]

Once again, however, that proposal presents us with two difficulties: one technical, the other political. The technical problem is that of drafting a law that will indicate to people, with reasonable precision, what they may say and what they may not. Phrases like 'decent' or 'civilised' leave everything to interpretation. A law stated in those terms would make it almost impossible for people to know in advance whether their statements were permitted or prohibited; they could be sure only after the court had decided. Nor would it be easy to infer from its past decisions what the future decisions of a court would be.

The political problem is how we are ever to achieve a reasonable degree of consensus on what it is acceptable and what it is unacceptable for people to say, remembering that we are legislating for a society of people with different sets of beliefs. The problem here is not merely that different individuals may have different views on what decency requires. It is also that different faiths, and different varieties of the same faith, may have different conceptions of the limits imposed by 'decency'. In other words, rather than 'decency' providing a criterion that people can recognise and embrace, independently of whatever beliefs they hold on religious matters, it may itself be a belief-dependent notion and so vary according to belief. Fundamentalists, for example, be they Muslim or Christian, are likely to possess a more severe view of what decency requires that those who are, in religious terms, 'liberals' or 'modernists'.

All of this may seem to make the attempt to exclude certain matters of substance from criticism seem hopeless as well as undesirable. However, there is a third possibility which might seem more promising. That option turns upon a distinction between the matter and the manner of what is said. Broadly it holds that people should not be prevented from saying things merely because others dislike the 'matter' of what they say, but that they may be prevented from saying things in an objectionable 'manner'. Thus, your taking exception to the substance of my opinions is not an acceptable reason for my being silenced; but I may be prevented from expressing those opinions in an unnecessarily disrespectful way.

This is another distinction that has been frequently invoked in relation to the English law of blasphemy. Stephen, for example, characterised the law as follows:

> Every publication is said to be blasphemous which contains any contemptuous, reviling, scurrilous or ludicrous matter relating to God, Jesus Christ, or the Bible, or the formularies of the Church of England as by law established. It is not blasphemous to speak or publish opinions hostile to the Christian religion, or to deny the existence of God, if the publication is couched in decent and temperate language. The test to be applied is as to the manner in which the doctrines are advocated and not as to the substance of the doctrines themselves.[32]

There is much that is attractive about dealing with this issue in terms of the distinction between matter and manner. For one thing it seems to offer a more workable distinction than appeals to 'decent' or 'civilised' discussion. Secondly, it would appear to offer us the best of both worlds. Freedom of expression would be limited but in a quite unobjectionable way. No opinion would have to remain unstated, no subject would be excluded from open discussion and none would be exempt from critical scrutiny. All that would be proscribed would be attacks upon beliefs that were formulated in an unnecessarily abusive manner, and there would seem little reason to champion unnecessary abuse. Thirdly, the very phenomenon of treating other people's beliefs 'disrespectfully' often seems to be a question of manner rather than matter. As I argued above, subjecting another's beliefs to sober and serious examination can hardly be represented as treating those beliefs, or their holders, disrespectfully. It is when matters of special reverence are subjected to ridicule, contempt, vilification, and the like, that people are most likely to object. If the demands of respect concern the manner rather the matter of one's treatment of another's beliefs, the principle of respect for beliefs will provide a secure normative underpinning for that distinction.

Does, then, this distinction between matter and manner provide an acceptable and workable standard for setting the boundary between freedom of expression and respect for beliefs? The distinction clearly has some merit. A sceptical academic treatise and an abusive vulgar lampoon may both deny the existence of God, but, although they agree in their matter, there would be a clear difference in their manner and a difference that is likely to be significant for those whose beliefs are under attack. The problem is that applying the distinction between matter and manner is rarely as straightforward as that. More often form and substance are so interrelated that it is not possible to treat one as a dispensable feature of the other. Manner and meaning are not wholly separable. Nor need a forceful and contemptuous manner be without justification. Religions are many and various and have been responsible for many of the worst, as well as some of the best, episodes in human history. If strong and colourful prose enables an argument to hit its target more effectively, and if we believe that a religion or cult deserves to be targeted, then we are likely to feel that this more effective medium is justified. Moreover, the exponents of religion have themselves not always been notable for the temperateness of their language. Those who possess a religious faith may be amongst the most reluctant to forsake the full armoury of language in opposing doctrines that they believe to be bogus and harmful or in condemning conduct that they regard as evil.[33]

Nor is it clear that this distinction has actually been followed in English law or that it would acceptable to those who want some legal restriction placed upon blasphemy. It is quite obvious that it was the matter, and not merely the manner, of James Kirkup's poem that led to the successful prosecution of *Gay News* and its editor in 1977. The same is true of many earlier cases of blasphemous libel, even though judges who presided over those cases claimed to be applying the distinction between matter and manner.[34] It is also difficult to apply the distinction to Rushdie's work. For one thing it is hard to know quite what should count as matter, and what as manner, in a novel. For another, it is quite clear that it is *what* Rushdie was understood to have suggested about Muhammad, the Qu'ran and other important aspects of Islam, and not merely *how* he stated those thoughts, that was found objectionable.

PUBLIC ORDER

Finally, a word about public order. The maintenance of public order is typically considered an uncontroversial obligation of governments. It is also widely regarded as an acceptable reason for curtailing freedom of expression. Even Mill was prepared to concede that the urgent need to prevent a riot should take precedence over freedom of expression. A government might claim that it is obliged to proscribe what members of its population find offensive or disrespectful simply to prevent disorder, violence and social conflict. That seems to have been part of the motivation for banning *The Satanic Verses* in India and Pakistan where people have died in demonstrations against the book. In Britain there have been suggestions that the sort of issue raised by the Rushdie affair might be most satisfactorily handled in terms of the maintenance of public order and the avoidance of social conflict. Thus, for example, in his response to the Rushdie affair, the Chief Rabbi of Britain has proposed that the law should prohibit 'the publication of anything likely to inflame, through obscene defamation, the feelings or beliefs of any section of society, or liable to provoke public disorder and violence'.[35]

Yet there is reason to be deeply unhappy with this sort of proposal. If the prospect of violent and disorderly reactions is sufficient reason to curtail a freedom, that freedom is placed at the mercy of others' willingness to react in violent and disorderly ways. The readier they are to respond violently, the more they can curtail the freedoms they find objectionable. The more aggressive and intemperate a group, the more protection it will receive; the more stoical and pacific a group, the less protection it will receive. That cannot be right.

If we are to distinguish between justified indignation and mere bully-boy tactics, we have to have some way of distinguishing between justifiable and unjustifiable (or excusable and inexcusable) disorder. If disorder occurs, or is likely to occur, we need some way of determining whether the responsibility for that lies with the speaker or writer (was he being unreasonably provocative?) or whether it lies with those who have resorted to disorder and violence (were they responding in an unreasonable way?).[36] That, in turn, requires us to return to questions of what, all things considered, constitutes unjustified offence or what, all things considered, constitutes intolerable disrespect for people's beliefs. We cannot therefore satisfactorily evade the issues that I have raised in this chapter by making public order our concern.

It may be, of course, that a violent reaction is likely to occur, even though it would be unjustified, and that a government may feel unable to prevent or to contain it except by disallowing what the reactors find objectionable. That government may then judge that it is duty-bound to maintain the public peace even though that entails preventing people saying what they ought to be free to say. However, it is still important to distinguish between (i) cases in which the fault lies with the speaker and in which a government merely prevents him from saying what he has no right to say, from (ii) cases in which the fault lies with the reactors and in which a government feels compelled to override people's rights of free expression only as the lesser of two evils. Clearly more is required to justify government action in the second case than in the first.

CONCLUSION

What, then, are we to conclude? In spite of the difficulties that the notion of respect for beliefs encounters, it is not a principle that is wholly without appeal. I have shown that, in any very strong form, the principle is unsustainable. If we interpret the principle less demandingly so that it is concerned with the manner rather than the matter of statements, it is still not without its problems and difficulties. However, the objections that it encounters in this weaker form are, perhaps, less imposing and less conclusive. If the principle is concerned more with the way something is said than with the substance of what is said, it does not run into the simple contradictions that characterise its stronger version, nor does it collide so readily with the concerns that underlie freedom of expression. Moreover, there is reason to object to remarks which are intentionally and gratuitously disrespectful, whether they concern religion or any other subject, and, of course, a whole range of terms and phrases exist in our language whose very purpose is to insult, humiliate, belittle, or wound.

There can, then, be cases in which someone's disrespectful treatment of another's beliefs is properly condemned. Whether we should translate that moral condemnation into legal condemnation is another question. Suppose that we do encounter a case in which people's complaints of disrespect are well-founded and in which the author of the disrespectful remarks can claim no countervailing justification for them. Are these 'wrongs' really of sufficient moment to warrant bringing in the 'rough engine' of law? If we draw only upon the idea of respect for beliefs, and do not allow that to be supplemented by claims about the *religious* wrongness of the author's words, is he guilty of very much more than bad manners or gross discourtesy? And, given the problems of definition that a law on this matter would face, and given the risk of serious and justified criticism being suppressed along with scurrilous and gratuitous insult, do we really want to have these matters decided upon by judges and courts? The conflicting interpretations that have been offered of Rushdie's *Satanic Verses* serve notice that these are likely to be 'hard cases' and ones which judges and lawyers will be poorly equipped to handle. My worries about translating the more modest version of the principle of respect for beliefs into law are of this more practical kind. They indicate that the safest course, as far as law is concerned, is to err on side of freedom of expression.

However, if we do abjure resort to law, we can still insist that those who avail themselves of the right of free expression are under a moral obligation to exercise it responsibly. That does not mean that it must never be exercised in a way which people will judge disrespectful. Clearly, if people are wrong, it is usually desirable, as well as justifiable, for others to tell them so, even if they themselves find that exceptionable. Even if people are not wrong, it may be no bad thing, as Mill argued, that from time to time they should have to confront challenges to their most cherished beliefs. But to recognise that is not to endorse indiscriminate abuse. Strong, derisive, colourful, hurtful language may on occasion, all things considered, be justified. But it may also, on occasion, all things considered, be unjustified.

The position that I am arguing for here then is that, legally, people should be entitled to do what, morally, they may be unjustified in doing. People ought not gratuitously to vilify the most cherished beliefs of others even though, legally, they should be unprevented from treating beliefs in that way – just as people should not call for the banning of books whose content they dislike, even though, legally, that is a call that they should be free to make. I would therefore be loath to see law, in the wake of the Rushdie affair, used to limit freedom of expression in the name of respect for beliefs. I would also want public bodies to withstand the use of other sorts of coercive tactics such as attempts to prevent books being held by public libraries. However, if we can demand a certain minimum of robustness from readers, we can also demand it of authors. That does not mean, of course, that they should have to endure threats of assassination or other forms of physical assault! But they cannot expect to be spared the vigorous protests of those who strongly object to their works.

For example, provided it does not form the prelude to something more sinister, I can see nothing wrong with people burning their own privately purchased copies of books to manifest their disgust at their content. Whatever the moral and practical limitations of the principle of respect for beliefs, it is notion that should not be wholly dispensed with and those who wield the pen should not feel themselves wholly free to disregard it.

NOTES

1. This chapter is a revised version of an article that first appeared in the *British Journal of Political Science* 20 (1990), 415–37. I am indebted to many people for discussions on the issues it raises and, in particular, to Kay Black, David George, Robert Goodin, Tim Gray, Barbara McGuinness, Susan Mendus, David Miller, Bhikhu Parekh, Andrew Reeve, and Albert Weale. Thanks are also due to John Horton and to the other participants in the Morrell Trust seminar at the University of York.

2. Salman Rushdie, *The Satanic Verses* (London: Viking/Penguin, 1988). For a useful collection of documents on the Rushdie affair, see Lisa Appignanesi and Sara Maitland (eds), *The Rushdie File* (London: Fourth Estate, 1989). Timothy Brennan, *Salman Rushdie and the Third World* (London: Macmillan, 1989), examines *The Satanic Verses* in the context of Rushdie's other writings. Three general accounts of the Rushdie affair and its background, the first two written from a Muslim and the third from a non-Muslim stance, are Shabbir Akhtar, *Be careful with Muhammad! The Salman Rushdie Affair* (London: Bellew, 1989), Ziauddin Sardar and Merryl Wyn Davies, *Distorted Imagination: Lessons from the Rushdie Affair* (London: Grey Seal, 1990), and Malise Ruthven, *A Satanic Affair: Salman Rushdie and the Rage of Islam* (London: Chatto & Windus, 1990). The Commission for Racial Equality, under the editorship of Bhikhu Parekh, has published three very valuable reports of seminars on the Rushdie affair: *Law, Blasphemy and the Multi-Faith Society, Free Speech,* and *Britain: a Plural Society* (London: CRE, 1990). The issues raised by the affair are also considered in Richard Webster, *A Brief History of Blasphemy: Liberalism, Censorship and the 'Satanic Verses'* (Southwold: Orwell Press, 1990); Nicholas Walter, *Blasphemy Ancient and Modern* (London: Rationalist Press Association, 1990); Simon Lee, *The Cost of Free Speech* (London: Faber & Faber, 1990). To date Rushdie has given two main defences of his position: 'In good faith', published in *The Independent on Sunday*, 4 February 1990, pp. 18–20, and 'Is nothing sacred?', The Herbert Read Memorial Lecture, 6 February 1990 (London: Granta, 1990). These are reprinted in Rushdie's collection of essays, *Imaginary Homelands* (London: Granta, 1991), pp. 393–429. That collection also contains his essay, 'Why I have embraced Islam', pp. 430–2, which originally appeared in *The Times*, 28 December 1990, p. 10. Doubts about whether Rushdie's decision to 'embrace' Islam really signalled a significant change in his beliefs seem confirmed by his own remarks in an interview reported in *The Guardian*, 21 September 1991, p. 23.

3. On 'overlapping consensus', see John Rawls, 'The idea of an overlapping consensus', *Oxford Journal of Legal Studies* 7 (1987), 1–25.

4.   Compare:
         Many writers often condescendingly imply that Muslims should become as
         tolerant as modern Christians. After all, the Christian faith has not been
         undermined. But the truth is, of course, too obviously the other way. The
         continual blasphemies against the Christian faith have totally undermined it. Any
         faith which compromises its internal temper of militant wrath is destined for the
         dustbin of history, for it can no longer preserve its faithful heritage in the face of
         the corrosive influences.
         The fact that post-Enlightenment Christians tolerate blasphemy is a matter for
         shame, not for pride. ...
         Those Muslims who find it intolerable to live in a United Kingdom
         contaminated with the Rushdie virus need to seriously consider the Islamic
         alternatives of emigration (*hijrah*) to the House of Islam or a declaration of holy
         war (*jehad*) on the House of Rejection. The latter may well seem a kind of hasty
         militancy that is out of the question, though, with God on one's side, one is never
         in the minority. And England, like all else, belongs to God. Shabbir Akhtar,
         Guardian, 27 February 1989 (*The Rushdie File*, pp. 240–1).

5.   Whether the truth or falsity of beliefs is really of no consequence here is a nice
         question. It is arguable that, if my offence is misplaced because it stems from false
         beliefs, it cannot provide adequate reason for limiting your freedom. However, even
         if we take that view in principle, we may still regard it as of little consequence in
         practice, since, in religious matters, there is such radical and unresolvable
         disagreement about which beliefs are true.

6.   Compare, 'The Rushdie affair is, in the last analysis, admittedly about fanaticism on
         behalf of God.' 'It is true of course that God is above human insult in one sense; but
         there is another equally valid sense in which the believer is morally obliged to
         vindicate the reputation of God and his spokesman against the militant calumnies of
         evil. Only then can he or she truly confess the faith. For faith is as faith does.'
         Shabbir Akhtar, *Be Careful with Muhammad!*, pp. 61, 103. In taking action against
         Gay News for blasphemous libel in 1977, Mrs Mary Whitehouse explained, 'I
         simply had to protect Our Lord', *New Statesman*, 15 July 1977, p. 74.

7.   For the history of the English law of blasphemy, see G.D. Nokes, *A History of the
         Crime of Blasphemy* (London: Sweet & Maxwell, 1928). See also the discussion by
         David Edwards in this volume.

8.   The British Government's considered position on the issues raised by the Rushdie
         affair was set out in a letter sent by John Patten, Minister of State at the Home
         Office, to a number of leading British Muslims, 4 July 1989. The full text of the
         letter was published in *The Times*, 5 July 1989, p. 13, and is reprinted in Bhikhu
         Parekh (ed.), *Law, Blasphemy and the Multi-Faith Society*, pp. 84–7.

9.   'Blasphemy, offensiveness and law', *British Journal of Political Science* 10 (1980),
         129–48. A few years ago, the Law Commission recommended that the common law
         offences of blasphemy and blasphemous libel should be abolished: The Law
         Commission, *Working Paper No. 79: Offences against Religion and Public Worship*
         (London: HMSO, 1981), and the Commission's subsequent Report to Parliament,
         Criminal Law: Offences against Religion and Public Worship (Law Com. no. 145)
         (London: HMSO, 1985). For other recent discussions of the law of blasphemy, in
         addition to those cited in notes 1 and 6 above, see Richard Buxton, 'The Case of
         Blasphemous Libel', *Criminal Law Review*, November 1978, 673–82; J.R. Spencer,
         'Blasphemy: the Law Commission's Working Paper', *Criminal Law Review*,
         December 1981, 810–20; St John A. Robilliard, *Religion and the Law* (Manchester:
         Manchester University Press, 1984), pp. 25–45; David Edwards, 'Toleration and the
         English blasphemy law', in John Horton and Susan Mendus (eds), *Aspects of*

Toleration (London: Methuen, 1985), pp. 75–98; Robert C. Post, 'Cultural heterogeneity and law: pornography, blasphemy, and the first amendment', *California Law Review* 76 (1988), 297–335. In Britain an attempt was made to prosecute Rushdie and the publishers of *The Satanic Verses* for blasphemous libel, but the High Court upheld the generally accepted view that the English common law of blasphemy related only to Christianity; see *R.* v. *Chief Metropolitan Stipendiary Magistrate, ex parte Choudhury*, [1991] 1 All ER 306.

10.   E.g. John Rawls, *A Theory of Justice* (Oxford: Oxford University Press, 1972); 'Kantian constructivism in moral theory', *Journal of Philosophy* 77 (1980), 515–72; Ronald Dworkin, *Taking Rights Seriously* (London: Duckworth, 1978); *A Matter of Principle* (Oxford: Clarendon Press, 1986), Part 3; Bruce A. Ackerman, *Social Justice in the Liberal State* (New Haven: Yale University Press, 1980).

11.   The following statements, prompted by the Rushdie affair, provide examples of opinions which imply a commitment to something like the principle of respect for beliefs.

... in our view, it [*The Satanic Verses*] is a mere collection of insults, sacrilege, blasphemy and obscenity against Islam. No individual with the slightest grain of self-respect can accept being insulted and it is a more serious matter when a whole world community is subject to outrageous abuse of its inviolable sanctities. Dr. Mughram Ali Al-Ghamdi, chairman of the UK Action Committee on Islamic Affairs; quoted in *The Rushdie File* p. 113.

The right to freedom of thought, opinion and expression should not be practised at the expense of the rights of others. Islam should not be degraded under the banner of freedom of thought. Cursing any divine religion (Islam, Christianity and Judaism) could not be excused on the basis of freedom of thought, expression and opinion; it is a low act which deserves to be condemned by the whole world. Declaration of the Islamic Conference Organisation, *The Times*, 18 March 1989.

The Labour Party is a secular political party in a secular state. Britain, however, is a multi-racial, multi-faith society. There must be respect and understanding for everybody from everybody. This must impose constraints and restraints on freedom of speech. Max Madden, *Tribune*, 7 April 1989, p. 1.

When a prophet is treated in a supercilious, dismissive or crude manner, what is at stake is not his honour – for he is dead and too big a person to be affected by insults. What is really at stake is the sense of self-respect and integrity of those living men and women who define their identity in terms of their allegiance to the prophet. Their pride, good opinion of themselves, dignity and self-esteem deserve to be protected and nurtured, especially when these are subjected to daily assaults by a hostile society. Bhikhu Parekh, *New Statesman and Society*, 24 March 1989, p. 33.

The laws of this country [Britain] were made before the Muslim peoples arrived .... Now they must adapt to us. Others must respect our faith. Pir Mahroof Hussain, quoted in *New Statesman and Society*, 2 June 1989, p. 14.

Faith is something to be respected and revered: not to be used as an opportunity to humiliate. Keith Vaz, *Independent*, 29 July 1989, p. 11.

One would think that, in a plural democracy, we would all generate respect rather than hatred for opposed yet conscientiously held convictions .... It can never be right to defend, in the name of liberalism, works that demean and humiliate human nature and tradition in any of their established forms.' Shabbir Akhtar, *Be Careful with Muhammad!*, p. 7.

12.   However, note that my offended reaction may be caused not by the fact that what you say amounts to disrespect for my beliefs, but simply by my taking exception to the substance of your remarks. For example, if you make abusive remarks about Christ, I may be offended, not because that constitutes disrespect for me as a Christian, but simply because you are abusing the Son of God.

13.   For a catalogue of offended conditions, see Joel Feinberg, *The Moral Limits of the Criminal Law*, vol. 2: *Offense to Others* (New York: Oxford University Press, 1985), pp. 10–13.

14.   On 'rights–based' moralities, see R. Dworkin, *Taking Rights Seriously,* pp. 169–73; J.L. Mackie, 'Can there be a right–based moral theory?', in Jeremy Waldron (ed.), *Theories of Rights* (Oxford: Oxford University Press, 1984), pp. 168–81.

15.   Rawls, 'Kantian constructivism in moral theory', p. 543.

16.   *The Rushdie File*, p. 28.

17.   E.g. 'You are aggrieved that some of us have condemned you without a hearing and asked for the ban without reading the book. Yes, I have not read it, nor do I intend to. I do not have to wade through a filthy drain to know what filth is. My first inadvertent step would tell me what I have stepped into.' Syed Shahabuddin, *The Rushdie File*, p. 47.

18.   In some measure this difficulty might be handled by subjecting offence to a test of reasonableness; see Jones, 'Blasphemy, offensiveness and law', p. 147, and *Report of the Committee on Obscenity and Film Censorship* (the 'Williams Report'), Cmnd 7772 (London: HMSO, 1979), pp. 122–5. However, not everyone would accept that 'reasonableness' is an appropriate test to apply to offence; e.g. Feinberg, *Offense to Others*, pp. 35–7.

19.   This issue presents a further complication. The example that I use here is deliberately one in which the difference in the two religions' susceptibilities to offence is explained by something extraneous to their bodies of belief – the extent to which each religion's adherents have been exposed to attack in the past and have become inured to those attacks. But it might also be that the different contents of different faiths makes the adherents of one faith more susceptible to offence than the adherents of another. In that case what would constitute 'equal' or 'equitable' treatment of different religions is much more complicated. See further my 'Rushdie, race and religion', pp. 691–2, and Bhikhu Parekh, 'The Rushdie affair: research agenda for political philosophy', pp. 702–4, both in *Political Studies* 38 (1990).

20.   The grounds for freedom of expression are examined in relation to the Rushdie affair in Jeremy Waldron, 'Too important for tact', *Times Literary Supplement*, March 10–16, 1989, pp. 248, 260, and Albert Weale, 'Freedom of speech vs freedom of religion?', in Bhikhu Parekh (ed.), *Free Speech*, pp. 49–58.

21.   For a contrary view, see the chapter by Susan Mendus in this volume.

22.   For an examination of the significance of revelation for the Rushdie affair, see Preston King, 'Rushdie and revelation', in Parekh (ed.), *Free Speech*, pp. 28–48.

23.   Bernard Williams, *Problems of the Self* (Cambridge: Cambridge University Press, 1973), p. 136.

24.   I have examined some aspects of this relation in 'Liberalism, belief and doubt', in Richard Bellamy (ed.), *Liberalism and Recent Legal and Social Philosophy* (ARSP, Beiheft 36) (Stuttgart: Steiner, 1989), pp. 51–69.

25.   *R.* v. *Lemon* [1979] 2 WLR 281 at 315. See also Weale, 'Freedom of speech vs freedom of religion?', pp. 55–8. For criticism of Lord Scarman's view, see the Law Commission, *Working Paper No 79: Offences against Religion and Public Worship*, pp. 78–80.

26. This may also explain why liberalism tends to concern itself much more with some sorts of belief than with others, an unevenness of concern which would seem odd if what mattered were beliefs as such. Why all the angst about moral and religious beliefs? Why not an equal concern with people's beliefs about the natural world or about art? Part of the answer would seem to be that moral and religious beliefs are 'life-shaping' and are therefore more directly relevant to the kind of rights that the deontological liberal wants to assert.

27. For example:

> For Unesco, as a world–wide forum for dialogue and understanding, freedom of creation, of opinion and of expression, with respect for convictions, beliefs and religions, is essential. ... It is every person's duty to respect other people's religions; it is also every person's duty to respect other people's freedom of expression. Frederico Mayor, Director–General of UNESCO; *The Rushdie File*, p. 125.

> Western emphasis on freedom of speech and tolerance is essential to civilisation. But reverence towards the traditions and ideals which other peoples hold dear is also an essential part of a healthy and happy society. H.B. Dehqani-Tafti, Bishop in Iran, Letter, *The Times*, 1 March 1989.

28. For example:

> ... censorship is wrong and any calls for censorship by any fundamentalist religious leaders should be resisted. Not because of any lack of respect for anyone's sincerely held personal faith. But because it cannot be right to have one set of views imposed on everyone else by force, punishment and the censor. Diane Abbott, Letter, *Guardian*, 16 February 1989 (*The Rushdie File*, p. 111).

> It is important that their [British Muslims'] spiritual values should be respected. ... They in turn, however, must not seek to impose their values either on their fellow Britons of other faiths or on the majority who acknowledge no faith at all. Editorial, *Independent*, 16 January 1989.

29. For example:

> It is not civilised to insult the religious sanctities of any people. We do not object to anyone writing critically about Islam – there are hundreds of such books in our libraries – but as you see these *Satanic Verses* belong to an entirely different genre. Spokesman for the Islamic Council; *The Rushdie File*, p. 78.

> That Rushdie has insulted us is evident. ... Of course, the rights of the individual, notably to free expression, are inalienable. Those of the community, notably the respect of its beliefs, are no less so. Moncef Marzouki; *The Rushdie File*, p. 182.

> Islam and Muslims are not against freedom of expression but they are against freedom to insult and injure the religious beliefs and sentiments of any community. Drs S.M. Khalil, I. Mojahid, and M.S. Khan, Letter, *Independent*, 3 March 1989.

> The Muslims did not object to anybody disagreeing with Islam but only to somebody insulting it. Whether this right to insult exists, is the issue. Shoaib Qureshi and Javed Khan, *The Politics of Satanic Verses* (Leicester: Muslim Community Studies Institute, 1989), p. 27.

30. No freedom can be absolute and, in a democratic society, the individual, whether a writer, an artist or an ordinary man in the street, must voluntarily restrain his freedom to stay within the universally accepted bounds of civilised conduct. If he does not, then he is asking for restrictions to be imposed upon him. Some argue that writers and artists are a special category and must enjoy unrestricted freedom

of expression. This notion must be challenged. No one who has read the book can deny that Mr Rushdie has transgressed all boundaries of decency and propriety in *The Satanic Verses* and for that he must be condemned. M. Akbar Ali, Letter, *Daily Telegraph*, 9 March 1989 (*The Rushdie File*, p. 217).

The book is not a threat to Muslims. It is a threat to decency. One cannot and should not malign or publish libellous statements against leaders of any faith. Islam can withstand any controversy and criticism. No religion should tolerate blasphemy. Shaikh Mohommad, Letter, *Independent*, 20 January 1989.

Freedom to criticise one religion from the basis of another is not under threat.... Muslims accept criticism but they will not tolerate vilification of the Prophet Mohamed. They in turn may criticise the beliefs of Christians but would never insult Jesus.... Criticism will be met, as it has been in the past, by "the ink of the scholars". But why should vilification be allowed? Surely it is not beyond the capability of intelligent people to distinguish between useful religious debate and deliberate distortion and insult. M. Hossain, Letter, *Independent*, 1 June 1989.

31. In *R.* v. *Ramsay and Foote* [1883], Lord Coleridge declared, 'I now lay it down as law, that, if the decencies of controversy are observed, even the fundamentals of religion may be attacked without the writer being guilty of blasphemy'. 15 Cox C. C. 231, at 238. However, he was not the first to interpret the law in that way. See also the essay by David Edwards in this volume.

32. *Stephen's Digest of the Criminal Law*, 9th edn (1950), article 214. This formulation of the law was endorsed by Lord Scarman in *R.* v. *Lemon* [1979], 2 WLR 281, at 315.

33. Compare:
     Religion is a luxuriant growth. Alongside major historical traditions is a tangled mass of lesser and newer ones, not always easily identifiable, fiercely competitive, some of them much given to litigation, and with beliefs that range from the profoundly impressive to the suspiciously barmy. Where does one draw the line? Is Ron Hubbard, for instance, a candidate for posthumous inviolability? And if not, why not? And what might be the consequences of protecting the reputation of religious founders who, in any sane and tolerant society, would deserve to be ridiculed? The Archbishop of York (commenting on a proposal to extend the law of libel to the founders of religious faiths), Letter, *The Times*, 1 March 1989.

34. See further, Jones, 'Blasphemy, offensiveness and law', 141–4.

35. Letter, *The Times*, 9 March 1989 (*The Rushdie File* pp. 215–6). Similarly, though rather more opaquely, the Archbishop of York has suggested dealing with the issues raised by the Rushdie affair by developing 'that aspect of the present law of blasphemy which focuses on the shaking of the fabric of society when widespread sensibilities are offended. Implicit in this is the belief that stable societies contain a sacral element, and that it is unwise to allow this sense of sacredness to be undermined by scurrilous attack'. Letter, *The Times*, 1 March 1989.

36. Note that, even if we judge that the speaker was speaking improperly, that need not be sufficient to condone a violent or disorderly reaction.

9 Muslims, Incitement to Hatred and the Law
Tariq Modood

There are many ways of considering the Muslim anger and protests against Salman Rushdie's book, *The Satanic Verses*. One of the most direct is to use the occasion to ask in what way the Muslim demand for the withdrawal of the book compares and connects with existing limits to free speech and why these were not adequate to resolve the crisis. Most of the discussion in this respect has focused on the law of blasphemy, and many people, including the Commission for Racial Equality (CRE) and the Deputy Leader of the Labour Party, have argued that the privileged position that law gives to Christianity (or perhaps to the Anglican Church only) is incompatible with racial equality and that law should be abolished or extended to cover other religions.[1] The law of blasphemy, however, is not the only law which in principle might protect Muslims but in fact fails to cover them. The Race Relations Act of 1976, including the offence of incitement to racial hatred, does not include religion as a component of the multiform concept of race consisting of differences and inferior treatment perceived to be based on 'colour, race, nationality (including citizenship) or ethnic or national origins'. The definition of a racial or ethnic group is wide but not without limits and this has meant that some minority religious groups such as Sikhs, Jews and Rastafarians enjoy some legal protection against discrimination and incitement to hatred (because they are deemed to meet the criteria of what constitutes an ethnic group) but Muslims do not.[2] This is a significant exclusion for Muslims, for not only does it weaken their rights in employment, housing and so on, but it deprives them of a further opportunity of protection against offensive literature. The sense that Muslims have that the existing laws do not adequately recognise them as a group and fail to meet their needs on the issue of group defamation has, therefore, some justification and needs to be considered in terms of the purpose and nature of incitement to group hatred legislation.

This is a topic which perhaps cannot be discussed without saying where one stands on the infamous *fatwa*. My view is that natural justice requires that a person cannot be sentenced without a trial and hence the *fatwa* cannot be, as its author the late Ayatollah Khomeini claimed, ' a verdict of execution'. At best, it is a learned, and for Shia Muslims (not very numerous in Britain) an authoritative, *opinion*. What is too readily forgotten in Western discussions is that the *fatwa* of 14 February 1989 was an immediate (indeed, too immediate) and direct response to the deaths of the ten anti-*Satanic Verses* demonstrators in Islamabad, Pakistan, on 12 February and the five deaths in Srinagar, India, on the 13th. The share of responsibility for these deaths by the parties named in the *fatwa*, namely the author and publishers of *The Satanic Verses*, is a question I cannot discuss here. Suffice it to say that the Tehran *fatwa* was cruel and unjust in its method even if one holds, as I personally do not, that the Qur'an sanctions capital punishment for blasphemous literature. I shall endeavour in the rest of this paper to discuss the issue of group libel as if the *fatwa* did not exist.[3]

THE LAW ON INCITEMENT TO HATRED AND GROUP DEFAMATION

Prior to the existence of any race relations legislation in Britain hateful speech could be dealt with only under the Public Order Act 1936; this meant that the offence could only be said to occur if the speech actually caused a breach of the peace or in the opinion of the police was likely to do so.[4] Section 6 of the Race Relations Act 1965 broadened this offence by not restricting the criteria to those of outcome but including the intentions of the speaker or writer in question: intending to stir up racial hatred, regardless of the measure of success, became an offence. This in effect meant (and this is how the courts interpreted the few cases that came before them) that stirring up racial hatred could not be construed as an action with an immediate outcome but as something which if not challenged undermined the official commitment to racial equality and led to racial conflict. This offence was further amended by the Race Relations Act 1976 and later incorporated in the Public Order Act 1986 (Northern Ireland, 1987) so that now a person is guilty if in the use of threatening, abusive or insulting words or behaviour or display of publication or distribution of written material:

(a) he intends thereby to stir up racial hatred (or arouse fear); or
(b) having regard to all the circumstances racial hatred is likely to be stirred up (or fear is likely to be aroused) thereby. (The words in brackets are in the Northern Ireland law only.)

The second half of this disjunction is important for, the offence having been earlier disconnected from any strict likelihood of the breach of the peace, it no longer depends on the speaker's/author's intentions or interpretation of his speech/text but on what a person may reasonably conclude is the likely effect on one or more racial groups, especially the group(s) referred to in the speech/text. If the group is likely to feel that as a group it is being rubbished, that old wounds are being reopened, enmities rekindled, images of domination invoked, then it can legitimately argue that the level of hate is being increased even if that is not the intention of the author and even if no specific act of violence is imminent. If this is a fair reading of the law in question surely we must conclude that despite the language of causation in which the offence is framed ('X incites Y to do something to Z'), what is at issue is in fact group defamation. For it seems to a non-lawyer like me that if a book uses unambiguously insulting and derogatory language to portray a group the author could be liable to prosecution on the basis of his insulting portrayal without any special inquiry into the actual consequences.

As I say, I am not a lawyer and I could not say with any confidence whether the case I have described is just within or just outside the law (so few cases are brought forward by the Attorney-General that the discussion is perhaps inevitably somewhat hypothetical).[5] My purpose is to try to bring out the rationale behind the law and here it is significant that for some time the CRE has been of the view that the law is necessary to avoid the feelings of humiliation, indignity and insecurity that minority groups would experience if subject to the unchecked use of inflammatory language.[6] Similarly, when the Home Office last reviewed the Public Order legislation, incitement to racial hatred was viewed in terms of the offence to minority groups occasioned by racialist speech.[7] The phrases that apply in Northern Ireland, enlarging the focus to include the fear in the breasts of the attacked, as well as the hatred in their potential attackers, are also significant.

My purpose can perhaps be furthered by a brief comparison with some other liberal democratic polities. The most interesting thing about the comparable offences in France, (West) Germany, the United States and Canada is that they cover a wider spectrum of social groups than those defined by race. In each of these countries religious groups are protected and in (West) Germany the law extends to cover cultural associations and political parties, for the offence is broadly conceived as 'an attack on human dignity'. In Canada women are included amongst groups whose dignity is protected by law, and Norway, Sweden, Denmark and Ireland prohibit incitement to hatred based on sexual orientation.[8] Secondly, each of these countries sees the nature of the offence in terms of group defamation. Indeed, in the USA it is treated as a piece of libel, and while libel law is limited by the constitutional right to free speech, nevertheless the Supreme Court in the 1952 decision in *Beauharnais* v. *Illinois* agreed that since an individual's dignity and reputation was associated with that of the group to which he or she belonged, there was no justification for treating group libel laws differently from the rules of private libel. While the *Beauharnais* decision has been gradually weakened by subsequent decisions there is some indication of growing public support for the view that 'hate propaganda undermines the very values which free speech is said to protect and that the prohibition of such material is not incompatible with the US Constitution'.[9] In a landmark decision, *R.* v. *Keegstra*, the Supreme Court of Canada in December 1990 found against a high-school teacher who was charged and convicted of communicating anti-Semitic statements to his students. The court argued, by a majority of five to four, that multiculturalism was an important political objective for which it was sometimes reasonable to restrict the expression of hatred against identifiable cultural groups and that in any case hate propaganda contradicted all the values, such as quest for truth, promotion of self-development, public debate and democratic participation which supported freedom of expression. One other point to notice is that the laws of group defamation in (West) Germany and France are more widely drawn, at least in the protection of the Jews, than in Britain, for the offence is not limited to abusive, insulting or threatening language but outlaws at least one proposition regardless of the manner in which it is put forward. This is the proposition that six million Jews did not die in Nazi gas-chambers; the propounding of which has been a criminal offence in both countries for some time, punishable by imprisonment in the case of (West) Germany and in France, too, since May 1990.[10]

It seems then on the basis of these brief comparative remarks that the United Kingdom is in an anomalous position amongst liberal democracies in confining its group libel laws only to racial groups and in not including religious groups (except in Northern Ireland where groups defined by reference to religious beliefs have been covered since 1970).[11] The distinction here, however, is not a clear-cut one. For as British courts recognise religious minorities such as Sikhs and Jews as ethnic groups, it has been argued that 'the advocacy of hatred against the Jewish community *on account of its religious beliefs* would amount to the stirring up of racial hatred against the Jewish community as a group', for the critical legal point is not that the hatred be directed to the racial features of a group but that it be directed to any distinctive feature of a group defined in law as a race.[12] Nevertheless, the greater protection afforded to (some) groups in France and (West) Germany comes as a double surprise. For, firstly, this restriction on hate literature especially in connection with the Holocaust, coexists with a virtual absence of anti-racial discrimination legislation and racial equality promotion (there is no equivalent, for instance, to Britain's Commission for Racial Equality); secondly, it belies the impression created by some commentators, such as the *Observer* and *New Statesman and Society* that the reason why in 1989 the French and West German governments took a more severe stand against anti-*Satanic Verses* protesters than did our own is that there is a greater libertarianism in the intellectual sphere in those countries. I shall return to the issue of which groups need protection, and what kind of literature ought to be banned, later. For the moment I would like to underline the point that legislation in other countries confirms and makes explicit what in Britain is perhaps only implicit, that the rationale of such legislation is not the danger of some immediate violence or breach of the peace but group defamation.

The above discussion I think helps us to see that the aim of this kind of law may at times be narrowly conceived but that it tends towards and its rationale depends upon a wider conception. The concern of the legislation may initially be limited to some of the earlier of the following points but the concept of incitement to hatred leads to a concern with them all:

(i) an immediate breach of the peace;

(ii) the aggressive intent of the speaker/author in the context of a possible breach of the peace;

(iii) the stirring up of racial hatred and antagonisms which if left unchecked could lead to serious social conflict and an eventual breakdown of public order;

(iv) speech and writing which have the same effects as (iii) even if the speaker/author had not intended it;

(v) group defamation as 'an attack upon human dignity'.

While (i) represents the position pre-1965 when there was no incitement to racial hatred offence as such and when it was simply a public order concern, (ii) constitutes the 1965 position, (iii) and (iv) represent the explicit context of the 1976 Act and finally, (v) represents what I take to be implicit in the use of that Act as opinion has developed on the matter so that it represents where we are today, or where we have nearly reached, and where other liberal democracies and Northern Ireland have already reached.

MUSLIM HONOUR AND LIBERAL LEGISLATION

It was noticeable from the placards of the anti-*Satanic Verses* demonstrators and from those interviewed on television that in trying to convey the nature of the insult and their hurt that words such as *honour* and *dignity* were more commonly used than *blasphemy*. Similarly, Shabbir Akhtar, described by the *Guardian* and the *Independent* as the most formidable Muslim fundamentalist intellectual ranged against Rushdie, begins his critique, entitled *Be Careful with Muhammad!*, by reminding all that one of the most basic duties of all Muslims is to guard the honour of their Prophet;[13] and it is interesting again, that when Akhtar discusses the question of legal remedies he concludes that it 'may well be that, in a secular society like Britain, the Muslims' best bet is to campaign for a law making certain kinds of conduct or publication socially unacceptable as opposed to religiously offensive'.[14] The honour and dignity that Muslims feel to be at stake, then, may be located in their religion but cannot be understood as a narrowly theological matter. Malise Ruthven has tried to bring out this aspect by describing it as a form of *izzat*.[15] *Izzat* is a form of honour important to Muslims, usually associated with the social standing or respectability a family may enjoy. The issue here, however, is *ghairat*: while *izzat* is about the respect others accord to one, *ghairat* is about the quality of one's pride or love – pride in one's religion or the Prophet. While *izzat* is something to be maintained, *ghairat* is something to be tested.[16] *The Satanic Verses*, then, is for many Muslims an unavoidable challenge to demonstrate their attachment to and love for their faith: their *imani ghairat*. And naturally the more the book is lauded as a literary masterpiece and so on, the greater the challenge, and greater the response required.

It may perhaps be all too clear how the honour of the Prophet is linked to the dignity of the followers, and so to group defamation, but I think it would be best to explore this a bit further by comparing it with cases of racial defamation that contemporary Western societies are more familiar with. Consider the following propositions:

1. Six million Jews did not die in Nazi gas-chambers.
2. American blacks have a lower IQ than American whites.

Each of these is regarded by many people, at least officially, as statements which are false or highly misleading, grossly disrespectful to a minority who have a right to be angry, perhaps inevitably violently so, because the statements belong to an ideology of domination and exploitation. Some would doubt whether these statements can have any place in legitimate intellectual enquiries and, as we have seen, to argue the first proposition in (West) Germany and France is to risk imprisonment.

Consider another proposition, which led to a successful legal prosecution in Britain in 1977:[17]

3. Jesus Christ was a homosexual.

Many people who strongly object to the propagation of (1) and (2) would not want the law to interfere with (3). The difference would lie in some or all the following features:

(i) the proposition is about an individual, not a group;
(ii) the proposition disputes a religious belief and does not defame a group;
(iii)there is not a historical or contemporary oppression linked to the proposition;
(iv) some Christians do not mind if the proposition was true, and many of those who do mind yet believe that those who wish to say such things have the right to do so.

How do these four differentiating features compare with:

4. Prophet Muhammad was a lewd, dishonest, dissembling power-seeker.

Proposition 3(i) applies to 4, and the charge against the individual in question is considerably more serious. 3(ii) too seems to carry over to 4 but I think we need to question whether it makes a valid distinction. It certainly does not sufficiently distinguish 4 from 1 and 2 if it is the case, as indeed it is, that there is a historical oppression linked to the proposition. Proposition 4 has been very much part of the medieval and early modern Christian diatribes against Islam and Muslims,[18] who have subsequently been dominated by the West, and in contemporary Britain find themselves suffering much anti-Muslim as well as racial prejudice, and of all minority groups are the worst off as measured by the usual indices of discrimination and disadvantage. As for (iv), Muslims cannot view the truth of 4 with any kind of equanimity, though, like contemporary Christians with 3, most are sufficiently confident of its falsehood to allow it to be a subject of reasoned inquiry as opposed to parody and unsubstantiated claims.

The similarity of type, then, between 4 and the first two propositions lies in showing that a defamation of the Prophet is indeed a defamation of Muslims. The link is the belief that the honour and good name of Muslims depends upon upholding the honour of the Prophet. For some liberals, willing to give oppressed minorities a sympathetic hearing but on guard to prevent unnecessary restrictions on free speech, this mediating belief is one belief too many. Michael Ignatieff, for example, has argued that it is important to distinguish between two incompatible conceptions of freedom: one which protects beliefs and ultimately leads to a theocratic state, and the other which protects individuals against expression of hatred such as racial defamation.[19] His view is that liberals cannot countenance the use of law to protect beliefs from insult, even though those beliefs may be central to a group of people, a religion or a way of life, but that he would protect the individuals who happen to be members of that religion or way of life. He, therefore would not have the honour of Muhammad or any other Muslim conceptions enjoy any kind of legal immunity from insult, but he would support a law to prosecute those who would shout 'you filthy Muslim' at Muslims. This distinction between beliefs and the individuals who may or may not hold those beliefs may work for the normal range of beliefs but there is at least one type of belief where it does not hold. That is the beliefs which form the self-definition of a group, for there cannot be membership of a group without some idea of the relevant groupness. Even those groups who are identified in terms of physical features, such as skin colour or sex, can only exist as groups as long as members do actually hold the belief that the physical attributes in question are what defines them. If all black people or all women ceased to define themselves in terms of their skin colour or sex, black people and women would cease to be groups, unless others, white people and men, had the power to maintain these groups; but, again, they could only do so by acting on a set of beliefs. A group exists only while some persons identify themselves and others in certain ways and this cannot be done without beliefs.

This is not a trivial logical point. In any case, some of the beliefs that a liberal state concerned to protect vulnerable minorities will have to concern itself with will be far from trivial. Look back at propositions 1 and 2. For besides beliefs which are what I might call part of the primary self-definition of a group, there are other beliefs which as it were have got historically or sociologically stuck upon a group for they are involved in its oppression, in its relationship with the oppressor. That piece of history, that piece of oppression can become so central to the psyche, to the life and continuing vulnerability of that group, that it can become part of its mode of being.[20] This is the case with the Holocaust to modern Jewry, and racial slavery to the African diaspora. Hence to protect those groups the liberal state must uphold the truth of and commitment to certain beliefs and protect them, if not from critical inquiry which promises to be respectful, at least from gratuitous and blatantly offensive attack; the beliefs in question are the negation of propositions 1 and 2.

And how are Muslims to be protected? Are recent events not enough evidence that the honour of the Prophet or the *imani ghairat* is as central to the Muslim psyche as the Holocaust and racial slavery is to others? Ignatieff's reservations, and I am sure that he is not alone, seem to be that the honour of the Prophet is not relevant to the prejudice, discrimination and harassment that Muslims experience in Britain; that it is not a focus of oppression and violence, so that however offended Muslims may be by abuse of the Prophet, it is not likely to make them feel physically insecure. He infers, therefore, that while 'You filthy Muslim' harms them, abuse of the Prophet only insults them and does not warrant legal intervention. Muslims will argue however that historically vilification of the Prophet and of their faith is central to how the West has expressed hatred for them and which has led to violence and expulsion on a large scale. It may be that the West thinks in a more secular mode now, but Muslims are not just outraged but fearful of what a revival of that old provocation can lead to. Muslims are also mindful of how medieval religious anti-Semitism provided much of the imagery and folk-memory that nourished modern racial anti-Semitism, and believe that religious anti-Islamism too will reinforce secular muslimphobia if left unchecked. The numerous attacks on mosques, the appearance of graffiti such as 'Gas the Muslims' (Bradford) and 'Kill a Muslim for Christmas' (London) and cases of discrimination in employment against Muslims suggests indeed that Muslims *qua* Muslims have become a target for secular racism.[21] In any case, no matter what the nature of the more usual defamation and discrimination may be, in order to resist it Muslims have to draw strength from the sources of their group pride, that is to say, from non-secular roots; and an attack upon those roots, even if it is not the most typical of the harassment Muslims currently experience, is the more devastating for it hits the group in a way which does most damage and undermines its strength as a group to resist attacks from any direction.[22] For these reasons as well as *imani ghairat*, given the choice between having to suffer a secularised 'You filthy Muslim' (i.e. one that was not shorthand for 'You filthy follower of the lewd, etc. Prophet') and insults upon the Prophet, many Muslims would prefer to have to live with the former – just as Jews might prefer to suffer contemporary insults rather than allow anything that defiles the memory of those who suffered and died in the Holocaust. Of course, not all Muslims are active believers and they may not weigh the two sorts of insult in the same way as the believer. But they know too that an abusive attack upon the believers by non-Muslims or in a non-Muslim society ultimately affects the dignity, pride, social status and safety of Muslims as a group and therefore of all Muslims. Under such an attack non-practising or lapsed Muslims, as we have seen in the events around us, instinctively rally round in community solidarity. The effect is just the same as when in Northern Ireland lapsed Catholics, who amongst themselves may be irreverent about their community's dogmas and rituals, are provoked to anger and community defence when Protestants or others taunt believers with images of the Virgin Mary as a whore. Such taunts are not part of the healthy clash of ideas that all beliefs ought to be subject to; they are an incitement to community hatred based upon an intimate knowledge of what will hurt and set the communities apart. It is for this reason that in Northern Ireland, though not in the rest of the United Kingdom, incitement to religious hatred is a criminal offence. If Muslims and other minorities are to be welcomed as a constituent community of Britain they too will need similar protection against group defamation.[23]

Liberals may well prefer, given the history of Europe out of which liberalism has arisen, that minority groups should not identify themselves so closely with a religion; that religion should not be a form of group self-definition. But is this anything more than an anti-religion prejudice? It is now widely acknowledged that despite how others may see them Muslims do not primarily see themselves in terms of colour or race and that religion is central to their ethnicity, to their group-beingness and to how they relate to other groups. Muslims are not alone in this: a similar situation holds not just with Jews and Catholics in some contexts, but also with Sikhs and Hindus. Whatever reservations liberals may have about giving public recognition and legal protection to religious groups, an anti-religion prejudice can itself be a form of racial discrimination, for religion is currently of greater personal and community importance to non-white than to white people in this country; hence, however racially neutral the principles of secularism may be in their formulation they will affect different groups in unequal ways. Muslims in particular feel that they suffer a double discrimination: they do not enjoy the legal protection favoured on the majority religion; and, not being a racial group, they are not recognised as a group protected by the incitement to racial hatred offence. *The Satanic Verses* crisis is not a clash 'between incompatible conceptions of freedom'. It is an attempt by Muslims, however inept in terms of public relations, and callous as regards the author of that book,[24] to press their claim to be recognised as an oppressed group in British society, as a group whose essential dignity must be respected by the rest of society. The important question then is: *who is to be protected by law?* Muslims believe that, in addition to the groups that already enjoy this protection they too are worthy enough to merit legal protection against group defamation. The Muslim protests are not so much a refusal to come to terms with modern creative literature and humanistic irreverence, not some form of opting out of the country which they have made their home, but a demand to be incorporated with the same kind of legal protection as other oppressed groups – a demand for a full membership in which society makes clear through law and other institutional means that gross defamation will not be tolerated.

FREE SPEECH AND FREE DISCOURSE

Space is not often given – it has to be taken. You have to create it, and when a group of people appears to be intolerant, to be demanding that the established norms be opened up a little, it is also a demand to *create a space in which a dialogue is possible*.[25] (My italics).

The above quote from Bhikhu Parekh – in a piece which because of his insights into the dynamics of multiculturalism deserves to be more widely available – links the intolerance of which campaigns for rights can be guilty with the objective which we should all have before us, a space in which dialogue is possible. R.G. Collingwood, when forced to justify what was superior about liberal democracy compared to the Nazis, placed the commitment to political debate, to the politics of persuasion, at the heart of his understanding of liberalism.[26] Free and open debate upon all matters of public concern did not, however, mean what some currently call 'freedom of expression'. Free debate is structured by a goal and by an important restraint. The goal is that all speech, all discourse should use every opportunity to convert non-agreement into at least some possibility of meaningful exchange: to avoid the *eristic* in favour of the *dialectic*. The paradigmatic examples of eristic reasoning are the early Socratic dialogues where no effort is made by Socrates to understand his opponent, nor to help his opponent to reach greater understanding, nor to seek some constructive common ground; instead, the *logos* is used to break up the opponent's understanding, to demonstrate Socrates' intellectual superiority and to exert intellectual power over his opponent. None of these dialogues leads anywhere, they all break down in bad temper. When students of philosophy are first introduced to these works, most are dismayed that philosophy can be so barren and surprised that Socrates does not sometimes get a physical beating. The dialectic, on the other hand, as demonstrated in the main part of *Republic*, uses questioning and criticism carried out cooperatively and constructively. Its ideal is to share understanding and through creative difference to improve understanding. The restraint which dialogue must work with is that arguments must not be pressed or criticisms ignored in a way that threaten the possibility of discourse. Collingwood recognises that the principal risk to civilised discourse is where one party rouses anger or fear or some other powerful disabling emotions in another, such that the latter is unable to exercise rational control over himself or herself and the dialogue collapses into uncivil conflict; indeed Collingwood calls such a provocation the use of 'force' and believes that it is essential to civilised relations that individuals do not provoke such conduct (the gradual elimination/reduction of force from our relations with each other being the mark of civility).[27]

Of course social life is not like a philosophy seminar and the law should not be used to make it so, and nor did Collingwood intend it so. The point is that the ideal of civilised discourse has built-in restraints and in the extreme case liberals may have to use law (where nothing else will do) to prevent the kind of abuse and provocation that would lead to a breakdown. As Susan Mendus has put it: 'Where free speech is employed in such a way as to destroy the possibility of communication, and of mutual understanding, then its *raison d'être* is destroyed.'[28] She sees in this idea a basis of a socialist conception of tolerance, of appreciating that people's existing ethnic and other group loyalties have to be respected, indeed welcomed, if they are to feel a sense of belonging and common citizenship that socialist solidarity seeks to create.[29]

Appeals to solidarity can sometimes lead to undue restrictions on free speech. I personally think that the National Union of Students' campaign of *No Platform for Racists and Fascists* in the 1980s is an example. Yet in the present situation some socialists are discovering libertarianism. John Mortimer and Hanif Kureishi are two who have declared that they can no longer support an incitement to racial hatred statute except where the incitement could be shown to lead directly to violence (i.e. the pre-1965 position) and others have made comments in the heat of the *Satanic Verses* conflict as if that were their position.[30] The libertarianism, whether genuine or born out of a moral panic or simply out of solidarity for a fellow artist, is out of character with all the mainstream British political philosophies which, at least since the time of T.H. Green, have been committed to balancing the rights of individuals with the good of the community. For it is only in the context of shared conventions and responsibilities that rights arise and can be met. And just as unbridled economic individualism can destroy the ethical base upon which it depends for the continuation of a public order, so similarly the artist without social responsibility, who provokes anger where there can be no dialogue, threatens the field of discourse itself. Twentieth-century liberal polities have successfully resisted the individualism of Herbert Spencer and John Stuart Mill, of Max Stirner and Nietzsche and recognised that where internalised restraints break down, social harmony and other goals must be protected by means of law. In the past decade or so we have seen the rise and fall of the latest brand of economic individualism; we should not succumb to the libertarianism which sees the artist as a Nietzschean *übermensch*, towering above conventional morality with perfect liberty to publish imaginative explorations regardless of social consequences. In most cases the necessary inhibitions will be acquired through habit, principle, sympathy and public censure; but where they are lacking and civility is threatened, the law may be the only recourse available.

THE NEED FOR PUBLIC ACCOUNTABILITY AND EQUALITY

Some people who may accept the substance of the foregoing arguments still believe that the best way to deal with most or all forms of group defamation is by non-legal means.[31] Of course, the law can only deal with the most extreme cases and even there its legitimacy depends upon cultural attitudes, forms of self and social restraint that have a much wider scope than the law itself. For the law to have any support at all, challenges to it must be relatively few; moral disapproval, public censure, acceptance by the political parties, the education system, the mass media, artists, publishers and so on is crucial. But for any of this to take place at least two conditions have to be fulfilled in connection with any group:

(a) its condition is thoroughly publicised and its sensibilities are widely understood;
(b) it can exercise sufficient pressure when rallied to prevent the defamation from being published.

In the absence of these two conditions, especially the second, the more powerful and more established groups will be able to manage without recourse to legal action, while weaker groups will be forced to put up with the libel or make a lot of protest and noise, make a nuisance of themselves and risk being labelled as intolerant in the process and thereby lose what public sympathy they initially had. And is not this more or less what happens? It is now well known that a Jewish lobby was able to prevent the going ahead of the stage production of Jim Allen's *Perdition* at the Royal Court Theatre with little adverse publicity; they were able to postpone twice a BBC *Desert Island Discs* interview with Lady Mosley; according to some press reports they were a contributory factor in the banning of the anti-Rushdie video *International Guerrillas*. British blacks do not have anything like the same influence though many public libraries and schools are careful not to give offence and the publisher of Noddy recently banished golliwogs from Toytown. American blacks are a more substantial lobby and were able, for example, in October 1989 to get an association of advertising agencies to collectively refuse to handle a 25 million-dollar advertising campaign by Bennetton because they thought it evoked images of black slavery. In 1967 Allen Lane, the publisher, surreptitiously burnt the entire stock of Sine's *Massacre* because some Christian booksellers found it deeply offensive.[32] Nine years later plans for *The Many Faces of Jesus*, a film on the sex life of the hero, had to be abandoned in the face of protests including those of the Queen and the Prime Minister of the day. If some of these examples are thought to belong to the pre-*Satanic Verses* era one should also consider the banning of the anti-Semitic *Lord Horror*, a novel based on the life of the traitor Lord Haw-Haw,[33] the withdrawal and pulping of the graphic novel *True Faith* by one of Robert Maxwell's companies because he learnt that it caused offence to some Christians;[34] the decision by the BBC to cancel the screening of *The Last Temptation of Christ* (a film banned from cinemas by many local authorities);[35] the seizure by Scotland Yard of records by *Niggas with Attitudes* on the grounds that the rap music 'could provoke racial hatred against whites and police';[36] the virtual banning of Robert Crumb's comic book, *My Troubles with Women* by the refusal of his usual distributors to handle it because 'it is degrading to women'.[37] These are all, of course, British examples but similar examples of state censorship, censorship by the powerful and censorship through pressure groups can be found, though often they receive little or no publicity, in each of the countries in which Muslims are vilified as being uniquely illiberal.[38]

It is indeed remarkable that in the same period of time that liberal intellectuals have rallied round 'I am not anti-Muslim but ...' speeches, they have endorsed a rising tide of 'politically correct' censorship, particularly on American campuses, without any sense of hypocrisy. Muslims, understandably, complain of double standards; far from taking exhortations to freedom of expressions to heart they are encouraged by what is possible.

It is because the absence of a law or some other publicly accountable procedure is inegalitarian and tends towards creating confrontational situations that the issue of group defamation cannot be left entirely to the process of informal pressure and public indignation. Perhaps a combination of a minimalist legal framework and a voluntary code of practice regulated by a semi-official body is a happy compromise. I am thinking of something like the equivalent of a Press Council. While that particular body has not been notably successful in its aims, perhaps in the less rough world of books, a Writers Council may be adequate.[39] Group defamation could be explicitly added to the following statement from the charter of PEN, the World Association of Writers, which could be used as a basis of its objectives:

> Since freedom implies voluntary restraint, members pledge themselves to oppose such evils of a free press as mendacious publication, deliberate falsehood and distortion of facts for political and personal ends.

Such restraint cannot in my view be entirely a matter of individual conscience. There has to be some public forum where these issues are discussed, principles laid down, specific charges examined, defences heard, apologies and retractions made and commitments about future behaviour given. In this way groups who feel despised or powerless can have their case heard and the same standards be applied to all groups. One has to be very careful of course in being able to distinguish defamation from legitimate criticism, for while freedom of expression is too gross a right and has to be seriously qualified by the protection of minorities and other civilised values, freedom of inquiry is too precious to lose. It is for this reason that I think the Anglo-Saxon instinct is to be preferred to the (West) German or French mode of protection. Defamation should ideally be confined to 'threatening, abusive or insulting' language or images, not to the presentation of arguments, however, outrageous, in the context of a discourse. I appreciate that this is something of an ideal and could not always be adhered to, and that a discourse itself is something that needs to be created and is at least partly dependent upon social equality and access to education, research, the media, publishers and so on. Yet ideals are important, for without them we are left uncertain as to what is at issue in a particular conflict and the direction we need to be moving in. Where reasoned discussion is possible, where dignity and mutual understanding can be maintained through sympathy and intellectual discipline in which insults have no place, then, in my opinion, even outrageous arguments amount to something less than defamation and must, because they can be, replied to differently than by proscription. This applies to arguments which embody the four sample propositions – though the four should be treated equally. Where the content of an argument is unpalatable, special attention needs to be given to its form and mode of presentation. The form of the argument must aspire to discourse: it must be an argument *with*, not *about* the minority group in question, and reasoned refutation must be possible. The ideal, as far as free speech is concerned, ought to be to create the conditions for *dialectical* inquiry and to prevent those conditions which lead to the breakdown of rational discourse into *eristical* conflict. *This* is the liberal ideal, not the impossible utopia offered by literary libertarians where everyone is free to abuse and insult everybody else, because words cease to wound and insults cease to hurt.

MUSLIMS AND MULTI-CULTURALISM

In a paper which is primarily about group dignity and the law but which has been concerned to interpret how Muslim demands connect with the rationale of existing legislation it may not be amiss to conclude with some remarks about Islam and the prospect of multiculturalism. I believe that the kind of legal and non-legal protection I have been discussing is necessary for Muslims to be symbolically and actually accepted and made a part of Britain; without that fundamental respect for their dignity they will become an increasingly alienated community at odds with their neighbours. Multiculturalism, however, is not simply a matter of accepting minorities; newcomers too need to be able to open up and welcome change.[40] This is a point worth making when present conflicts and policies are threatening to make Islam in this country a religion of the ghetto. The current temper of British Asian Muslims, partly as a consequence of the injuring and harassing power of *The Satanic Verses*, is not to seek the common ground, the universal in the particular, but to emphasise difference. Whereas at one time the Muslim creed used to be displayed, say at multifaith events at schools, as 'there is no god but God, and Muhammad is his Prophet'. We are now beginning to have 'There is no God but Allah...' which is not only bad translation ('Allah' is not the name of God, it means God), it is bad theology and bad multiculturalism. Two centuries of European domination and the immediacy of racism has of course badly bruised Muslims' self-confidence. Such self-confidence is returning but currently is at the stage of assertive independence rather than of a dialogue amongst equals. What happens at this stage, however, could prevent us from arriving at such a dialogue.

It is important for all – Muslims and non-Muslims – to be reminded that the narrow 'fundamentalist' Islam that is currently in some prominence is not all there is to be said for Islam. At its best it has been the ethical inspiration and the ground of solidarity that has at times given its adherents the power of not just physical conquest but a dynamic in which other civilisations are probed for understanding. The Arabic word for knowledge, *ilm* is second only to *Allah* in its frequency of appearance in the Qur'an. Even before the Arabian Peninsula had been mastered Muhammad emphasised the centrality of the temper of inquiry and urged the need to learn from all cultures: 'Seek knowledge, even unto China'. Moreover, the Qur'an is explicit that its message is not new and is not to be set apart from other religions: it is the culmination of the Prophetic tradition and is in direct continuity with all previous revelations, and encompasses all that is true in other faiths. This gave the early Muslims not only the confidence in themselves but the confidence to seek common ground with other faiths and synthesis with other cultures. Indeed there has not yet been a major Muslim society that has not been heavily dependent upon intelligent borrowing from other traditions of thought and social organisation, whether they be Greek, Persian, Indian or Western European. This is not something to be ashamed of for in each case Muslims have given as well as taken. And taken not in the way of imitation but creative reformulation. As evidence that the flow of traffic has not all been one way, Muslims take pride that it was Muslim medieval culture that provided the historical foundations of the Renaissance of Europe – something that Europeans have systematically erased from their consciousness because of the pain to their self-image.

Since the eighteenth century, since Shah Waliullah and Hegel, we have had to give up uncomplex conceptions of universality, and the search for creating what is of universal value in historically varied contexts has been at the centre of Muslim and European philosophical projects; but who can doubt that the latter has made far greater intellectual progress. Muslims, as they once did with Greek learning, have to come to terms with this body of thought – even though it is not always easy from a position of political inequality to learn from a culture which in its hegemonic arrogance all too readily sees non-European cultures, not least religious, as relics of primitivism.[41] This can be made easier if the West is willing to learn as well as teach. I think there are several aspects of Muslim historical experience from which the West can learn. It can, for example, learn or re-learn a respect for religion; for that historical experience embodies a record of tolerance of religious and cultural minorities such as the Jews which far exceeds that of Christendom and modern Europe.[42] Muslims continue to have a concept not just of tolerance but of respect for religion as such, including the religious beliefs of others, which seems to be disappearing in the West, where, as Michael Dummett, one of Britain's leading philosophers, observed, the assumption amongst intellectuals is that 'religious believers may properly be affronted, indeed deserve to be affronted'.[43] It is for this reason that most Muslims hope that the outcome of the Rushdie affair will be an extension of respect for all religious believers, not merely the abolition of the current law of blasphemy in a strengthening of a secular hegemony.[44]

The celebration of cultural synthesis, of hybridity, in *The Satanic Verses* should be of the deep significance to British Muslims that it was meant to be. Yet that book and the battles that have been fought around it has made the development of a confident outward-looking British Islam less rather than more likely. In that are lessons about Muslims, incitement to hatred and the law.

NOTES

1. Subsequent to the conference presentation the CRE has initiated a public debate on legislating against incitement to religious hatred and discrimination on religious grounds (Commission for Racial Equality, *Second Review of the Race Relations Act*, June 1991, pp. 58–61). These issues were, however, notable by their absence in the Labour Party's *Charter of Rights – Guaranteeing Individual Liberty in a Free Society*, March 1991. For a well-argued set of proposals see Sebastian Poulter, 'Towards Legislative Reform of the Blasphemy and Racial Hatred Laws', *Public Law*, 1991, pp. 371–85.

2. The House of Lords judgment on *Mandala* v. *Dowell Lee* (1983) contains the fullest statement of what the law understands to be an ethnic group. Legal judgments have included Sikhs, Jews, Gypsies, Rastafarians and others within the term but *Nyazi* v. *Rymans Ltd* 1988 specifically excluded Muslims. In 1991, the Appeal Court, by a majority decision, overruled the recognition of Rastafarians as an ethnic group and *CRE* v. *Precision* made it clear that discrimination against Muslims (as opposed to say, Pakistanis) is not unlawful. For a discussion of some of the issues that Muslim assertiveness raises for anti-racists, see my *Muslims, Race and Equality: Some Post-Rushdie Affair Reflections, Third Text*, 11, Summer 1990.

3. For an account of some of the ethnographic background see my 'British Asian Muslims and the Rushdie Affair', *Political Quarterly*, vol. 61, 2, April 1990, pp. 143–60. For Muslim criticism of the *fatwa* see *The Position of the Islamic Society for the Promotion of Religious Tolerance in the UK in the Rushdie Affair*, n.d. and Ziauddin Sardar and Merryl Wyn Davies, *Distorted Imagination* (London: Grey Seal, 1990). For a defence of the jurisprudential validity of the *fatwa* see the introduction to M.M. Ahsan and A.R. Kidwai (eds), *Sacrilege versus Civility: Muslim Perspectives on the 'Satanic Verses' Affair* (Leicester: Islamic Foundation, 1991); this volume contains a chronology of the affair to February 1991 and the most comprehensive bibliography available, though the annotations are of a mixed quality and from a narrowly orthodox Muslim viewpoint.

4. I am indebted for the bulk of some of the factual information on which this section is based to Eric Barendt, *Freedom of Speech* (Oxford: Clarendon Press, 1985), pp. 161–7. In revising my paper for publication I have also found helpful the report on group defamation by a sub-committee of the Law and Parliamentary Committee of the Board of Deputies of British Jews, June 1991.

5. In 1985 there were seven racial hatred prosecutions (three successful), 12 in 1986 (ten successful); under the new law there were three in 1988 and several anti-Jewish hatred prosecutions were in the pipeline in 1990: Robert Silver, 'Ban Race Gibes With New Law', *The Times*, 11 June 1991, p. 31.

6. Home Affairs Committee, *The Law Relating to Public Order*, vol. II, House of Commons, 1980, pp. 99–101. The TUC and the Board of Deputies of British Jews in their oral evidence to the Committee explicitly endorsed the CRE's view.

7. Home office, *Review of the Public Order Act 1936 and Related Legislation*, para. 107.

8.　In 1989 the Saskatchewan Court of Appeal upheld the judgment against the Engineering Students' Society, University of Saskatchewan, for producing newspapers which 'ridiculed, belittled and affronted the dignity of women because of their sex'. I owe the references to legislation on sexual orientation to Robert Wintemute.

9.　Board of Deputies, op. cit., p. 13.

10.　Patrick Marnham, 'Just Between Friends, Let's Hate Them'. *Independent*, 19 May 1990, p. 17.

11.　Simon Lee, 'First Introductory Paper', *Law, Blasphemy and the Multi-Faith Society*. Commission for Racial Equality and the Inter-faith Network for the UK. 1990, pp. 13–16. See also his contribution to *Law, Respect for Religious Identity and the Multi-Faith Society*, The Inter-faith Network for the UK and the Commission for Racial Equality, 1990.

12.　Board of Deputies, op. cit, p. 46; my emphasis.

13.　Bellew Publishing, 1989, p. 1.

14.　Shabbir Akhtar, 'Is Freedom Holy to Liberals? Some remarks on the Purpose of Law', *Free Speech*, Commission for Racial Equality, p. 24.

15.　Malise Ruthven, *A Satanic Affair* (London: Chatto & Windus, 1990), pp. 73–5.

16.　Allowing for cultural translation, it may be said that a case of national *ghairat* was the British response to the invasion of the Falklands.

17.　*Whitehouse* v. *Gay News*. Strictly speaking, James Kirkup's poem did not attribute homosexuality to Jesus, rather it imagined the crucified Christ as a suitable object of homosexual lust.

18.　Norman Daniels, *Islam and the West*: vol. 1, *Making of an Image, 1000–1300 A.D.* (1961); vol. 2. *Islam, Europe and Empire*; Karen Armstrong, *Holy War* (London: Macmillan, 1988).

19.　Michael Ignatieff, 'Defenders of Rushdies Tied in Knots', *Observer*, 2 April 1989 and 'Protect People, Not What They Believe', *Observer*, 11 February 1990.

20.　For a further elaboration of the concepts of the mode of being and the mode of oppression, see my 'Catching Up with Jesse Jackson; Being Oppressed and Being Somebody', *New Community*, October 1990.

21.　Sometime in 1989 a total stranger came up to me on a domestic British Airways flight to tell me all Muslims should be gathered together in one place and a nuclear bomb dropped on them.

22.　For the importance of group pride to ethnic and racial equality see the article cited in note 20.

23.　Simon Lee has sketched how this could be done by using article 20 (2) of the International Covenant on Civil and Political Rights, to which the UK is already a signatory, in 'Protecting Both Gods and Books' *Independent*, 9 March 1990. See also *Law, Respect for Religious Identity and the Multi-Faith Society*, op. cit., and Commission for Racial Equality, 1991, op. cit.

24.　In this regard Western liberals all too readily forget the 30 or so deaths in anti-*Satanic Verses* riots in Islamabad, Srinagar and Bombay when they assess Muslim attitudes to the author.

25.　'Identities on Parade', *Marxism Today*, June 1989, p. 29.

26.　R.G. Collingwood, *New Leviathan* (Oxford: Clarendon Press, 1942).

27.　*Ibid.*, 35.41–35.45.

28.　Susan Mendus, 'The Tigers of Wrath and the Horses of Instruction', Chapter 12 in this volume.

29.　Susan Mendus, *Toleration and the Limits of Liberalism* (London: Macmillan, 1989), pp. 154–62. Elsewhere in this volume Debbie Fitzmaurice argues that the fact of pluralism has to make us consciously value autonomy; I would say that it increases our appreciation of the value of belonging. See my 'On Not Being White in Britain: Discrimination, Diversity and Commonality', in M.J. Taylor and M. Leicester (eds), *Ethics, Ethnicity and Education* (London: Kogan Page, 1992).

30. For example, *The Crime of Blasphemy – Why It Should Be Abolished*, International Committee for the Defence of Salman Rushdie and His Publishers, London, 1989, which includes various black groups as among its signatories insists that there should be no restriction of any kind on the discussion of any subject (p. 6).

31. Simon Lee, 'First Introductory Paper', op. cit. pp. 17 and 19–20; Peter Jones 'Respecting Beliefs and Rebuking Rushdie', Chapter 8 in this volume.

32. For this and the next example I am indebted to an exciting book on aspects of the Rushdie affair, Richard Webster, *A Short History of Blasphemy* (Southwold: Orwell Press, 1990), pp. 26–7.

33. *Sunday Telegraph*, 8 September 1991, p. 3.

34. *Muslim News*, 19 April 1991, p. 3.

35. The BBC denied that the film was withdrawn at the last moment because of a fear of the law. Peter Rosier, head of Corporate Affairs and Press Relations was quoted as saying: 'It is not a legal thing at all. We had a lot of people who have contacted us. It is perfectly plain from the volume of letters and phone calls that we have had that this film will cause some considerable distress to people', *Muslim News*, no. 33, November 1991, p. 1. This is exactly the sort of sensitivity that was looked for by the 60,000 British Muslims who signed a petition asking Penguin to withdraw *The Satanic Verses* months before the Bradford book-burning, let alone the *fatwa*.

36. *Daily Mail*, 5 June 1991, p. 5.

37. Francis Wheen's Diary, *Independent on Sunday*, 14 October 1990.

38. The most bizarre example of pressure-group censorship is National Stuttering Project having got the US distributors of the British film *A Fish Called Wanda* to cut out a scene in the film in which a character is mocked because of his stutter (The Weasel, 'Up and Down the City Road', *Independent Magazine*, 7 September 1991).

39. Albert Weale, 'Freedom of Religion?' *Free Speech*, Commission for Racial Equality, February 1990, p. 58.

40. See my article mentioned in note 29.

41. For a recent excellent example of a Muslim militant engaging with modern Western ideas, see Shabbir Akhtar, *A Faith For All Seasons, Islam and Western Modernity* (London: Bellew Publishing, 1990).

42. India, of course, is the glaring counter-example to this historical record of toleration, the best examples of which are in the Middle-East, Central Asia, Northern Africa and Spain where Christian and Jewish minorities flourished for centuries.

43. *Independent on Sunday*, 11 February 1990.

44. Most Muslims would endorse the following: 'Muslims have no wish to lend their shoulders to those who want to pursue their own secular crusade against the Anglican Church or to get involved with the problem of Christian unbelief. For one thing, Christian sanctities are also their own and Muslims do not think it is an honourable way to gain one's right by seeking or acquiescing to the abolition of other peoples' rights'. M.H. Faruqi, 'For Muslims, the Law of Indifference', *Impact International*, vol. 21, 1&2, 13 September 1991, p. 7.

45. It has of course led to an unprecedented level of Muslim activism, not least amongst the youth, as evidenced by flourishing Islamic university societies and the numerous new magazines, and perhaps in this there is some hope.

10 The History of Blasphemy and the Rushdie Affair

David Edwards

Among the startling consequences of the publication of Salman Rushdie's *The Satanic Verses* in 1988 was not only a renewed practical interest in the English blasphemy law, but also the apparent paradox whereby this apparently illiberal remnant of an ancient jurisdiction was urged as the basis for a more comprehensive law which would be a necessary complement of a multicultural and pluralistic society. The vehement and bitter strife sparked off by the publication went far beyond what is usually denoted by the term controversy. Even in Britain the various protagonists and antagonists cannot be reduced into two coherent camps; the range of argument is testimony to cultural pluralism of a sort, if not always edifying throughout its variety. The outrage expressed by British Muslims over Rushdie's work did not impact upon a uniform, homogeneous, secular, liberal culture, but one which already had great complexity and diversity woven into its traditions before the ethnic settlements in Britain of recent generations – the range of the response to the controversy sufficiently demonstrates this.[1] Questions of pluralism and cultural diversity have long been issues for the law in England, though the controversy over *The Satanic Verses* manifestly raises such issues in an unprecedented way. In particular, the history of the ancient blasphemy laws, dating back over many centuries, illustrates a long development of pluralism in religious, intellectual and cultural life.[2]

The history of the English blasphemy laws developed through successive stages, each of which expressed and regulated different understandings of the coherence and diversity of society. It may be doubted whether the spirit even of the earliest stages of the law is yet entirely superseded. J.S. Mill felt that the suffocating social conformity of mid-Victorian times derived inspiration from old traditions of theological uniformity;[3] Richard Webster's recent work on the Rushdie affair asserts that there has been a 'deep internalization' of the repressive aspects of the Christian culture of the West over the past thousand years.[4] In what follows I shall review the different stages of the English blasphemy law, the way in which the development of that law reflected and influenced cultural transformations, and then consider the apparent paradox, that the extension of what seems to be an instrument of cultural repression is claimed as the basis for a successful plural society.

In all probability, blasphemy has been a punishable offence in England since the conversion of the Anglo-Saxons to Christianity in the dark ages. The medieval culture constituted by the dominance of the Catholic Church saw no significant challenges to its orthodoxy prior to the fourteenth century. After the suppression of heathenism the offence of blasphemy was generally a casual and routine matter, made up of cases of gross impiety, cursing, lack of respect, rather than a fundamental assault on theological doctrines. But in the late middle ages the history of the blasphemy laws merges with the story of a more systematic persecution of heresy.

To understand the medieval blasphemy laws, it is necessary to have a general idea of what the relevant characteristics of the Christian religion were taken to be, and secondly of the nature of the jurisdiction that enforced the laws. The first aspect is far better known than the second, but needs to be repeated for the sake of completeness. Richard Webster, in his book on the Rushdie affair, suggests that the remote origins of the 'liberal' reaction in defence of Rushdie ultimately derives from these theocratic structures.[5]

Both Christianity and Islam derive much of their conception of the sacred from Judaism, and in particular that complete intolerance of affronts to God which is so different in degree and principle from the scruples of many other religions. The early history of Christianity, however, stands in the sharpest contrast to that of Islam. For three centuries Christianity was subject to periodic bouts of persecution, and convictions about blasphemous idolatry gave the persecuted religion the steel to survive and grow stronger. To the intolerance inseparable from such beliefs, as much as to other qualities, Christianity owed its eventual triumph. In the complex tangle of early Christian thought we find the same mixture of intolerance and liberating ideals which is to be found, for instance, in seventeenth-century Puritanism and radicalism. Christians denounced the political and religious ideology of the Roman Empire, they claimed that theirs was the exclusive way to salvation. Even during the period when their faith was outlawed the Christians were aggressive and provocative in reviling the idolatrous beliefs of their neighbours.[6] Heretical versions of Christianity were condemned in terms just as strong. Even heretics who suffered death for their faith were denounced as destined to hellfire for their errors. Before ever there was a Christian ascendency there was a ferocious denunciation of heresy and a stream of proscribed opinions. With that ascendency came a vigorous use of secular power to suppress paganism. The old Christian abhorrence of capital punishment was abandoned, leaving only the mockery of the use of fire to cause death for extreme religious offences, in order to prevent the shedding of blood.

Needless to say, for a fair estimation of Christianity in its early centuries much else needs to be taken into account but this implicit intolerance is clearly relevant to the formation of the later blasphemy laws. Christian thought in these early centuries formed an ethical culture which was to dominate European thought on such legal matters as incest, adultery, homosexuality, abortion, polygamy and divorce. Attitudes towards blasphemy also tended towards persecution because of a 'belief that God not only abominates the act of the misbeliever, but will not hold us guiltless if we leave him unmolested'.[7] This guilt might have consequences not only in the after-life, but in visitations on earth. The Old Testament is full of events where God has visited divine anger on those guilty of religious offences and those who connived at them. When Christianity was a persecuted religion such catastrophies as famine, earthquake and pestilence were attributed to the Christians' mocking of pagan gods, just as the Christians ascribed these disasters to divine vengeance on their persecutors.[8] Blasphemy is the most obvious provocation to such divine judgments, but there was also a belief that other religious and moral offences called down retribution. The Emperor Justinian claimed that a succession of disasters was a reason for punishing homosexual behaviour. As late as 1666 the disasters of plague and fire in London stirred the House of Commons to examine books tending to blasphemy and atheism and so put Thomas Hobbes in jeopardy. Because such beliefs in divine visitation are so foreign to our world-view we may tend to exaggerate the elements of conscious wish-fulfilment which are no doubt close to such beliefs and underestimate their former plausibility as an explanation of the course of events.

These concepts inherited from the early centuries of Christianity, together with later modifications, led the people of medieval England to live under a quasi-theocracy as pervasive, and sometimes as rigorous, as that of contemporary Iran.[9] Apart from the small number of Jews, the whole population was subject to the ecclesiastical authorities and the jurisdiction of the Courts Christian. This jurisdiction claimed an authority quite independent of the secular power, though it was often dependent on the latter for purposes of enforcement.

The spiritual courts had miscellaneous functions but the most important were concerned with the suppression of sinful behaviour. Modern controversies about the relationship of crime and sin are altogether removed from the presupposition of this jurisdiction. Sin *was* crime, and its definition, detection and suppression was a central task of the Church authorities. They did not undertake the hopeless task of punishing all moral defects and dispositions, nor did they think that sin could be cured by means of legal sanctions. But sinful behaviour was punishable as crime. This in large measure is the origin of the notion of 'Christian morality', which derives in part from the concrete activities of the Church courts.

The Church courts claimed a formidable jurisdiction, even allowing that the actual control they exercised might be moderate or intermittent. The purpose of the jurisdiction was to subject virtually the whole population to a detailed discipline of moral conduct and religious belief. Naturally an integral aspect of the latter was the maintenance of the veneration on which the whole jurisdiction rested. The Church courts could, perhaps, have connived at drunkenness or adultery, but to have ignored blasphemy and heresy would have been suicidal to this authority. In punishing blasphemy the Church courts were not merely

suppressing sin, but asserting the coherence and integrity of their whole jurisdiction.

The jurisdiction of the Courts Christian arose from, and tried to maintain the
coherence of, a culture permeated by powerful and authoritative judgements on
sin and religion. It adapted to the challenge of a serious and radical heresy by
closer alliance with the civil power and by invoking the death penalty. From
1400, in their campaign against the Lollards, the Church courts effectively had
powers of life and death. The clergy had a free hand to define heresy as they
thought fit, while the civil power was bound to execute obstinate heretics.

Despite sporadic episodes of heresy, the theocratic jurisdiction of the Church
courts presided over an impressive regime of cultural homogeneity by the end of
the middle ages – certainly in comparison with what was to come. The doctrine
and morality which it enforced and defended had the prestige of great antiquity
and the strength of coherence. The coming of the Reformation to England did not
see the extinction of this jurisdiction, but its erosion and increasing confusion.
The attempt to enforce a strict and coherent orthodoxy perished with Mary Tudor.
The crime of blasphemy had its roots in an age of orthodoxy, with a jurisdiction
ready and able to strike at all opinion which it regarded as damnable sin and a
peril to salvation.

The division of English society into Protestant and Catholic, together with the
constitutional changes which both caused and resulted from this division,
rendered the rigorous enforcement of an orthodoxy impossible, or drastically
impolitic. This itself is a cultural transformation of enormous consequence, and
the operation of the blasphemy laws reflects and exemplifies it, from the
beginning of Elizabeth's reign the old ecclesiastical courts continued their
time–honoured jurisdiction over minor offences and immoralities, while the
Court of High Commission proceeded against more serious cases, particularly the
suppression of heresy, blasphemy and seditious books. Even to contemporaries, it
seemed arbitrary in its proceedings and punishments. But its jurisdiction over
heresy was confined in such a manner that the doctrinal questions at issue
between Protestants and Catholics were excluded from *criminal* charges of
heresy. Needless to say, strong partisans on either side regarded each other's doctrines as blasphemous, but neither view was adopted by the criminal law. To this
extent legally enforced orthodoxy was relaxed to tolerate some diversity of
religious opinion. Beyond these bounds the punishment for blasphemy was as
harsh as ever, but the criminal law could no longer be seen as the instrument of
rooting out all damnable heresy or the enforcement of an orthodoxy necessary for
salvation.

The Court of High Commission fell in 1640 with the crash of Charles I's
government, and the following decades of the 1640s and 50s witnessed the
greatest display of cultural diversity, toleration and pluralism yet seen in English
history.[10] This was certainly not because these were generally regarded as
intrinsically valuable – probably all ranks of society agreed in holding the reverse

– but because the instruments of government broke down and revolutionary ferment and old allegiances were equally hard to repress. The divergent cultures of the old regime, of Puritanism and of the radical underground adapted or burgeoned in the new climate. From the latter group in particular came a hubbub of speculation on social, political, ethical and theological issues. Controversy and polemic abounded with the collapse of the institutions of censorship, accompanied by visionary invective and apocalyptic fulminations.

Because the Parliamentary regime was unable to agree upon, or at any rate to impose an official religious settlement, because the army disagreed with the Parliamentary majority, because Cromwell and other influential leaders sympathised with the notion of toleration of Protestant sects, a considerable *de facto* pluralism prevailed in England for two decades. The claims of 'conscience' and the religion of the 'God-within' expanded within this more tolerant framework. This was probably scandalous to the majority of the population, at least in its toleration of the most bizarre manifestations of religious enthusiasm, but lack of agreement on the orthodox alternative, and the realities of political circumstances, gave scope for this unwanted state of affairs. Provisions for the suppression of blasphemy were improvised to deal with the most outrageous departures from conventional Christianity, but these were not equal to the desired restoration of decorum. Toleration and the abandonment of the ideal of orthodoxy were so marked a feature of Cromwell's rule that Jews were allowed to settle in England for the first time in over three centuries, and toleration was extended to a non-Christian faith.

Webster suggests that the development of the spiritual nucleus of the 'God-within' and its secular consequences is what marks off European culture so decisively from Islam, and which explains much of the mutual incomprehension shown in the Rushdie affair between a culture which accords such centrality to the sacred text and tradition and one which is so emancipated from such external authority.[11] Of course, mystical spirituality, whether Islamic or Christian, tends to form such a nucleus, but this is not the religion of the many. We should be careful in equating 'Puritanism' with the religion of the 'God-within', and be aware of the parallel and reinforcing tendencies of the Enlightenment (particularly in Catholic countries). Yet, after all qualifications and amplification, surely the formation of this spiritual nucleus does indeed indicate a great cultural distinction with innumerable ramifications for the relations of these cultures, some of which are evident in the Rushdie controversy.

The restoration of the monarchy in 1660 could only be partly a restoration of the old constitution of church and state – the revolutions in society and culture prevented more. Ecclesiastical courts retained authority in name only. In consequence the common law was obliged to step into the breach if the various transgressions which had been punishable under the old jurisdiction were to remain crimes. The Court of King's Bench assumed the responsibility of protecting the moral welfare of the state, and since it defended 'Christianity' as part of this moral welfare, the punishment of blasphemy became part of common law jurisdiction.

The trial of John Taylor for blasphemy in 1676 is of significance because it establishes a character to the crime of blasphemy which was to endure for over two centuries. Taylor's reviling of God, Jesus and religion were said by the Lord Chief Justice, Sir Matthew Hale, to be

> not only an offence against God and religion, but a crime against the laws, State and Government, and therefore punishable in this Court; that to say religion is a cheat is to dissolve all those obligations whereby civil societies are preserved; and Christianity being parcel of the laws of England, therefore to reproach the Christian religion is to speak in subversion of the law.[12]

Hale's dictum marks a clear shift between the treatment of blasphemy as a crime against God or an orthodoxy relevant to salvation and blasphemy as a crime against civil obligation. Part of the jurisdiction of the common law, Hale implies, is the preservation of its own integrity and authority. Reverence for the truth of Christianity is an integral part of that authority, and therefore the common law must retaliate against attacks on Christianity as an attack on itself. In a country recently torn by political, social and cultural strife, yet still despite all variations overwhelmingly Christian, this is a stress not on the divisiveness of theological orthodoxy but the unifying theme of civil obligation. Christianity in Hale's usage, has to do with the sense of duty which subjects ought to possess; perhaps it impresses on them particular duties, or perhaps it gives a general conception of right conduct, with the idea of duty as a part of this. Perhaps Hale's term 'parcel' implies that Christianity, rather than being a department or segment of the law, is the tie which binds the part together. Christianity gives to the system of laws a mandate and sanction which they could not do without.

It could also be that the Hale meant to advance the view that the specific practices of individual civil societies bore a relation to the moral code of a particular religion and that the specific provisions of English law were so related to Christianity. There is much to be said for this; indeed if we take 'Christianity' to be the moral code enforced by the defunct Courts Christian, it cannot be denied. To take, for example, the case of sexual crimes – homosexual acts, adultery, fornication, procuring, abortion – the rationale of punishing these was to be seen in the context of moral and religious ideas that forbade them. So the Christian moral tradition indeed did give meaning to the practice of such criminal laws. Moreover, England had an established religion and all manner of public ceremonies from the Coronation to the oaths for the giving of evidence in Courts were associated with Christian belief. Consequently there is a threefold ground which makes intelligble Hale's dictum incorporating the old ecclesiastical offence of blasphemy in the common law. Civil institutions were supposed to require the general sense of obligation that the sanction of religion alone could give; a 'Christian' ethic was essential for the justification of the traditional collection of laws relating to morals; the English constitution incorporated customs and institutions which were supposed to depend on the truth of the Christian religion and therefore the latter was entitled to protection.

Belief in the general grounds of Hale's reasoning was almost universal among his contemporaries. Even the most liberal-minded accepted its general tenor, if not some of the supposed implications. Far from contradicting the political ideal of universal religious toleration and cultural pluralism, it might be seen as a corollary of that ideal. This was so in the work of John Locke. After arguing that even idolaters should not be excluded from toleration, Locke stipulates 'those are not at all to be tolerated who deny the being of God. Promises, covenants and oaths, which are the bond of human society, can have no hold upon an atheist. The taking away of God, though but even in thought, dissolves all'.[13] This is the view that religious pluralism itself rests upon the compunctions and restraints of civil society, which in turn depend upon theistic conceptions too universal to be related to any particular religion, and that atheism therefore subverts religious toleration along with all other rights. The common law offence of blasphemy, like that enforced by the old Church courts consequently had a distinctive relation to the jurisdiction as a whole. It no longer had a relation to the attempt to guide individual souls to salvation, but it did have a relation to the coherence and integrity of the entire jurisdiction.

Almost two centuries were to elapse before civil disabilities in English law were removed to the degree suggested by Locke's theoretical treatment of toleration. The common law crime of blasphemy was far more repressive in its operation than the legitimate protection of a theistic ground of civil obligation advanced in his theory. Moreover, in the two centuries following Hale's judgement the character of the blasphemy law gradually became more and more ambiguous. The spirit of that judgement seems to be that all fundamental attacks on Christianity are criminal offences, no matter how pure the misguided motives of the offender or discreet the language employed. In fact, all the cases which were actually prosecuted and punished as blasphemy at common law would have been offensive to the pious sensitivities of contemporaries. Some were intentionally outrageous, some simply failed to go to extreme lengths of discretion and circumlocution. But the degree of offence is not necessarily proportionate to the degree to which religion is undermined in the crucial respect indicated in Hale's judgement – the degree to which an attack on religion tends 'to dissolve all the obligations whereby civil societies are preserved'. Any telling critique of Christianity might be subversive on the premises of this judgement, regardless of its temperateness of expression or the degree of learning shown in its argument.

The two centuries which elapsed after Hale's judgment saw both increasing pluralism in the forms of Christianity legally permitted in England and cultural adaptations to this fact. The courts showed an inclination to accommodate the claims of academic theological discussion – though the impetus of such discussion does not recognise the sort of bounds that the theory of the theological underpinning of civil obligation requires. Moreover the legal recognition of different sects and the emancipation of 'conscience' from sacred texts or formal institutions had a profound effect on English political culture. Even the judicial bench conceded in cases of blasphemy a legal right to the enjoyment of free opinions. It was left in the difficult position of recognising this right, but denying any right to express it. To accommodate the changes in political culture which reflected growing religious pluralism and its legal recognition, the doctrine crept into the law that the crucial offence in blasphemy was the manner, not the matter of utterance.

The simple rigour of Hale's judgment was increasingly inconsistent with the social and political culture of Victorian England. Of course Victorian society was replete with taboos and social inhibitions heavily curbing both conduct and expression. But there was also an increasing suspicion of the regulation of free discussion by the public authorities. Even where the majority approved the punishment of convicted blasphemers, this was regarded as a justifiable departure from a general public culture founded on a supposed right to free discussion – particularly in religious matters, where conscience gave a distinctive sanction to freedom. I say 'supposed right', because on a strict construction of the existing common law of blasphemy no such right existed. But the popular view was that England was a free country, and the judges, only influenced by this prejudice in less degree, had allowed the law to become ambiguous to accommodate such a view.

The harshness of the workings of the blasphemy law were illustrated in the case of Thomas Pooley, an obscure and half-demented Cornish labourer whose imprisonment outraged J.S. Mill and the historian H.T. Buckle.[14] The public controversy between the latter and the prosecutor in the case, J.D. Coleridge, illustrated the mid-Victorian disquiet about the practical enforcement of the law, if not the principle of the law itself. When, in 1883, Coleridge was Lord Chief Justice, he gave a new formulation to the common law offence: ' ... if the decencies of controversy are observed, even the fundamentals of religion may be attacked without the writer being guilty of blasphemy'.[15] This dictum effectively resolved the ambiguity in the law of blasphemy. Just as centuries before the offence of blasphemy had ceased to be an integral part of a jurisdiction whose *raison d'être* was the enforcement of an orthodoxy essential to salvation, so the offence had ceased to protect what had been regarded as the essential sanction of the authority of the system of laws and the ground of civil obligation. The blasphemy law was now concerned with 'decency' in the treatment of Christianity, the manner of attacks on that religion rather than the matter of the assertion against it and protection to the feelings of Christians and 'sympathizers with the Christian religion' within these limits.

Judicial opinion on Coleridge's ruling was by no means unanimous. His chief critic was the eminent jurist and historian of the English criminal law James Fitzjames Stephen. The latter criticised the judgment as a defective interpretation of the law, its history and as a potential new lease of life to a law which, in Stephen's opinion, was so radically bad that it required legislative abolition.[16] Stephen was able to show that only strained logic could deduce from the abolition of disabilities of Jews and different classes of Christians that the law now gave latitude to the public advocacy of atheism. Indeed, Coleridge's conclusion cannot be derived from those changes in the Statute law to which he makes reference in his ruling. Rather the conclusion is derived from something at the same time more momentous and impalpable, a change in the political culture and the growing prevalence of an outlook in society that was too pluralistic for any more extensive interpretation of the blasphemy laws. The controversy over Pooley's case could not have failed to make Coleridge aware of such an attitude.

Whatever the shortcomings of Coleridge's interpretation of the blasphemy law in 1883, and despite initial dissent from the judicial bench, his ruling came to be the principle on which blasphemy cases continued to be tried until 1992. From the time of that ruling the peculiar link between the law of blasphemy and the character of a particular jurisdiction was broken. The old system of ecclesiastical jurisdiction would have been senseless without proscribing blasphemy as a crime. When that system perished, Hale took cognisance of the crime as a common law offence because religious belief was held to be essential to that recognition of obligation on which law, state and government rested. From 1883 no jurisdiction (except perhaps that exercised by the Church courts over Anglican clergymen) punished blasphemy because it was in need of a divine sanction. The effective change in the blasphemy law, together with the Judicial Oaths Act of 1888, saw the end of that long tradition which required a super-mundane origin for obligation and oaths. There finally prevailed the recognition that non-believers might have sufficient incentive to truthfulness and fidelity to the law from a sense of their own integrity or from dread of penal sanctions of a very earthly nature.[17]

The lack of any prosecutions under the blasphemy law after 1922 led many, including judges, to consider that the law was defunct. However, in 1976 the proposal by the Danish film-maker, J.J. Thorsen, to make a pornographic film in Britain about a fantasised sex-life of Jesus led to an outcry which made him desist. The Prime Minister and the Archbishop of Canterbury referred to the possibility of a prosecution under the common law of blasphemy; the Queen let it be known that she viewed the project as 'obnoxious'. Shortly afterwards Mary Whitehouse undertook a private prosecution against *Gay News*, the homosexual newspaper, and its editor, Denis Lemon. They had published a poem by James Kirkup which involved a fantasy of homosexual intercourse with the crucified corpse of Jesus. The trial judge ruled that the common law offence was still current and Lemon became the first person to be convicted of this crime in over half a century.

The Thorsen episode and *Gay News* case not surprisingly gave rise to great controversy, and this forms one of the strands continued in the greater complexity of the debates concerning *The Satanic Verses*. An attempt to abolish the offence of blasphemy on the grounds that laws on obscenity, indecency and conduct likely to lead to a breach of the peace were adequate safeguards for decency and order was overwhelmingly defeated in the House of Lords. The Law Commission produced a working paper proposing that in place of the offence of blasphemy there be a new offence of using threatening, insulting or abusive words in a place of worship. In response to this, the then Archbishop of Canterbury, Dr Runcie, suggested that the law of blasphemy not only be retained but extended to religious other than Christianity 'with the object of protecting the fundamental, sacred beliefs of all religious people from deep and hurtful attack', though he acknowledged the difficulty of defining those religions which should receive legal protection. When the *Gay News* appeal was dismissed from the House of Lords, Lord Scarman's judgment advanced the view that the scope of the offence should be extended by new legislation. In his judgment he says:

> The offence belongs to a group of criminal offences designed to safeguard the internal tranquillity of the Kingdom. In an increasingly plural society such as that of modern Britain, it is necessary not only to respect the differing religious beliefs, feelings and practices of all but also to protect them from scurrility, vilification and contempt ... It would be intolerable if, by allowing an author or publisher to plead the excellence of his motives and the right of free speech, he could evade the penalties of the law, even though his words were blasphemous in the sense of constituting an outrage upon the religious feelings of his fellow citizens. This is no way forward for a successful plural society.[18]

It seems paradoxical, when viewed in the light of the history of the blasphemy laws of England, to arrive at a point where not only the retention but also the extension of these laws is argued for in terms of fostering the conditions of a successful plural society. The old ecclesiastical jurisdiction had been obliged to renounce the enforcement of doctrinal orthodoxy when diversity in religious convictions reached the point where repression had become untenable. The common-law jurisdiction had been gradually altered in character in order to avoid the restrictive consequences of the austere doctrine of the reliance of civil obligation on religious belief. Diversity of beliefs and values, both in matters of substance and of expression, had so widened that even the enforcement of the blasphemy law to maintain the decencies of controversy long fell into disuse. The transformations of earlier statutes would seem to have been brought about by the pressure of increasing plurality of belief and modes of conduct and the complementary extension of liberty, so that what once was regarded as at best straining the bounds of tolerance came to be regarded with comparative equanimity. I have traced how the ingenuity of generations of judges tended to accommodate the blasphemy law to changed cultural circumstances. Judicial amplification of the law, by contrast, extending it to cover non-Christian religions, would seem to be an illegitimate act equivalent to retrospective legislation. Consequently any extension of the blasphemy law requires new legislative enactment.[19]

The case for extending the blasphemy law of course depends on the argument that the principle of the current blasphemy law is sound, and that failure to so extend the law is inequitable, a denial of rights and likely to be socially pernicious. The character of the religious pluralism prevailing in England is now quite different from that traced in the evolution of the blasphemy laws over the centuries. True, it derives in part from that diversity in religious opinions foreshadowed in Victorian times and brought out so acutely in the Thorsen and *Gay News* cases, but it also derives from the transplantation to England of the religious cultures of other continents, the context of the Rushdie affair. If the religious sensitivities of Christians are to be given circumstantial legal protection, to the degree that the treatment of religion should be decent and restrained in manner, should this protection not extend to followers of Islam? Since 1883 the reasons for a circumstantial legal protection of Christianity and it alone have not been clear. A case might be made out that even after this date Christianity has stood in a distinct relation to English law. A majority of the population believed Christianity to be true; a greater majority have 'sympathised' with Christianity; Christian tradition has been the origin of many legally enforced practices. Whatever force such considerations may have, they are more and more attenuated with the passing of each decade. Most cogently, if the *raison d'être* of the current blasphemy law is the protection of Christian believers and sympathisers from offence, then since susceptibility to such offence extends equally to Islam, its adherents are equally in need of legal protection.

Indeed it has been argued that Islam is more in need than Christianity of legal protection, owing in part to the relatively weak social and informal pressure that Muslims are able to bring to bear in English society. Certainly the degree of influence previously mentioned in the Thorsen affair is not at the disposal of English Muslims. This kind of inequality is clear, but a subtler inequality is suggested by Richard Webster with regard to the operation of social inhibitions against blasphemy. He speaks of an 'impalpable injustice' in the relative susceptibility of Christianity and Islam to blasphemy in contemporary England, besides the 'palpable injustice' that only the former has legal protection against blasphemy. This impalpable inequality is supposed to be due to the degree of internalised repression of blasphemous thought and utterance among the British people which renders a blasphemy law protecting Christianity largely superfluous.[20] Moreover he appears to think that this internalised repression derives from the past operation of the law, and that a legacy of inhibition obviates the possibility of the floodgates of blasphemy against Christianity being opened by particular blasphemous incidents. Certainly the inequality of recourse to informal social pressure between the adherents of Christianity and Islam is a fact which adds to the case for the legal protection of the latter, so far as the principle of a blasphemy law is sound. But I find the idea of the impalpable injustice much less convincing. The 'floodgate' theory was never the rationale of the English blasphemy law. Internalised repression, in the sense of psychological inhibition and reluctance to engage in blasphemy, was cultivated to a far greater degree in the religious upbringing of past generations than is generated by contemporary standards of tact and good manners. I doubt that the period since 1922 has seen any diminution of anti-Christian blasphemy, despite the fact that there has only been one conviction in an English court. What has diminished, rather, is the proneness of Christians to take the same degree of offence, to seek redress at law, or indeed for the legal system to think of criminal blasphemy as an important matter. Indeed, what seems to distinguish contemporary attitudes to religion from those of past generations is indifference and broadmindedness rather than any subtlety or degree of inhibition with regard to religious sensitivities. Naturally, this has its limits, as the *Gay News* case demonstrates, where Mary Whitehouse's sense of what went beyond the limit was shared by a jury. To the general degree that Christianity is protected by the inhibitions of tact and good manners, the disinclination of most people to affront the religious beliefs of others, so is Islam. The problem, of course, is that some people do not share these inhibitions, and it is this rather than any impalpable injustice that generates the questions of the retention and extension of the blasphemy laws.

The chief inequality between Christians and Muslims in contemporary England does not lack palpability and goes far beyond the latter not having the sort of influence marshalled in the Thorsen affair. It derives, setting aside all nuances of pluralism, from Muslims being a minority within a comparatively (but only comparatively) homogeneous majority culture. The Rushdie controversy intensified this to the degree that many Muslims felt not only an acute sense of being a minority, but a besieged minority. All this is well brought out in Tariq Modood's essay, in which he addresses issues which go far beyond the scope of this chapter.[21] Clearly Rushdie's defamation of Muhammad is widely regarded by British Muslims as not only blasphemous, but also in its dissemination and reception an attack on their honour and dignity as a group. This certainly marks out the Rushdie affair from all the cases prosecuted for blasphemy in the history of the English law. Not even Mary Whitehouse's *Gay News* prosecution could be regarded as motivated by the desire to defend a minority group. Nonetheless, the anxiety expressed before that case, that the point was being reached where nothing was held sacred at all, does hint at a sense of helpless frustration not entirely removed from the later exasperation of Muslims. Indeed, this is the context which makes Lord Scarman's judgment in his House of Lords ruling have greater weight. The sort of legal recourse for Muslims implied in that judgment by means of an adaptation and extension of the blasphemy laws is not grounded on the notion of group defamation which Tariq Modood believes to be at the heart of Muslim hurt in the Rushdie affair, but would still redress the sense of injustice felt by them.

Even the strongest accentuation of the hurt to the collective feelings of honour and dignity of British Muslims involved in the Rushdie affair cannot avoid the fact that the focus of this hurt was an act of perceived blasphemy. The honour of the believers is consequential on the honour accorded to Muhammad and the Islamic faith. Any vindication of group honour by means of the instrument of an extended blasphemy law would have an indirect relation to such a law. The form of protection such a law could offer would be the enforcement of a circumstantial restraint on the treatment of the essentials of the Islamic faith. This would require decency of manner in those handling such essentials, since the law does not and could not uphold the truth of doctrines or the holiness of substantive beliefs. Such a law can only endeavour to protect the feelings of believers; it cannot directly vindicate group honour or attempt the absurdity of protecting holiness. This incongruity between the logic of the law and what believers would wish to protect or vindicate has long been present in the operation of the English blasphemy law. Mrs Whitehouse wished to protect Jesus; the law could only redress an outrage on her own feelings and those of others. From the origin of the common law of blasphemy, the Christian experience of holiness which is the true context of blasphemy was displaced first by concern to protect the idea of a sanction of civil obligation and then by the need to enforce a circumstantial decency in the treatment of Christianity. An extended blasphemy law could offer no direct defence of Islamic conceptions of truth, holiness or honour, only a comparable circumstantial restraint in the treatment of the fundamentals of the Islamic faith.

If the principle of the current blasphemy law is sound, then the proposals of such figures as Lord Scarman and Lord Runcie to extend the scope of the law to the protection of religions other than Christianity seem to be cogent. But is this principle sound? The proposal to extend legal protection against blasphemy to various religions appears, on the surface at least, to run counter to the character of a plural society. Such a society is marked by the same diversity in religious commitment and indifference as is displayed in all other aspects of life. The claims of religions seem to be matters for personal choice and the exercise of liberty, and these tend to produce ever greater variety of opinion. Where such variety exists, controversy and antagonism seem inevitable, since religious matters, like those involving sexual conduct or politics are matters of strong feeling. No doubt vehement and intemperate expression concerning religious matters is often and perhaps generally to be deplored. But why should expression on religious matters be the subject of special legal restraint? This question is particularly pressing in a pluralistic society which cannot appeal to any orthodoxy constraining the convictions of individuals. It would seem that such pluralism rests the decision over the claims of religion to special scrupulousness of treatment with individuals, and that any coercion in this matter is a denial of pluralism.

However, such a view is surely a superficial and insensitive interpretation of those characteristics which distinguish religious belief.[22] Religious belief is generally connected with upbringing in childhood, and this and the claims of group identity and tradition are emphatically brought out in the example of

British Muslims. Whether such belief is a confirmation of childhood learning or the result of later conversion, it is not chosen but rather is the recognition of what, to the believer, is reality. What is involved in religious belief is a transformed understanding of the self – it is not a self moving among different options and settling on one of them. For those who interpret their lives in relation to what is seen as sacred, this relationship constitutes a recognition of ultimate value and is the most powerful conviction it is possible to hold. These characteristics of religious belief, which differentiate it from other forms of choice or belief, are the reasons why religious freedom is accorded a special status in national constitutions and international declarations of rights. Advocates of an extension of the blasphemy law infer from this peculiar character and importance of religious belief and the correspondingly unique vulnerability of believers the conclusion that the corollary of this is that all believers should be protected from outrage against their most deeply held convictions.

Any extension of the blasphemy law now current in English common law must have as its purpose the protection of religious believers from offence. Plainly the law cannot be based on the defence of the truth of religions each of which denies the truth of the others. The development of the English law of blasphemy may be seen as paradoxical. Of course, over the centuries and decades the scope of the law has become less and less restrictive, yet on the other hand the law may be seen as becoming increasingly illiberal in that it came to focus exclusively on the satisfaction of the injured feelings of believers without supposing that blasphemy causes any further harm. The older stages of the law certainly assumed that further harm was done by blasphemous utterances – incurring divine retribution, the erosion of an orthodoxy essential to the salvation of the people, the subversion of the conditions of civil association and the sanction of the system of law. But the present blasphemy law is solely concerned with the satisfaction of outrage against religious feelings, and any extension of it would have to be confined to a similar concern. This does seem to be inconsistent with the general tenor of liberalism which alone makes sense of placing value on a diverse and plural society, and only the attribution of special value to religion as previously outlined can make sense of the apparent paradox.

A more extensive notion of harm in relation to the blasphemy law has appeared among those proposing a widening of the law in the wake of the Rushdie affair. It is to be seen, for example, in Tariq Modood's argument. He considers reform of the law not only in order to protect believers against the outrage of specifically religious feelings, but also to vindicate group dignity and honour. As I have suggested, any extension of the current spirit of the blasphemy law to include Islam will focus on the first harm and address the second only indirectly. But Modood also discusses a third form of harm alleged to arise from works like *The Satanic Verses*. This is a threat to the future safety of Muslims which is supposed to be the cumulative effect of vehemently anti-Islamic polemic. Just as anti-Semitic writings prepared the way for the Holocaust, so anti-

Islamic writings are seen as a threat to the future safety of Muslims. The consid-erations involved in deliberating the force of these claims are beyond the scope of this paper. However, two points may be noted. First, if this threat is to be regarded as a likely consequence of works such as *The Satanic Verses*, it constitutes a different sort of harm from that involved in injuring the feelings of believers. Indeed some would contest whether the latter case actually constituted harm (since they regard such feelings as being of debatable worth). Yet on any view of harm the alleged tendency to threaten safety is incontestably harmful. Secondly, it is the plausibility of this threat and the weighing of the particular contribution made to it by each publication which is the chief issue raised by these arguments for legislative reform. Assessing the plausibility of the threat is a matter of very complex historical and political judgement. Weighing the con-structive injury done by a particular publication is equally problematic. Undoubtedly, for example, there is some connection between Karl Marx's anti-religious writings and the horrific persecution of believers (Christian, Muslim and others) under Communist regimes several decades later. But even with historical hindsight, the degree of responsibility of the former for the latter is controversial and difficult to determine. All those with any regard for values of pluralism and freedom of opinion must insist on the satisfaction of stringent criteria concerning the plausibility of the threat and the judgement of publications as acts of instigation contributing to that threat if these considerations are to be the basis of an extension of the criminal law.[23]

What I have called the current spirit of the blasphemy law is not prompted by these considerations, but is concerned with the prevention of offence and the according of a minimum circumstantial respect to religious belief. In his paper 'Respecting Beliefs and Rebuking Rushdie' Peter Jones places a clear analytical distinction between the prevention of offence and the according of respect to beliefs as grounds for any extension of the blasphemy law.[24] Certainly he is right to distinguish utilitarian and rights-based explanations of the rationale of the law. But in tracing the reactions to the Rushdie affair and considering the claims advanced for the extension of the blasphemy law, if these ontological explanations are set aside, I think that the distinctions between the two principles of curbing offence and according respect to beliefs can be over-emphasised. The notion that people are self-originating sources of claims, if it is to be the basis for an extension of the blasphemy law, cannot avoid the conclusion that what is claimed by such advocates is a circumstantial protection from offence. Similarly, the claim to be protected from offence cannot, in any equitable legal system, be reduced to a claimed entitlement to be defended against the mere fact of mental pain, regardless of the value to be placed on the occasion of such susceptibility to pain. Offence, if it is to be a basis for legal enactment, cannot designate a simple empirical fact; it must be accorded a normative status. This is especially true in a pluralistic society where, characteristically, the enacting of law is unlikely to be by a particular set of believers for the benefit of the same set of believers. Here the question must be formulated along such lines as: 'Though I don't believe in that, do I nonetheless perceive in the belief sufficient value to justify the punishment of those who grossly offend those who do believe in it?' Consequently, I feel that in deliberating the extension of the blasphemy law respect for beliefs and the avoiding of offence are not two different and alternative sets of principle, but rather are interrelated aspects of one argument which is put forward by the advocates of such an extension. The actions of Muslims in going out of their way to read *The Satanic Verses* and then publicising the particulars of the affront they felt on the grounds that they were offended do not seem to me to be paradoxical. They were exercised by what they perceived not only as a lack of respect but also an outrage on their religious feelings, and the 'offence' they felt was not a merely personal anguish or inner mental state which could be mitigated by avoidance, but the breach of what they regarded as a normative claim.

I feel obliged to regard both offence and respect for beliefs as necessary aspects of the case for the extension of the blasphemy law. Moreover, just as offence must be translated from a mere report of mental upset and made into a normative claim in order to merit circumstantial legal protection, so particular religious beliefs must advance a claim to be worthy of respect in order to merit circumstantial legal protection. This surely is a corollary of a pluralistic society where the truth of particular religious beliefs is necessarily disputed. It is indeed true that religious beliefs may be respected in the sense that they are accorded religious toleration, and that believers are entitled to profess and practise such beliefs, without interference and molestation. Like Peter Jones, I disagree with Lord Scarman's inference that respecting the right to religious freedom of individuals necessarily implies legally enforceable limitation on the manner of criticism or portrayal of their beliefs by others.[25] As I have previously indicated, I think that the priority properly accorded to the right to religious belief and observance in international law may suggest further rights, but the latter do not follow by any direct and necessary inference. The 'respect' which is involved in the mere toleration of the profession of different religious beliefs is not itself sufficient to yield the conclusion that all religions are consequently entitled to esteem and a legally enforced minimum deference. The sort of respect which is involved in extending the sanctions of the criminal law to the protection of a religion must surely imply a recognition of merit, esteem and value from those who do not share belief in the particular religion. That religious belief *per se* is not entitled to such respect is clear from the history of the whole human race. What relevant respect is due to the religion of the Thugs, or of the Aztecs or other civilizations of ancient Meso-America?[26] In England today there is no consensus of respect for the religious beliefs of the Rastafarians, Scientologists, the Unification Church, Voodooists and Satanists. These would seem to be religions just as traditional Christianity or Islam are religions. But even this is open to dispute. A statutory definition of religion would be difficult; none of the international treaties of human rights define the character of a religion. Whether the definition was prescribed by statute or left to the practice of the courts anomalies are likely – Scientology's claims may be found less authentic than those of the Unification Church; the line of adjudication is indistinct.[27] A far greater problem, I think, arises when what is deliberated is not the religious character of a sect or belief, but rather the degree of respect that ought to be accorded to sects and beliefs which cannot be set aside on the grounds that they are not religions. The extension of the blasphemy law must involve a legal recognition of 'respect-worthiness' to different religions, and this must involve an attribution of worth which it is difficult to see being extended to all religions. This appears to be an invidious distinction in any pluralistic society, but one which is inseparable from the extension of the English blasphemy law.

A pluralistic society must accord value to freedom of expression, since plurality of ideas, tastes, lifestyles and sentiments has little substance or rationale without this. Nonetheless, within this vague general sphere it is the freedom to express opinions which has the greatest claim to unrestricted liberty, since free expression and debate over opinions bears a conceptual relation to the capacity to reveal truth by withstanding testing and scrutiny. Since 1883 the law of blasphemy became reconciled to these claims of free expression of opinion in religious matters, but it adapted in order to enforce decency of manner in such expression. Peter Jones has forcefully presented the case that respect for religious beliefs in no way precludes their public contestation. Indeed, characteristically religious beliefs do pose truth claims, and attempts to protect them from challenge are actually subversive of the seriousness of these claims. Moreover, unlike other forms of expression (of the sort, for example, of the *Gay News* poem or Rushdie's novel) argument provides dissentients with the remedy of counter-argument.

Beyond agreeing with the case presented by Peter Jones that respect for religious beliefs does not preclude, but rather implies this contestation where there is diversity of beliefs about religion, I wish to give consideration to the actual benefit which religious belief may gain from controversy. Mention has already been made of the transformation of spiritual life in seventeenth-century England with the intensification of what Richard Webster styles the religion of the 'God-within'. This was, at least in part, associated with the development of religious pluralism and the slackening of the rigour of the blasphemy law. A similar development, combining great controversy and offended religious feeling with a regenerated religious vision, was seen in the nineteenth century with the investigation of the life of Jesus using the then new techniques of historical scholarship as the basis of a critical examination of the gospels. Some of these investigations were motivated by hatred of Christianity, and imputed to Jesus such characteristics as fraud, ambition, fanaticism and duplicity.[28] But without these investigations, and the controversy which they provoked, Christian thought and spirituality would have become ossified and unable to come to terms with a world of which a highly developed historical consciousness is an integral part.

These are examples of how religious thought has benefited from an increasingly pluralistic setting of argument and discourse.

With regard to England, the relaxation of legal constraints permitted such stimulation, and conversely the widening of debate led to the modification of legal restraint. Nineteenth-century theological argument contributed to the development of the current character of the law of blasphemy, with its regulation of the manner, not the matter, of discourse. Is it sufficient to allow the discussion of all opinions regarding religious belief provided that circumstantial decency is observed? The problem which arises from a stress on such circumstantial restraint is that religious utterance often takes a form where such restraint effectively amounts to a prohibition of authentic expression of opinion. Religious advocacy in particular shows a degree of antagonism and vehemence that has never been exceeded. The passionate propagation of religion, or denial of one, inevitably invites offence. Of course, certain idioms and traditions of religion emphasise this much more than others. Vehemence and invective have been a strain of Christian tradition (as previously indicated) since the early centuries of the Christian faith, and this in turn derives from Old Testament roots. No matter how repugnant such forms of religious expression (and also the anti-religious responses modelled on them) may seem to those who do not share the beliefs out of which they grow, any restrictive emphasis on decency actually prohibits the authentic expression of such belief. Whether contempt, scorn and ridicule are deserved or properly deployed depends on the merits of the argument itself, which the law avowedly does not judge. Surely any regard for the value of pluralism must pause before endorsing an enforcement of a degree of 'decency' and prevention of offence which would itself generate offence and curtail the expression of ideas, no matter how much we may personally deplore them.[29]

Contestation of religious ideas has, then, sometimes enriched religious thought even though this has generated great offence – offence taken at the substance of ideas rather than inflammatory modes of expression. Furthermore, even deliberately inflamed religious arguments are an integral part of the spectrum of religious ideas. But beyond either category come forms of 'expression' which are not the advancing of an opinion, because no argument is presented, and no point of purchase is offered for counter-argument. It is impossible to 'get to grips' with this kind of expression. Such characteristically is the case with films, poems and novels – at least to the degree that these latter two media are not reduced to a merely didactic function.

The outrage provoked by such expression differs from the advancing of even the most obnoxious opinion, since here there is no opportunity for counter-argument. Resentment is left powerless and speechless because when the source of offence is a mere image, this is impervious to denial, let alone refutation. Although the current blasphemy law prohibits indecency in arguments against the Christian religion, it may be doubted whether any successful prosecution could now be mounted fitting this description. We may infer from the Thorsen and *Gay News* cases that what the law currently protects is neither the doctrines of Christianity nor its claim to decency of treatment in argument, but rather Christian images of piety against obscene vilification. This, it seems to me, is the form of protection those who wished to see a prosecution against Salman Rushdie under an extended blasphemy law wished to extend to Islam.

When outrage is necessarily speechless, there is danger of recourse to violence.[30] Where those offended are judged to have good cause to feel wounded by desecrations that are in no way arguments and left with no means of rejoinder short of violence I see no point of principle why the law should not intervene on their behalf. This view depends on the arguments concerning the distinctive character of religious conviction previously outlined and is limited by the consideration that the religion so protected should be worthy of respect. The blasphemy law as presently formulated is too restrictive from the point of view of a pluralistic society in prohibiting even 'indecency' in argument. My own view is that the law should punish only obscene forms of expression which offer no opportunity for counter-argument. I accept that to regard such characteristics as especially obnoxious is culturally conditioned (though not therefore without a reasoned basis) and that there is no reason why this should correspond to the special susceptibilities of any and every religion. But all reasoning on this subject must arise from some cultural context and it is impossible for any legal code to accept all the different criteria of offensiveness which might be advanced by particular religions – here pluralism must meet a limit.

The history of the English blasphemy law shows the metamorphosis of religious ideas, the transformation of jurisdictions and conceptions of law, and the evolution of a complex and pluralistic culture. The Rushdie affair poses the question of the further direction in which this culture will evolve and the place, if any, a blasphemy law will have in it. The history of that law, with its continual narrowing and formalisation and virtual obsolescence, might indicate that it has no future. The previous discussion suggests that is not necessarily so, and that extension of the law (despite undoubted and formidable difficulties) might complement rather than contradict this pluralistic culture.

NOTES

1. See: Salman Rushdie, *The Satanic Verses* (London: Viking/Penguin, 1988); Shabbir Akhtar, *Be Careful with Muhammad!* (London: Bellew, 1989); Malise Ruthven, *A Satanic Affair: Salman Rushdie and the Rage of Islam* (London: Chatto & Windus, 1990); Richard Webster, *A Brief History of Blasphemy* (Southwold: Orwell Press, 1990); Fay Weldon, *Sacred Cows* (London: Chatto & Windus, 1989).

2. For the history of the crime of blasphemy in England see: C.M. Aspland, *The Law*

of Blasphemy (London: Stevens & Haynes, 1884); C. Bradlaugh, *The Laws relating to Blasphemy and Heresy* (London: Freethought, 1878); H. Bradlaugh-Bonner, *Penalties upon Opinion*, 3rd edn, (London: Watts, 1934); G.D. Nokes, *A History of the Crime of Blasphemy* (London: Sweet & Maxwell, 1928); Sir J.F. Stephen, *A History of the Criminal Law of England* vol. 2 (London: Macmillan, 1883).

3.   J.S. Mill, *Utilitarianism, On Liberty and Considerations on Representative Government*, ed. H.B. Acton (London: Dent, 1972), pp. 91, 92.

4.   Webster, op.cit., p. 14.

5.   Ibid., pp. 54, 55.

6.   See Elaine Pagels, *Adam, Eve and the Serpent* (Harmondsworth: Penguin, 1988), chapter 2, for the extent of early Christian opposition not only to Paganism but the dominant social and political ideas of the Roman Empire.

7.   J.S. Mill, op.cit., p. 147.

8.   W.E.H. Lecky, *History of European Morals from Augustus to Charlemagne,* vol. 1 (London: Longmans, Green, 1899), p. 408.

9.   Sir J.F. Stephen, op.cit., chapter 25.

10.   Christopher Hill, *The World Turned Upside Down* (Harmondsworth: Penguin, 1975); W.K. Jordan, *The Development of Religious Toleration in England*, vol. III (London: Allen & Unwin, 1965).

11.   Webster, op.cit., pp. 30, 31.

12.   Quoted in Bradlaugh-Bonner, op.cit., pp. 30, 31.

13.   John Locke, *A Letter Concerning Toleration*, in John Horton and Susan Mendus (eds), *John Locke 'A Letter Concerning Toleration' in Focus* (London: Routledge, 1991), p. 47.

14.   Mill's comments are to be found in J.S. Mill, op.cit., p. 90, Buckle's in *The Miscellaneous and Posthumous Works of Henry Thomas Buckle* vol. 1, (London: Longmans, Green, 1885), pp. 116–22.

15.   Quoted in Bradlaugh-Bonner, op.cit., pp. 103, 104.

16.   J.F. Stephen, 'Blasphemy and blasphemous libel', *Fortnightly Review*, 207 New Series, March 1884.

17.   A generation earlier, the lack of such reform gave rise to Mill's bitter outburst in *On Liberty*; see J.S. Mill, op.cit., pp. 90, 91.

18.   Lord Scarman's House of Lords Judgement in *R.v. Lemon*, WLR, 2, 1979, 281.

19.   This point is made in Sebastian Poulter's article 'Towards Legislative Reforms of the Blasphemy and Racial Hatred Laws', *Public Law*, 1991, p. 373.

20.   Webster, op.cit., p. 31.

21.   Tariq Modood, 'Muslims, Incitement to Hatred and the Law', Chapter 9 in this volume.

22.   The distinctiveness of the characteristics of religion and their relation to toleration is emphasised in Dr George Carey, *Tolerating Religion*, J.B. and W.B. Morrell Memorial Address on Toleration, York, 1991.

23.   Tariq Modood, op.cit.

24.   Peter Jones, 'Respecting Beliefs and Rebuking Rushdie', Chapter 8 in this volume.

25.   Peter Jones, op.cit., pp. 126–30. Sebastian Poulter offers a slightly more guarded case than Lord Scarman when he states that 'Freedom of religion is also a valuable human right and it may be doubted whether it can be fully enjoyed in practice if the state allows religious beliefs to be vilified and insulted in a gratuitous manner' (Poulter, op.cit., p. 376).

26.   This is not to deny the profundity of the problems and experiences which gave rise to them. See Ptolemy Tomkins, *This Tree Grows Out of Hell; Mesoamerica and the Search for the Magical Body* (New York: Harper Collins, 1990).

27.   Sebastian Poulter states that 'On the basis of past precedents [the courts] would

probably recognise Buddhism and the Unification Church but exclude scientology and secular humanism'. Precedents from English, Australian and US courts are cited. (Poulter, op.cit., pp. 379, 380).

28. Albert Schweitzer, *The Quest for the Historical Jesus* (London: Adam and Charles Black, 1910).

29. In his proposal for the legal reform of the blasphemy and racial hatred laws, Sebastian Poulter advances 'vilification' as the chief concept: 'Vilification seems a good portmanteau term for summarising the type of conduct which is to be outlawed. It conveys the flavour of abusive, disparaging words or actions which are designed to slander or render loathsome one group or their beliefs in the eyes of others' (Poulter, *op.cit.*, p. 378). To illustrate how this would limit authentic expression of religious belief, I suggest that the reader imagines how drastic an expurgation of the Old Testament would need to be in order to take out those passages which 'render loathsome' the beliefs of others. For some contemporary believers this is the divinely inspired model of religious discourse. They sincerely believe that other religious creeds lead to everlasting damnation. How can they view such creeds as other than loathsome; are they to be required to keep silent about what they regard as the most important of all issues?

30. The relation of speech and violence is a recurrent theme in the political philosophy of Hannah Arendt. In *The Human Condition* (Chicago: Chicago University Press, 1958) she distinguishes many uses of speech – as argument, persuasion, answering, talking back, measuring up to whatever has happened (p. 26). I have tended to concentrate on speech as argument, but all these modes of speech are struck mute by the sort of obscene blasphemy I am discussing. She further suggests that when all human togetherness is lost (and even strident argument presupposes some 'togetherness') speechless violence is apt to replace both speech and action (p. 180)

11 *Fatwa* and Fiction: Censorship and Toleration

Glen Newey

In February 1989 the Ayatollah Khomeini issued a *fatwa* against Salman Rushdie, calling both for Rushdie's death and the withdrawal of *The Satanic Verses* globally (it had already been banned in Iran). While the Imam's partisans were vociferous in their condemnation of the novel and its author, Western liberals were no less implacably convinced that both the ban and the death sentence flouted all they held most dear. The apathy which had greeted, for example, the judicial murder of thousands of Iranian subjects by their own government, transformed itself after the *fatwa* into righteous indignation at the Ayatollah's contempt for western values. These issues of the Iranian regime's human rights abuses and the death threat will not be pursued in this paper. It is not evident, after all, that they are best discussed as questions of *toleration* – to describe such actions as merely intolerant sounds bathetic. This ordinary-language point suggests that there are limits to the extension of the term and, in particular, that our reasons for disapproving morally of certain actions may not best be expressed by describing them as intolerant. The analysis below will attempt to explain these limits in terms of a general structure for the notion of toleration.

In the dispute between Western liberals and Muslim fundamentalists, the battle-lines were clearly drawn. But the relationship of toleration to the controversy was less clear, if only because accusations of intolerance were levelled by each side against the other. While liberals were quite clear that the banning of the book, not to mention the death sentence, was an act of the utmost intolerance, Muslims in this country were equally certain that publication was symptomatic of a wider intolerance towards religious and ethnic minorities in British society. According to this view of the matter, publishing the novel could only be seen in context as a calculated insult towards a group which already regarded itself as an embattled minority in a predominantly white Christian or secular culture.

In what follows I will examine these conflicting claims as interpretations of the principle of toleration. The aim will not be so much to decide which side in the dispute was right, but to discover what the Rushdie affair shows about the idea of toleration. I begin with some preliminary remarks about the conceptual structure of toleration, in an attempt to clarify the status of the claims mentioned above. After that I apply the analysis to the *Satanic Verses* dispute, then offer some general conclusions about the relationship between toleration and censorship.

As with all practical reasons, whatever reasons there are for acting tolerantly are only recognisable as action-guiding because they can figure in the actual deliberations of agents. We are not confronted with entirely general, abstract considerations about, say, the nature of agency, which somehow can be identified as requiring or commending the practice of toleration.[1] It is important to appreciate that acting tolerantly must proceed, in some sense, from the interests and values of the tolerators themselves.

This much, perhaps, is obvious. But even these very general remarks should serve to dispel some confusion about what toleration is, or can be. As has been noted,[2] there is no room left, once these observations are taken into account, for so-called 'vulgar' relativism – the conjunction of the claims, first, that conceptions of (moral) value are culturally, historically, etc. specific, with no assumption that real or imagined conflict between them can be rationally arbitrated; and second, a general principle of toleration to the effect that the maximum cultural diversity ought to be permitted or encouraged. The problem with this is that the relativism of values in the first claim is coupled with a non-relativistic assumption in the second, since the principle of toleration is held to apply quite generally. Keeping in view the situatedness of tolerators, and of the values which lead them to regard toleration as desirable, is one way of understanding the limits on the practice of toleration.

As several commentators have remarked,[3] it is a necessary condition of acting tolerantly in any situation that there is some practice of which the tolerator disapproves: toleration cannot be extended to practices which one finds entirely unexceptionable. This being so, any circumstances in which the question of toleration arises must involve moral or, more broadly, value-based beliefs of some kind. It is in this connection that the situation of tolerators, their historical and cultural circumstances, is of relevance to the question. If toleration presupposes an evaluative attitude, and all such attitudes are contingent, there is no possibility of any generalised principle of toleration. To tolerate is necessarily to adopt a contingent and contestable attitude.

This point also comes out when we consider a further necessary condition of toleration, that those exercising it should be capable, or at least believe themselves capable, of preventing, inhibiting or hindering the practices of which they disapprove – a further sense in which the issue necessarily involves questions of practical agency. This raises questions about power and its exercise. Power is about the implementation of disputable conceptions of value; if there were no dispute, there would be no need for its exercise. Consequently those in power are faced with a choice between values. As is true of agency in general, there is content in the idea of exercising power only if so doing can effect results in the world, states of affairs owing their existence to its exercise.

The fact that a group of would-be tolerators has to enjoy some position of power in society need not mean, though it can, that this group occupies some absolute position of power or domination over the group of whose activities they disapprove. There can be situations in which toleration takes the form of reciprocal agreements by different groups (each for example exercising hegemony within its own sphere of influence) not to interfere with the activities of the other; or, in contrast with this sort of mutual stand-off, one group merely decides that it cannot impose its values on another without incurring (in its own estimation) unacceptable costs – a possibility ignored by discussions which assimilate all cases of toleration to those where one side is dominant, and has in consequence only reasons of principle for refraining from imposing its will.

But even where there are these radical asymmetries of power between groups, it may be hard to distinguish between examples of pure or principled toleration and the more pragmatic case. This is clearly true of the utilitarian calculus. More interestingly, the distinction can also become difficult to draw in cases where the dominant group is not motivated exclusively by thoughts of efficiency, but is also working within a pluralistic set of values. When this is so, the commitment to pluralism may lead the group in power to behave tolerantly not purely because it sees this as the right thing to do, but because there are moral costs in enforcement. These moral costs relate not to practical administration but, for example, to side-constraints on what those in power, according to their own value-system, may do. Such a possibility suggests that the evaluative beliefs in question must be at least diverse enough to support both the original attitude of disapproval and some reason, drawn from within the value-system, for refraining from coercion. There is also usually – though it is debatable whether this is required by the notion of toleration – some consideration which inhibits the group from permitting other kinds of action.

Bearing this in mind, we seem to be left with a three-part structure for toleration, composed of the following elements:

1. a principle justifying disapproval of the other group's activities;

2. a consideration inhibiting the group in power from restraining the activity by force;

3. an explanation of the conditions under which the restraint mentioned in 2 is justified, which may or may not be identical with the principle mentioned in 1 above.

It should be said, however, that the basic three-part format allows for considerable variation in the forms of justification which toleration may receive, depending on the closeness of the relationship between the reasons for disapproval and the reasons for non-coercion. I set out some of the possibilities below.

In an *integrated* theory of toleration, there is some fundamental principle, such as that of equal respect, which provides the grounds for toleration in certain cases (as well as, in other cases, explaining why some kinds of action should *not* be tolerated), together with some supplementary moral principle providing grounds for disapproving of the tolerated activity. Some forms of religious toleration fit into this pattern.

A *fully integrated* theory allows that there can be lesser violations of the fundamental principle which should be tolerated, because restraint would itself involve a more serious breach of the principle; in other words, the reasons for the disapproval are articulated (at least in some cases) in terms of the principle itself. Thus an action breaching equal respect may be tolerated because coercive prevention of the action would violate the principle more seriously (such as by interfering with persons' privacy or physical integrity). Some might, for example, disapprove of abortion because of its violation of the foetus's physical integrity, but also believe that it should be tolerated because its prohibition would involve a more serious violation of the woman's rights. Nonetheless, certain breaches of the principle are held to be *in*tolerable; murder or rape provide obvious examples.

In a *diverse* theory, the fundamental principle which imposes limits on toleration (so that breaches of equal respect, say, are beyond the bounds of toleration) is supplemented by some further consideration which, when the fundamental principle itself is not breached, gives grounds for tolerating certain kinds of action; in addition, reasons can be given for disapproving of the actions in question which do not invoke the basic principle. Thus someone might hold that medical research on animals was undersirable because of the pain caused but believe it was justified because of the human benefits it secured; this does not invoke the fundamental principle – though the latter would come into play if experimentation on *human* subjects were under consideration.

Clearly these possibilities are not exhaustive, and are presented mainly for expository purposes. As well as a reason for tolerating certain kinds of action and restricting toleration in other cases, these theories require some reason for disapproving of the action to be tolerated in the first place, as explained above: this generates the three-part structure. Raphael supposes that this leads to paradox.

> If toleration implies moral disapproval of what you tolerate, and if the criterion of moral approval is conformity to the principle of respect for persons, then toleration presupposes that what you tolerate does not conform to the principle of respect for persons. But on the other hand, so it is suggested, we ought not to tolerate whatever contravenes the principle of respect for persons. So how can there be toleration at all?[4]

This alleged paradox does not arise from the nature of equal respect itself as the fundamental moral principle, but from the very idea of there being some such unitary principle. Given an account of morality in which equal respect, or some other principle, enjoys this overriding status, it follows that whatever incurs justifiable disapproval must breach the fundamental principle itself. The paradox emerges directly once it is accepted that the sole grounds for the original disapproval are that the fundamental principle has been breached.

It should be clear however from the account of integrated and diverse theories of toleration above that the paradox dissolves in the absence of any such single and universal principle. This is immediately clear in the case of diverse theories, where the grounds for toleration, such as some form of side-constraint, are different from the grounds for limiting toleration. But even in integrated theories, where this is not so, it is still true that the reasons for disapproving the action in question are distinct from the grounds for toleration – someone might disapprove of, say, some form of sexual practice on religious grounds, and yet hold that it should nevertheless not be prohibited, because this would violate equal respect. Even in a fully integrated theory, Raphael's paradox is answered by the possibility of not preventing lesser breaches of the principle because of the moral costs of coercion (where the costs are reckoned in terms of the principle itself).

Raphael's own solution distinguishes between duties of 'perfect' and 'imperfect' obligation.[5] In these terms, the difference between tolerable and intolerable wrongdoing consists in the fact that we are always obliged to restrain wrong actions of the former, but not the latter category. It is however doubtful whether this distinction coincides, as Raphael seems to think, with that between duties entailing correlative obligations and duties which do not.[6] After all, if rights are involved in cases of tolerable wrongdoing, it is not merely that one is not obliged to prevent the activity, as an 'imperfect' obligation, but that there is some obligation *not* to prevent it. This idea is more in keeping with a view of toleration as a good in itself, rather than a mere *pis aller*. But it is hard to believe that this insight can only be accommodated within a framework of obligation – that, in other words, in issues involving toleration, it must always be either morally required or prohibited. The two-level structure need not be embodied in a set of required interventions on the one hand and required restraints on the other. One alternative, which recognises a limit on moral rationalisation, is to regard toleration as a virtue of character, and its worth as consisting in actions motivated by or expressing this virtue.

In what follows I examine the implications of the above remarks for censorship policy, and ask in particular whether a permissive attitude towards artistic censorship is necessarily a tolerant one. There has been a strong lobby in favour of minimal artistic censorship, or none at all, over the past few decades, and this has become established as a standard liberal philosophical position. Minimal censorship can fairly be called 'liberal', I think, as its inspiration largely comes from the arguments in chapter 2 of Mill's *On Liberty*, a work in the mainstream of classical liberalism: as such it relies on claims about the value of free expression, cultural diversity and individual self-development. The position recognises certain marginal restrictions of freedom of expression, essentially dictated by Mill's harm principle. Thus incitement is the primary ground for censorship in Mill's view, and this has been reflected in legislation on such matters as defamation and incitement to racial hatred (though in the UK other residual restrictions persist, in the laws against blasphemy). Beyond these limitations, however, the liberal position regards freedom of artistic expression as absolute.

How far can this position be regarded as a *tolerant* one? It is usual to think of liberalism as being a philosophy advocating both freedom of expression and toleration. But the comments made so far leave uncertain the relationship between freedom of expression as a value and the three-part structure of toleration. More specifically, it is uncertain whether encroachments on this freedom are held to be tolerable or not. If they are, then what I have called the standard liberal position on censorship seems to be compromised. But if they are not, we need some explanation, in terms of the restraining moral principle (such as equal respect) or some other relevant evaluative consideration, of why artistic expression should enjoy this absolute immunity. Most pressingly, we need to determine whether this immunity remains where artistic activity breaches the principle itself – whether, for instance, incitement falls into this category, and whether the exceptions can be limited to cases of incitement if it does.

These issues are well exemplified by the *Satanic Verses* dispute. The Ayatollah's *fatwa*, and subsequent calls by Muslims in Britain and elsewhere for the book's withdrawal, brought into question the standard liberal identification of a commitment to toleration with minimal censorship. As I have already remarked, the controversy, in one of its aspects, consisted in opposed practical interpretations of the principle of toleration. While defenders of publication branded the *fatwa* and its supporters as intolerant, Muslims maintained that its continued availability was an act of intolerance against the Islamic community both in Britain and abroad.

As far as this went, the dispute involved mutual accusations of intolerance. This need not mean that one side or the other, in so far as its case rested on claims about toleration, must have been misusing the term. Both claims may, after all, have been true – though no doubt it would be difficult or even impossible for any individual to live simultaneously within both of the cultures which gave rise to them. But if this is right, and the Muslim claim of intolerance is justified, the liberal identification cannot be exceptionlessly true. It is, then, important to assess the merits of the Muslim claims about intolerance, and the Western response.

In essence the Muslims' grievance was that the novel, as they saw it, deliberately insulted their religion and its prophet. To sanction its publication was in their view to condone and perpetuate this insult when they had offered no comparable insult to the Christian religion or to secular opinion in Britain. To the extent that these complaints took the form of claims about toleration, then, they appeared to rest on some principle of equality of respect: publication was an act of intolerance because it offended one cultural group, while offering no similar offence to the non-Muslim majority.

Of course, there is no reason to think that the Muslims' sense of grievance would have been assuaged in any way if someone, to even things up, had published a comparable attack on the predominantly Christian and white majority: presumably the principle of equal respect is not honoured if it results, practically, in an equality of *dis*respect. The idea is rather that there is some minimal level of consideration due to all, and that the principle is violated if this level is not reached. On the Muslim view of toleration, then, as interpreted here, we are morally required to respect others' most deeply-held beliefs, and this requirement was violated by the attack on the Islamic religion allegedly contained in the novel.

Bearing this in mind, we can see how this appeal to the principle of equality of respect might be thought of as paradoxical in the way discussed by Raphael. We seem to be faced with the conclusion that publication breached the principle and should therefore not be tolerated; but, on the other hand, restraining publication marks a failure to tolerate an action of which, if the Muslim claims are right, they had valid grounds for disapproving. So either way toleration seems to be ruled out, and Raphael's paradox applies.

But the issue is less clear than this. Here the appearance of paradox arises from the assumption that *any* circumstances in which a group feels moral disapproval at the activities of another are such that toleration is called for: so the Muslim demands for the novel to be banned must be intolerant. But if, as the supporters of the *fatwa* implicitly claimed, publication breached the principle of equal respect, then the calls for a ban could be taken as consistent with the three-part structure of toleration discussed earlier.

This could be true of any of the three forms of theory distinguished earlier. In an integrated theory, for example, if what supports a policy of toleration is the claim that coercion is contrary to the principle of equal respect, it can be maintained that this principle, as the basis for toleration, cannot consistently be invoked to defend attacks on equal respect itself – though an advocate of a fully integrated theory may allow that certain forms of toleration do countenance (relatively minor) breaches of the principle. But as long as there are grounds for moral disapproval other than breaches of this principle, there can be genuine examples of toleration supported by equal respect, contrary to Raphael's paradox. This does not, however, mean that every legitimate cause of moral disapproval must be tolerated. There are actions which attack the very moral principle which provides a rationale for toleration itself.

It may be said in response that there is a distinction between accepting that a particular form of activity violates equal respect, and believing that one is justified in intervening to prevent such violations. Even if publication did manifest inadequate concern for Muslims' religious sensibilities, this does not prove that the novel should be banned as they advocated. Even within a strictly Kantian moral theory, it does not follow from the fact that the moral law has been broken that we are justified in using coercion to prevent such actions. Similarly, the notion of a moral right does not in itself justify our breaching some rights in order to protect others (though of course allowance may be made in rights theory for this possibility).

This response is right as far as it goes. But the preceding argument was meant to show not that considerations about toleration *prove* that the novel should be withdrawn, but only that calls for its censorship were not incompatible with the structure of toleration as presented above. Whether or not the Muslim claims about equal respect are found to be convincing, there is at least the need for the defender of the standard liberal position to show why the considerations which require restraint from interference in certain cases of toleration do not require restraining publication in this case. If equal respect is what requires toleration or non-censorship in other cases, we need some explanation of why respect for the same principle does not demand censorship in this situation.

It is of course possible just to deny that the Muslim appeal to equal respect is justified. One of the problems, however, with this line of argument is that modern liberalism, when confronted with disputes of this kind, has looked for some impartial means of arbitration between the protagonists, and found it in the principle of equal respect. Larmore, for example, has taken the principle to be of sufficient generality to serve as a basis for liberal neutrality (though he concedes that there may be marginal conceptions of value which reject the principle7). On this account, neutral liberalism is founded on the equality of persons in respect of certain fundamental moral claims or entitlements due to them as persons. But there is nothing in the notion of a parity of moral entitlements between persons to suggest that neutrality, under this conception, must require a complete absence of restrictions on, say, artistic freedom of expression, as liberals often seem to have supposed. Until the nature of the equality of respect due to persons is spelled out in more detail there can be no assumption that the notion will have any such consequence.

The problem faced by the liberal is that the generality of the principle, which enables it to serve as a basis for neutrality, is likely to disappear once this detail is elaborated. As long as equality of respect remains uninterpreted, it can be thought of (as Larmore does) as being unexceptionable enough to command nearly universal assent. But giving practical effect to the principle – for example in deciding what, politically, should be the legal limits on how persons may behave towards one another – is going to require decisions about values and the priorities between them. It is hard to see how this detail can be provided without forfeiting the across-the-board applicability of neutrality in its original, unelaborated form. If it cannot, there is little chance that liberal neutrality will serve as a means of arbitrating between competing values and the groups espousing them. For this reason, where there are deep conflicts between values and cultures, and appeal to equal respect may not be able to resolve them – or at least, not in a way acceptable to the standard, permissive view of censorship.

There is, however, an alternative to the neutralist strategy for the liberal, which consists in rejecting the idea of any such impartial point of assessment. Indeed it is odd, in view of liberalism's historical commitment to pluralism, that it should have thought it possible or even desirable to produce such a standard of judgement. Part of what pluralism involves is an acceptance of diverse conceptions of value, and that other value-based commitments than one's own can form an acceptable conception of the good life. But if liberalism is to avoid relapsing into the vulgar relativism mentioned earlier, it will have to acknowledge that pluralism is a partial and limited value-based commitment in itself. There is no fully neutral standpoint from which all values are both perceived as forming part of acceptable ideals of the good life for different persons, and at the same time are assessed impartially against each other for the purpose of reaching political decisions – a process which, if anything does, involves choosing between values in practical action. On this understanding pluralism views the system – any system – of political decision-making as a non-neutral instrument for implementing certain conceptions of value. Liberalism's commitment to pluralism is thus manifested in its holding power as a particular ideology, one which accords supreme value to (a specific conception of) the person, and value to other ideals in so far as they are or can be those which persons pursue.

This is certainly one conception of value; but there are others, which do not ascribe supreme value to persons. There is, moreover, a wider sense of pluralism, which embodies the apparent aspirations of neutrality, but which by definition could not function as an ideology for reaching political decisions in the way neutrality intends. This is because the wider version of pluralism expresses a certain relationship between ideologies. On this wider view, pluralism consists in the diversity of possible ideals of value which can exist in society. It reflects the continuing competition and rivalry between these diverse ideals, and their seeking to give themselves practical effect by securing political power. Pluralism, in this extended sense, is witnessed in this competition and in the possibility that different ideologies may gain power. But this notion of pluralism could not itself form part of an ideology, as it expresses the relationship between ideologies in competition for political power.

The wider conception of pluralism holds that value is so heterogeneous that it cannot be encapsulated in any single evaluative system, or at least in any such system's institutional expression. As a result the neutralist aim is recognised as being unattainable, and pluralism is seen instead as being expressed through political competition rather than being encapsulated in any specific ideology. This form of pluralism is reflected in the claim made earlier about the role of power relationships in the practice of toleration. Any ideology, even one espousing the more limited form of pluralism distinguished above, will have to exercise power, if at all, through its own values, and in so far as it does will have to decide questions of practical toleration from the standpoint of its own value-system. The situatedness of tolerators comes out, in part, through their exercising power in competition with other ideologies, and in their implementing contestable ideals of value.

These considerations about liberalism and neutrality help, I think, to indicate the limits of toleration – not in the sense identified earlier, that any theory of toleration must give an account of the intolerable, but a conceptual limit set by tolerators' cultural and historical circumstances. Censorship provides a useful illustration of the point: material can only be considered for censorship if it offends in some way against the values of the potential censors. Toleration, according to the conclusions reached earlier, must embody a form of moral disapproval, and this involves subscribing to particular values. But if this is so, and toleration can only be exercised by those in power, we have to take into account the fact that would-be tolerators are *situated* already in a particular conception of value – otherwise there would be no standpoint from which to disapprove of a given action in the first place.

These remarks are not meant to suggest that since the Muslims in Britain were a small minority in an overwhelmingly non-Islamic society, their actions by definition could not be branded as intolerant. But if it is a condition of exercising power that a group has at least some dimly-articulated values – even if these do not go much beyond the retention of power itself – any situation in which toleration can be extended towards another group in society necessarily precludes the impartiality sought by neutrality. Even if power is held by pluralistically-minded liberals, it is far from clear that there is any means of deciding a controversy such as that over *The Satanic Verses* in an entirely neutral fashion, given the opposing values at stake and the correspondingly diverse conceptions of practical toleration which they support. There is little reason to think that in such a case non-censorship is invariably the tolerant course of action.

It may be said that the desired neutrality is a procedural notion[8] which can be understood, for example, in terms of a impartial democratic political structure open to universal participation. What guarantees neutrality, on this view, is not the outcome of the procedure, but the fairness of the procedure itself. According to this procedural account, neutrality *qua* respect for persons is embodied in democratic processes, so the global perspective is, after all, available: and this means that we have a procedure for deciding between values, one which can in principle answer questions of practical toleration.

Whatever the merits of this answer as an interpretation of democratic procedures in general, it is hard to believe that it will be able to handle disputes like that over *The Satanic Verses*. This point can be illustrated with reference to Rawls's *A Theory of Justice*, the most cogent form of neutralist strategy yet devised. Behind the veil of ignorance, Rawls argues, no one would choose a society with repressive religious legislation because, once the veil is lifted, they might find they belonged to some other religious sect, which was disadvantaged by those laws. But, even if this form of procedure would indeed be chosen, it is still doubtful whether the arrangements behind the veil of ignorance would lead to the desired liberal conclusion. Given that there will be some persons with strong religious convictions in the projected society, it is not obvious that the rational calculator in the Original Position must favour a set of social arrangements wholly free of provision for censorship. Someone in the Original Position might well reason that if, when the veil is lifted, he or she turns out to be one of these persons, it would be desirable if there was some legal redress against publications which offend their fundamental beliefs.

It may be objected that any rational agent would realise that there was a plurality of religious beliefs and so would not know what form of laws to enact. If so, perhaps the best bet would be to reject censorship in any form. But why should those in the Original Position tie their hands in this way? There may be little point, given the known diversity of belief, in introducing censorship to protect a specific religion at this stage. But there would equally be no reason to rule out the possibility of such censorship when the veil was lifted.

Perhaps this is why Rawls appeals to the sanctity of conscience as the ultimate surety against repressive laws on religion, though freedom of conscience is to be limited 'when there is a reasonable expectation that not doing so will damage the public order which the government should maintain'.[9] It is not very clear how the reasonableness or otherwise of such an expectation is established, and by whom this is to be decided in the event of dispute. Nor does the sanctity of conscience preclude censorship on religious grounds. Someone in the Original Position might conclude that if she or he proved to hold strong religious beliefs, it would be a good idea to censor material offensive to them. He or she might of course also look at the matter from the standpoint of someone hoping to publish such material. But this need not involve any conscientious motive in itself, and it is doubtful whether even the maximin decision-theoretic apparatus favoured by Rawls must result in a regime of total non-censorship. The 'best worst' option might be taken as that society where persons' religious sensibilities were not exposed to gratuitous offence.

In this discussion I have taken the principle of equal respect as that grounding the three-level structure of toleration presented earlier, i.e. as the principle referred to under 1 in the structure. Other moral principles could naturally be offered as candidates for 'grounding' toleration. Equal respect was worth examining as a foundational concept, because it could be seen as the principle tacitly appealed to by Muslims in their objections to *The Satanic Verses*, and because of its important role in justifying certain varieties of modern liberalism. In a diverse theory, for example, it would be possible to hold that there were considerations supporting artistic freedom which should nonetheless be overridden by other, weightier reasons for censorship in certain cases; or, in an integrated theory, that the reasons (for example, of public order) supporting permissiveness in some situations also supported censorship in others.

In either case, equal respect (or some other basic principle) could still provide grounds for limiting toleration. It might be thought that the more diversified structure gave support to the liberal side in the *Satanic Verses* dispute. Thus the

Muslim claim that publication was an act of intolerance against the Islamic community would fail, on this account, because the claim rested on an appeal to the principle of equal respect. It could not be objected that breaching equal respect was an act of intolerance, because with the more diversified structure for toleration, equal respect would not be the moral principle the satisfaction of which was required for toleration. There would be some other grounds for thinking that toleration should in certain situations be exercised. But it would no longer be relevant that publication breached equal respect, since that principle would not be the grounds on which toleration was regarded as a good.

This objection does not however show that the Muslim claims about intolerance were false; merely that, with this altered structure and the role of equal respect within it, the claims could not be supported by reference to that principle. But there may be other moral considerations supporting toleration, such as that intolerance infringed persons' rights, and it would have to be shown that the Muslim claims could not be restated in these terms. In this example the Muslim objections might be reformulable in terms of rights. A full examination of alternative foundations for the principle would obviously demand much lengthier treatment than it can receive here. The point, though, remains that the conceptual link between toleration and permissive policies on censorship is not guaranteed even with this alternative structuring for the principle.

It is, indeed, difficult to think of any moral principle which would guarantee the standard liberal position on censorship. Liberalism allows for exceptions to permissiveness when there is the threat of personal defamation or incitement to cause harm to persons, as has already been noted. But judgements about the implications of such wrongs for censorship policy are essentially contestable. It is not that defamation or harm might, in marginal cases, be regarded as goods, but that it is open to dispute both what underlying moral principles, if any, are being invoked in such judgements and what practical implications they have. As a result, the hoped-for neutral justification for the standard position seems not to be available. Its only guarantee will be, presumably, a general commitment, along the lines presented by Mill, to freedom of discussion and intellectual creativity. This is doubtless a more viable line of argument than that pursued by the neutralist liberal; but at the same time, it abandons any attempt at value-neutral justification.

It will also have to answer potentially embarrassing questions about how the general commitment can accommodate the familiar liberal exceptions to freedom of expression, while allowing no censorship beyond this. For example, the Williams Committee on Obscenity and Film Censorship, while broadly sympathetic to Mill's arguments, took the view that '[t]he harm condition by itself would not necessarily produce very liberal results'[10]; but even the additional principle that 'each person is the best judge of whether he or she is being harmed'[11], while ruling out some forms of paternalism, leaves ample scope for censorship. Muslim protesters against *The Satanic Verses* were quite convinced

that they had been harmed by the book's publication. By focusing on the paternalistic motive for censorship, the report assumes that the (subjectively-
perceived) harms caused to a person will either be negligible or provide
inadequate grounds for censorship. But it is often impossible for a person
suffering such harms merely to ignore them. While there may be forms of
objectionable behaviour where this sort of response is appropriate, it is partly
constitutive of at least certain forms of moral disapproval that this is not a
practical option. This may be true, for instance, where the person is closely
identified with the concerns which he or she perceives as being harmed; in such
cases taking action may be seen as practically necessary.

These considerations apply with particular force to works with the avowed
intention of causing offence, as was true, or could reasonably have been supposed
to be true, in the case of *The Satanic Verses*. At about the same time as the *fatwa*
was issued, a private prosecution was brought against the director of a private
London art gallery for displaying a sculpture adorned with earrings made from
(legally obtained) freeze-dried human embryos. Acting on a direction from the
judge that they were to decide not the standards of public taste but of public
decency, the jury found the defendants guilty as charged. Both the gallery owner
and the sculptor were fined, and the sculpture removed from public display.

This legal action, like the *Satanic Verses* case, raised issues of artistic freedom
and censorship. As with the novel, the intention of the sculpture seemed to be, at
least in part, to cause offence or shock. The statement made by the sculpture
would have been quite different if the earrings had not been made from real
human embryos, but were facsimiles made from ceramic or some other material.
If the sculpture had been intended merely to make a point about the cheapening
of human life, an imitation of this kind would have served equally well. But the
use of real embryos was surely meant to reinforce this point by making the
sculpture itself an example of this very depreciation, by its own frivolous use of
real embryos for the purposes of something comparatively trivial, namely an
artistic work. To understand the point of using real embryos is thus to grasp a
self-referential point about the work's own relative worth. Assuming a non-
contingent link between the cheapening of human life and the feeling of revul-
sion, this moral response must be essential to understanding the intentions behind
the sculpture as I have interpreted them.

If this is so, it is hard to see how the defender of the standard liberal position
can merely appeal to freedom of expression as some kind of absolute or non-
negotiable value. The same considerations as those which dictate the exceptions
allowed by Millian liberalism to artistic freedom support also the moral objections to the sculpture and the calls for its removal from exhibition. Offence – the
criterion suggested by the Williams committee in preference to the older 'deprave
and corrupt' test for deciding a work's acceptability for publication – does not, at
the very least, obviously support a permissive attitude towards the sculpture's
display. Indeed, if as I have suggested the moral offence caused by the work was

an intrinsic part of its artistic aims, the criterion seems to support its censorship. The extent to which liberalism can consistently defend its display, while preserving the residual restrictions, depends on what is thought to justify the latter. But it is not easy to think of any criterion, whether of offence or harm or corruption, which would not under some interpretations lead to greater restrictions than the standard position. Which interpretation of the appropriate restrictions prevails is, in the nature of the case, a political question.

It is thus possible that the exceptions allowed by the Millian position to free expression will go beyond the marginal restrictions envisaged by classical liberalism. The argument of this paper has suggested that in defending familiar liberal policies like freedom of expression the justificatory role of toleration may be more limited than some liberals have thought. It has not been an aim of this paper to argue that either of the examples cited are cases where censorship must be imposed. But it has argued that one purported class of reasons for refraining from censorship, namely that such a policy is tolerant, fails in some important cases to support this conclusion. Once the three-part structure for toleration is accepted, there is the possibility that the foundational moral concepts will apply to a given practical problem in such a way that toleration cannot simply be identified with freedom of expression.

Reasons for tolerating are generally reasons for forbearance – their force lies in the wrongness of interference rather than the rightness of the actions tolerated. At the same time, this dimension of wrongness suggests that toleration's justificatory scope is limited. Neither the general three-part structure distinguished above, nor the addition to it of a particular moral principle such as equal respect, is enough to tell us by itself whether or not a particular form of action should be tolerated. In the case of censorship policy, the cost of publication has to be weighed against the cost of its restraint. There may of course be the familiar Millian goods to be had from publication, though it is unclear that these are best described as goods of *toleration*. If the question of toleration arises at all, these goods must be partly offset if not cancelled by the costs or harms incurred by publication.

It therefore seems doubtful whether there can be any principled defence of free publication, with only the residual exceptions, which essentially relies on the notion of toleration. Cases may arise where the justification for the free market in ideas will come from the Millian good of publication, rather than the evil of its restraint. Sometimes these distinct considerations seem to be conflated in liberal writing. But there may be situations where the only evil in restraint is precisely its preclusion of the Millian goods, rather than the breach of some general principle such as equal respect. And it may be true that publication breaches the principle, even though it promotes these goods. It is hard to see what in the notion of toleration, beyond an absolute commitment to freedom of publication, could provide a consistent rationale for the liberal position; this paper has moreover argued that such a commitment may not be as definitively tolerant as liberals have supposed.

NOTES

1. Some forms of neutrality might be taken as claiming this; for example, the procedural arguments in John Rawls's *A Theory of Justice* (Oxford: Oxford University Press 1971).
2. See the discussion of this notion in Bernard Williams, *Morality: An Introduction to Ethics* (London: Penguin, 1973), pp.34ff.
3. See, for example, Peter Nicholson, 'Toleration as a Moral Ideal', in J.Horton and S.Mendus (eds), *Aspects of Toleration* (London: Methuen, 1985); D.D.Raphael, 'The Intolerable', in S.Mendus (ed.), *Justifying Toleration* (Cambridge: Cambridge University Press, 1988).
4. Raphael, op.cit. p.142.
5. Ibid., pp.143f.
6. Ibid., p.145.
7. Charles Larmore, *Patterns of Moral Complexity* (Cambridge: Cambridge University Press, 1987), pp.59ff.
8. Ibid., p.44.
9. Rawls, op. cit., p.213.
10. *Report of the Committee on Obscenity and Film Censorship*, Cmnd 772 (London: HMSO, 1979), p.57.
11. Ibid.

12 The Tigers of Wrath and the Horses of Instruction[1]

Susan Mendus

Reading through the vast and still burgeoning literature on the Rushdie affair, it is surprisingly difficult to establish precisely what the debate is about: in part it is about how to read novels; in part it is about the nature of Islamic fundamentalism; in part it is about the preservation of cultural identity in a multicultural society. Most pervasively, however, it is a debate about the values which inform modern liberal societies – a debate in which liberal culture, with its emphasis on rationality, choice and the sovereignty of the individual, is pitted against cultures which emphasise sanctity, tradition, and group identity.

Fay Weldon asks:

> Who is there left of us brave enough to state what we believe? That, say, the Bible is a superior revelatory work to the Koran – or at any rate reveals a kinder, more interesting, less vengeful, less cruel God, one worth studying, worshipping? ... One you can interpret? All you can do with the Koran is learn it by heart.[2]

The emphasis here is on rationality – on the need to submit texts to scrutiny and interpretation. And religions and cultures are deemed superior in so far as they do admit of interpretation – of 'thoughts, perceptions, and increasing understanding'. Similarly, the role of choice is prominent in the debate. On 9 March 1989 a meeting of women called by Southall Black Sisters and Southall women's section of the Labour Party issued a statement which declared:

> We will not be dictated to by fundamentalists. Our lives will not be defined by community leaders.
> We will take up our right to determine our own destinies, not limited by religion, culture, or nationality.[3]

Here the emphasis is on the control of one's own destiny, and the desire, even the right, of the individual to shake off the shackles of cultural heritage.

Finally, the debate has been informed by a distinction between societies in which the individual is sovereign and societies or cultures which give greater emphasis to group identity (often an identity which is forged through identity of belief). Michael Ignatieff writes;

> In theocratic States like Iran, the law guarantees the inviolability of certain sacred doctrines. In free societies, the law does not protect doctrines as such; it protects individuals – through the law of libel, or the law against incitement to racial hatred.[4]

In so far as the law declines to protect doctrines as such, it also declines to protect the 'social glue' which binds groups together and makes them a coherent whole. For better or worse, it supports the sovereignty of the individual against the identity of the group.

Here then are three themes which lie at the heart of the Rushdie debate: rationality versus sanctity, choice versus tradition, and the sovereignty of the individual versus the identity of the group. In much of the literature the tensions inherent in these distinctions have been presented as battles between the forces of light and darkness; between the rationality and tolerance of liberalism, and the bigotry of fundamentalism; between the horses of instruction and the tigers of wrath.

Two responses to this state of affairs suggest themselves: firstly it might be argued that Western liberal democracies do not, after all, have a monopoly on rationality. This is a line of argument favoured by Shabbir Akhtar, who has urged the necessity for 'a reasonable, intellectually adequate defence of "the virtues of fundamentalism",. There has, he says 'been an unargued assumption on the part of the press, and indeed of academic writing, that fundamentalism has no intellectual basis. People should be allowed to defend the better side of fundamentalism'.[5] In other words, he claims that fundamentalism has been misrepresented as unthinking and anti-intellectual, when it is not so: the apparent struggle between the tigers of wrath and the horses of instruction is in fact illusory, for fundamentalism is also a rational doctrine, and one which admits of interpretation. A second strategy is that which provides a defence of tradition, sanctity and group identity against the dominant values of liberalism. This defence concedes that there is a battle, but asserts that it is a battle in which the tigers of wrath may yet turn out to be wiser than the horses of instruction.

In what follows I shall suggest that the two strategies are in fact quite similar: attempts to defend fundamentalism as rational may involve appeal to precisely the same kinds of consideration as attempts to invoke values of tradition or group identity. In part, therefore, my argument will be an argument for contextualisation. It will echo Alasdair MacIntyre's theme – 'progress in rationality is achieved only from a point of view'.[6] To the extent that it does this, it is a defence which aligns itself with opponents of the Enlightenment; with anti-Kantians; with the philosophical tigers of wrath.

At the same time, however, my account will invoke rather than reject some basic Kantian tenets – notably Kant's commitment to emotional love as the prerequisite of morality, where morality is nevertheless a rational enterprise. I shall argue that the tigers of wrath must not be completely uninstructed and that arguments for contextualisation, and claims that 'progress in rationality is achieved only from a point of view', need not lead us either to a vicious relativism or to maudlin and ineffective nostalgia for times past.

The terms in which the Rushdie debate have been conducted, and which are exemplified by the earlier quotations, point to a dilemma for modern liberals in multicultural societies: either we say that 'our' values (liberal values) are better, more rational than any others, and refuse to countenance any curtailment of the free speech which those other values dictate; or (with MacIntyre) we spurn rationality, embrace relativism, yearn for a return to lost days, and render ourselves impotent against those who would undermine our commitment to values such as toleration and free speech. The former is a kind of cultural arrogance; the latter, a kind of cultural apathy and, at the limit, cultural suicide. If the tigers of wrath triumph, then we must conclude that really we stand for nothing defensible, and we stand alone. If the horses of instruction triumph, then we must conclude that we do stand for something – we stand for our own values, but again we stand alone. Either way we seem isolated and unable to communicate effectively with others. But in a modern, multicultural society, isolation and separatism are our problems, so they can hardly be our solutions.

This essay aims to marry the tigers of wrath with the horses of instruction: it suggests that although progress in rationality really is achieved only from a point of view, we can still hope to find ways of living one with another. Since its aim is ambitious, it will almost certainly fail, but I hope that it will throw up some interesting ideas en route.

HOW RATIONAL ARE THE HORSES OF INSTRUCTION?

My first question, then, is 'How rational are the horses of instruction?' Put less cryptically, it is the question; 'How much of a defence will appeal to rationality provide for liberal commitment to free speech?' At the beginning I quoted Fay Weldon. Ms Weldon's assertion hints at important and familiar claims about the justification of free speech in liberal societies. It implies the possibility of intellectual progress, and a justification of free speech in terms of its tendency to facilitate such progress. Her distinction between studying and interpreting on the one hand, and 'learning by heart' on the other, is reminiscent of John Stuart Mill's distinction between a faith which allows itself to be put to the test in the free market place of ideas, and a creed which 'remains outside the mind, encrusting and petrifying it against all other influences addressed to the higher parts of our nature'.[7] In both these cases the distinction drawn is between those who submit their beliefs to scrutiny and those who engage in unthinking compliance and acceptance. And the clear judgement is not only that the latter are inferior to the former, but that the latter are inferior precisely because they reject rationality – 'the higher parts of our nature' in Mill's terms, or 'thoughts, perceptions and increasing understanding' in Weldon's. The defence of free speech is thus linked to a belief in the possibility of progress and improvement: free speech is necessary in order to move from a state of benighted acceptance to a state of critical awareness.

Connectedly, both writers imply that societies are superior in so far as they free individuals from passive conformity into a world of rational and individual decision-making. The reason for this is not simply that such rational decision-making will herald progress, it is also that human beings are essentially rational creatures – fulfilled to the extent that they employ their rationality in critical assessment of the socialisation to which they have been submitted. Thus Mill speaks frequently and scathingly of the 'numbing conformity' of nineteenth-century Victorian Britain, and draws unfavourable comparisons between that society and his ideal society of vibrant individuals, all of whom are thinking for themselves and critically evaluating the mores of their social and cultural world. Similarly, Fay Weldon extols the virtues of assessment, evaluation and interpretation. In both cases, the rational is contrasted with 'received opinion', and human beings are seen as beautiful and rational butterflies struggling to escape from the suffocating cocoon of custom, tradition and habit. Again, the debate is one between the forces of light and the forces of darkness; between the horses of instruction and the tigers of wrath. Finally, the quotation points to a defence of free speech in terms of its tendency to deliver truth. Fay Weldon's reference to the superior revelatory powers of the Bible echoes Mill's claim that freedom of thought and discussion is the surest path to truth.

There are therefore three lines of thought implicit in the Weldon claim, and familiar in liberal thinking generally: firstly, that free speech is necessary for progress; secondly that free speech is necessary for human fulfilment; and thirdly that free speech is necessary for the attainment of truth. All three make reference to rationality: progress consists in increased understanding; human fulfilment consists in the employment of rational faculties, which are the essential faculties of human beings; and truth is something discovered via rational argument. In this section I shall consider whether these appeals to rationality can deliver an adequate defence of an extensive free speech principle. And I begin, briefly, with the claim that free speech is important because of its tendency to deliver truth.

Much has been written about the inadequacies of Mill's defence of free speech in terms of truth: his belief that truth will triumph in the market place of ideas appears naively optimistic and also neglectful of other values, such as racial harmony and sexual equality. We have no guarantee whatever that free discussion will issue in truth, but often we do have reason to believe that free discussion will exacerbate racial tensions, will undermine the self-respect of disadvantaged groups, or will debase the values of some cultures. Faced with these threats, it is not obvious that truth either is or should be the paramount consideration.

Additionally, of course, the areas in which free speech is most problematic – areas of moral, political and religious debate – are precisely the ones where the concept of truth is extremely controversial. As Eric Barendt has put it:

> The argument for a free speech principle from truth is said [by Mill] to be particularly applicable to types of expression which can only rarely, if ever, establish truths with the same degree of assurance that obtains in mathematics or the natural sciences.[8]

So in the first place, it requires argument to show that free speech should be valued more highly than civil order or racial harmony, and in the second place, it is far from clear that the cases in which free speech is most problematic are cases in which truth is at issue. I shall not dwell on these points, as I do not believe that they are the central ones in the Rushdie debate. I shall simply add one further consideration, which is that historically, defences of free speech in terms of truth have supported policies of intolerance as well as policies of toleration: where the pursuit of truth is what justifies free speech, then the attainment of truth is what justifies repression – at least in the eyes of would-be persecutors. For this reason, if no other, defences of free speech in terms of truth strike me as dangerously two-edged.

But if free speech is not to be pursued in the name of truth, then its justification must lie elsewhere. This introduces the second argument referred to earlier – the claim that free speech is a necessary condition of human fulfilment. On this account, free expression of opinion is guaranteed because of what human beings essentially are: rational creatures. When we peel away the layers of habit produced by socialisation, we will reveal the essential nature of human beings – their capacity for rationality, independent of time and circumstance. Free speech is therefore required because human beings are rational creatures capable of assessing arguments and employing judgement about them.

This argument is connected with the argument from progress, since both emphasise fixedness and similarity. Just as the argument from human nature supposes a core 'self' which is essentially rational, and distinct from the self produced by socialisation, so the argument from progress supposes a set of fixed problems whose solution we approach by the application of rationality. We make progress in understanding the world via rational investigation, and simultaneously we develop our own true nature by employing our rational faculties. Thus Mill speaks not only of 'higher' parts of our nature (meaning intellectual parts), but also of the importance of freedom in the interests of 'progress' or 'the growth of civilization'. On this view, Muslim fundamentalists are seen as defending a quite arbitrary stopping-place on the route of progress. Their views are backward, primitive and, most importantly, they are views which deny the essential nature of human beings as rational creatures.

Two lines of criticism are pertinent here: the first (associated with the writings of Quentin Skinner) questions whether there are 'perennial problems' in social and political philosophy. What the study of the history of ideas reveals, according to Skinner, is not the essential sameness, but rather 'the essential variety of viable moral assumptions and political commitments'.[9] These different assumptions will generate different moral and political questions, and different conclusions as to what counts as rational. By assuming that there are perennial problems and that the history of political thought is evolutionary, we are led to the erroneous conclusion that our own concerns are the same as those of other times, and that we have arrived at a superior set of answers to one, timeless set of problems in political philosophy.

Secondly, and connectedly, such an account of moral and political philosophy covertly assumes that our own moral and political system is an improvement on those which have gone before – that we stand at the apex of an evolutionary process, which can be judged by fixed and value-free criteria of rationality. But as one writer has put it,

> a common criterion of reasonableness is not necessary in order to explain [differences of moral belief]. To call one set of beliefs irrational often obscures what disagreement amounts to in this context; that the disagreement is itself an expression or a product of a moral judgement.[10]

Thus the questions which are central to us may vary depending on the moral and political assumptions we make, and these moral assumptions can in turn determine what counts as rational, rather than being subject to an overarching and value-free judgement of rationality.

Blasphemy itself is an instructive example here: in the liberal tradition, and in English law, blasphemy is objectionable because of the offence which it causes to individuals (in the case of English law, to Christian believers). Where the blasphemy laws are invoked, therefore, they are invoked in an attempt to protect believers, not in an attempt to protect beliefs. This is the force of Ignatieff's distinction: 'In theocratic states like Iran, the law guarantees the inviolability of certain sacred doctrines. In free societies, the law does not protect doctrines as such, it protects individuals'.[11]

But it requires argument to show that 'free' societies are thereby more rational or better. In a culture in which religious beliefs are central, it is far from clear that it is rational to allow them to be interpreted in the way in which the English blasphemy law is interpreted. Shabbir Akhtar writes:

> The fact the post-Enlightenment Christians tolerate blasphemy is a matter for shame, not for pride. It is true, of course, that God can defend himself, but a believer must vindicate the reputation of God and his spokesmen against the militant calumnies of evil.[12]

In English law, which emphasises individuals, the wrong that is done by blasphemy is the wrong of offending individuals. In the eyes of Muslim (and many Christian) believers, however, the wrong that is done by blasphemy is a wrong against God. Similarly, where blasphemy is tolerated the result is not simply that individual believers are distressed: it is that God is mocked. Where we begin with the belief that the individual is most important, we will find it rational to conclude that blasphemous acts are damaging to the extent that they damage individuals, and conversely that censorship is damaging to the extent that it restricts or suppresses individual development. By contrast, where we begin with the belief that God is most important, we will find it rational to conclude that blasphemy is wrong because it scorns God, and conversely that censorship is a necessary means of affording protection to that which is sacred. Put differently, the basic question for liberals is 'How can we justify individual free speech?'; whereas the basic question for Muslims is 'How can we vindicate the reputation of God?' It is not obvious that the former is more rational than the latter. It is clear only that there are more or less rational strategies to pursue once the basic question has been identified.

I said earlier that discussions of the Rushdie affair tend to be cast in terms of an opposition between the forces of light and the forces of darkness; or between the horses of instruction and the tigers of wrath. Fay Weldon's claim that the God of the Bible is a better God than the God of the Qur'an rests on the belief that the former, unlike the latter, admits of rational investigation and interpretation. It assumes both that the God of the Bible is superior to the God of the Qur'an, and that interpretation of the Bible is superior to mere belief in the Qur'an. These assumptions generate not only characteristically liberal views about the importance of free speech but also, and most importantly, specific views about the wrong which is done by intolerance. For example, they allow that free speech may be restricted in cases where it is likely to cause profound offence or civil unrest. By contrast, if we do not assume an evolutionary view of morality, then the wrong of intolerance will also be understood differently: it will be the wrong of spurning a whole way of life or system of belief. It follows that not only is the justification of toleration drawn differently in the different cases, but also that what counts as intolerance is understood differently. By beginning with the question 'What justifies free speech?' we place the burden of proof on those who would restrict speech. By beginning with the question 'How should we vindicate the reputation of God?' we place the burden of proof on those who would mock God. And again, it is not clear that the former starting point is any more rational than the latter.

These lines of thought may appear to imply that 'to understand all is to forgive all'. In the Rushdie case they may seem to lead to something like the following conclusion: there is, in the end, no way of rationally resolving moral disagreement. Moral beliefs are not determined by interests, but are themselves what determine interests. We therefore have no means of assessing the different moral claims made by members of different groups. In other words, the Bible is not, after all, superior to the Qur'an. Our local prejudices deliver a judgement in favour of the Bible; the local prejudices of Muslim fundamentalists deliver a judgement in favour of the Qur'an. And that is all that can be said about the matter.

But this extreme relativist conclusion is hardly helpful in a multicultural society where differing values must coexist in some kind of harmony, however uneasy. Nor is it, I think, the correct conclusion to draw. The considerations adduced above are simply intended to cast doubt on the claim that free speech may be justified by reference to the concept of truth on the one hand, or the concept of rationality on the other. To reject those assumptions is not thereby to claim that there is no such thing as truth. It is only to claim that questions of truth are not always the most important questions. Similarly, the claim that rationality must be understood within a context, need not be taken to imply that literally anything goes. It implies only that, in deciding what goes, we should take account of the fact that moral judgements influence our beliefs about what is rational, just as much as beliefs about what is rational influence our moral judgements.

I shall return to these points later and say a little more about their implications for the Rushdie affair. For the moment, all I am concerned to indicate is that questions of truth or of rationality will not take us all the way in defences of free speech: the horses of instruction have an understanding of rationality which will not necessarily commend itself to the tigers of wrath.

HOW WISE ARE THE TIGERS OF WRATH?

In his recent book, *Contingency, Irony and Solidarity*, Richard Rorty makes reference to two kinds of writer in social and political philosophy:

> the one tells us that we need not speak only the language of the tribe, that we may find our own words, that we may have a responsibility to ourselves to find them. The other tells us that that responsibility is not the only one we have. Both are right, but there is no way to make both speak a single language.[13]

In the previous section I expressed scepticism about the claim that we may find our own language distinct from the language of the tribe, and suggested that the language we speak and the values we hold may be in large part a function of 'the tribe'. But this claim appears both unhelpful and false when we turn back to the second quotation I used at the beginning of the paper – the demand by Southall Black Sisters. Their statement takes the form of a declaration that they will find their own language distinct from the language of the tribe – that they, at least, will not be determined by socialisation. The claim harks back to Mill's assertion that the ideal for human beings is precisely to 'determine what part of recorded experience is properly applicable to their own circumstances and character'. My earlier criticism of this stance was not so much an attempt to deny that that can happen, as a scepticism about whether, when it does happen, the end result is a more rational state of affairs. It was a worry about whether the Bible may be recommended *tout court* as a better (more rational, more civilised) alternative than the Qur'an. By contrast, the demand made by the Southall Black Sisters is simply that this is their chosen or preferred alternative – not that it is thereby better or more rational. Moreover, they demand this as their right. Unlike Mill, they do not insist upon it as the duty of everyone, nor do their claims contain any commitment to rationality or to progress. My argument in the previous section was intended to cast doubt on the claim that free speech is justified by reference to rationality, to truth or to progress independent of prior moral beliefs. But the Southall declaration insists on the importance, not of truth or of progress, but of individual autonomy. Where the argument from rationality is sometimes used to imply that there is a truth which is the same for all, or a standard of rationality which may be applied to all, this argument allows that different people might choose different ways of life.

Nevertheless, the Southall declaration raises pressing questions about the balance to be struck between different moralities in multicultural societies, and about the role of choice in morality. Specifically, it raises the question of whether free speech should be defended, not because it leads to truth, nor because it leads to progress, but because it enables people to choose the moral and religious beliefs which best suit them – it enables them to develop their autonomy, where the availability of choices is a necessary condition of individual autonomy.

In this section I shall discuss two arguments which are relevant to the autonomy question, but which appear to lead to incompatible conclusions. The first is Bernard Williams's claim that, *pace* the Southall declaration, moral values are not chosen. The second is Joseph Raz's claim that in a multicultural society such as ours, members of minority groups must be encouraged to choose the values of the dominant group. If free speech and toleration are to be justified by reference to the importance of individual autonomy, then we need to know whether values are indeed possible objects of choice. Williams thinks not. He says:

> There are points of resemblance between moral and factual convictions; and I suspect it to be true of moral, as it certainly is of factual convictions, that we cannot take very seriously a profession of them if we are given to understand that a speaker has just decided to adopt them ... We see a man's genuine convictions as coming from somewhere deeper in him than that.[14]

Williams's target here is an aspect of Kantian rationalism: in the Kantian tradition it is often claimed that people should be encouraged to 'decide' upon their moral beliefs, meaning that the beliefs they hold ought to be the result of rational enquiry: they ought to be the consequence of active deliberation, not the consequence of prejudice, tradition or brute emotion. Again, socialisation is understood as something which masks an individual's true nature. But Williams's suggestion implies that there is a sense in which socialisation does not mask an individual's true nature; it *is* an individual's true nature; 'by what is only an apparent paradox, what we see as coming from deeper in him, he – that is the deciding 'he' – may see as coming from outside him'.[15] The desire not to be constrained by a social context, by 'prejudice' or tradition, should not lead us to suppose that we should aspire to a choice made completely independent of those things. Put differently, we should not believe that choice within a context is but a pale shadow of what we aspire to – choice unrestricted by any context and dictated by pure rationality alone.

It is this point which Joseph Raz gestures towards in his apparently conflicting claim that 'for those who live in an autonomy supporting environment there is no choice but to be autonomous' and that therefore members of minority groups must be brought 'humanely and decently' to valuing autonomy.[16] At first glance it appears that while Williams is insisting upon the lack of choice in moral matters (on the passivity of moral life), Raz is insisting on the necessity of choice. In fact, however, the difference between the two is less acute than it appears: Raz's claim is intended to emphasise the importance of social circumstances as determinants of flourishing: for people who live in a Western liberal democracy, where liberal values dominate, it is futile to attempt to flourish in any other way than by accepting at least some liberal values. Such acceptance will not, as Williams points out, be a matter of simple decision-taking, nor will it be the result of rational consideration and judgement. The defence of the need for choice in such a society is simply that choice is already a central value of the society. If people expect to flourish, then they must come to terms with that fact.

Several consequences spring from this argument: the first is that it implies an understanding of moral change as something distinct from moral progress. Whereas the argument from rationality pitted light against darkness, this argument simply reflects on differences, and also acknowledges that in the move from one set of moral values to another there may be not merely difference but loss. The second consequence is that it does not assume a concept of rationality distinct from social circumstances: quite the reverse, for the importance of social circumstances is precisely what forces the need for moral change.

But if moral values are not the objects of decision or choice, and if there is genuine loss in the move from one set of values to another, then the focus of attention must shift away from our original question, 'What justifies free speech?' We need to do less by way of defending our own values, and more by way of understanding the values of other groups. We need, in other words, to understand precisely what will be lost when values are replaced, and precisely what wrong is done by attempting to compel changes in value. Equally, however, we must be aware that change is needed, and is needed precisely because the values of the tribe are so important. The recognition that socialisation goes all the way down should not lead us to believe that nothing can be done to change moral values. On the contrary, it impresses upon us the importance of seeing that something is done.

THE LION AND THE LAMB

What conclusions are to be drawn from these discussions of rationality, choice and the sovereignty of the individual? In the liberal tradition, defences of the toleration of free speech tend to be couched in terms of truth, of rationality, and of individual choice. However, the claim that the *telos* of toleration is truth carries little force in cases where what is at issue is the toleration of moral or religious beliefs. The focus of attention thus shifts to the concepts of rationality and choice. In the former case it was argued that rationality requires reference to prior moral beliefs: there is no rational vantage point devoid of moral belief – no 'view from nowhere'. Additionally, it was suggested that moral and religious beliefs do not admit of choice or decision, but are to some extent 'given' by social circumstance.

These points, however, need to be set against the demands of the Southall declaration – the demand by members of minority groups that they be allowed to shape their own destiny and decide upon the forms their lives will take: 'We will not be dictated to by fundamentalists. Our lives will not be defined by community leaders'. It is tempting to interpret this demand as a proof that liberal standards are better, more rational than any other, since they are the standards which people will choose when once they are released from the constraints of fundamentalist socialisation. But equally it may be interpreted as the only appropriate response to the requirements of a different kind of socialisation – the socialisation inherent in a Western liberal democracy. In other words, the Southall declaration is not a refutation, but a confirmation of the belief that the individual is subject to the group – in this case to the influences of the dominant culture, as well as to the influences of the minority culture.

If this is correct, then it suggests an alternative account of the value of toleration – one which does not appeal to truth, to progress, or to individualist conceptions of rationality and choice, but which emphasises the individual's need to locate himself within a group. On this account, the wrong which is done by intolerance is not the denial of rational decision-making, or of choice, but the wrong of exclusion.

Richard Rorty has recently argued for the possibility of a certain kind of 'liberal utopia'. He says:

> In my utopia, human solidarity would be seen not as a fact to be recognized by clearing away prejudice, or burrowing down to previously hidden depths but, rather, as a goal to be achieved. It is to be achieved not by inquiry but by imagination, the imaginative ability to see strange people as fellow sufferers. Solidarity is not discovered by reflection but created. It is created by increasing our sensitivity to the particular details of the pain and humiliation of other, unfamiliar sorts of people.[17]

Rorty's argument shifts the focus of debate in three distinct but connected ways, all of which are hinted at in the earlier discussion: by emphasising solidarity, he urges a move from individual to social considerations; by emphasising imagination he urges a move from reason to emotion; and by emphasising humiliation he urges a move from the rights of the tolerators to the wrongs suffered by the oppressed. However, Rorty's reference to the wrong of humiliation strikes me as insufficiently strong.

Earlier I argued that defences of free speech in terms of rationality and choice are defective because the moral beliefs which we hold, and which define what we are, are not primarily objects of choice, nor are they the deliverances of an abstract rationality. It follows from this that there is a strong sense in which what we are is given rather than chosen. This is most obviously the case where what we are is a matter of ethnic identity, or of gender. But it is also true in the areas of moral and religious belief, which are equally incapable of being given up simply by act of will or on the basis of 'rational' argument. Moreover, beliefs of this sort define what we are, in the sense of specifying where we belong. If they are undermined or despised, we ourselves are also undermined and despised. But that is not, it seems to me, simply a case of individual humiliation. I shall conclude with a short example, which may help to explain what I mean.

It is often argued (and successfully) that racist or sexist literature should be restricted or banned. The reasons given for this are various: sometimes it is claimed that such literature is profoundly offensive (to blacks or women); sometimes that it is disruptive of the good order and harmony of society; sometimes that it serves to undermine the autonomy of the members of the groups in question. All these arguments are fundamentally individualist. They acknowledge that the standing of the group as a whole is threatened by the literature in question, but their primary focus is the state of mind of the individual who happens to belong to that group. (It is individual women whose autonomy is jeopardised by the proliferation of pornographic material, and it is therefore in the interests of individual women, or in deference to their feelings, that such literature should be restricted.) The question of whether material should be restricted thus becomes a matter of balancing the autonomy of the pornographer against the autonomy of women; or the rights of the pornographer against the feelings of (some) women. If the free speech argument wins, then it is not simply the case that the women in question are humiliated, in the sense of being offended, distressed or upset. Nor is it necessarily the case that the autonomy of any particular woman is threatened (though often it is). Rather, it is the case that what one essentially is is scorned. If socialisation goes all the way down, then the toleration of pornography may be interpreted as a statement of the worthlessness of women. The situation is only exacerbated if that toleration is justified by appeal to rationality, since it then reinforces the judgement of worthlessness.

Where we take 'what one essentially is' as referring to membership of groups, then the situation is made yet more complex: the Southall women may be Muslims, whose identity is determined by their membership of the Muslim community. They are also women, whose identity is determined by their gender. They inhabit a Western pluralist society, and their identity is formed by that membership too. When what we are is defined by reference to groups, and when the groups themselves contain inconsistent values, then the demands of solidarity become increasingly painful. That pain cannot be eased by constant appeal to rationality and choice, for both these concepts operate only against backgrounds which are given and understood. Equally, however, it cannot be eased by categorising people in terms which refer only to their group membership. The humiliation which is felt by fundamentalist Muslims is the humiliation inherent in the rejection of a whole way of life – the rejection of what one essentially is.

Free speech, I suggest, is important in so far as it increases the possibility of mutual understanding. The wrong which is standardly done by the denial of free speech must therefore be understood in these terms too, and these terms will both justify and set limits to toleration in liberal societies. But mutual understanding, like self-knowledge, is something which must be created, not discovered. To defend free speech by reference to rationality is to suppose that there is a truth which will emerge in the free market-place of ideas. Against this I have suggested that often there is no such truth, and that even if there were, we should be wary of supposing that it will always emerge in that way. Similarly, to defend free speech by reference to rationality is to ignore the extent to which rationality is itself context-dependent. And to defend free speech by reference to autonomy or individual choice is to ignore the sense in which we are not self-made, but self-made only within certain limits: the limits provided by our membership of often diverse and inconsistent groups.

What is needed therefore is a commitment to freedom of speech as one of the conditions for obtaining a better understanding of different groups. In Kant's terms, we must understand speech not simply as expression, but as communication. The justification of free speech will then be that it enhances rather than thwarts the possibilities of communication between different people. Additionally, however, the conditions of communication, and of morality generally, include our capacity for emotional love – our ability to recognise the needs of others and their similarities to us. Where free speech is employed in such a way as to destroy the possibility of communication, and of mutual understanding, then its *raison d'être* is destroyed. It is in this way that we come to ask whether the tigers of wrath are wiser than the horses of instruction, when the question we should be asking is 'How can the lion lie down with the lamb?'

NOTES

1.   The title is taken from William Blake's *Proverbs of Hell*, in which Blake tells us

that 'the tigers of wrath are wiser than the horses of instruction'. Blake's claim here is part of his general onslaught against Reason, and reflects his belief that Reason may not be the most reliable way of discovering Truth. I am grateful to Professor Jacques Berthoud and Professor David Moody for helping me to understand Blake's text.

2. Fay Weldon, *Sacred Cows* (London: Chatto & Windus, 1989), p.33.
3. As quoted in Lisa Appignanesi and Sara Maitland (eds), *The Rushdie File* (London: Fourth Estate, 1989), pp.241–2.
4. As quoted in Appignanesi and Maitland, op.cit., p.251.
5. As quoted in Appignanesi and Maitland, op.cit., p.229.
6. See Alasdair MacIntyre, *Whose Justice? Which Rationality?* (London: Duckworth, 1988).
7. John Stuart Mill, *On Liberty*, 1859, chapter 2, 'Of the Liberty of Thought and Discussion'.
8. Eric Barendt, *Freedom of Speech* (Oxford: Clarendon Press, 1985), p.11.
9. Quentin Skinner, 'A Reply to my Critics', in James Tully (ed.), *Meaning and Context: Quentin Skinner and his Critics* (Oxford and Cambridge: Polity, 1988), pp.231–88.
10. D.Z. Phillips, 'Allegiance and Change in Morality', in *Through a Darkening Glass* (Oxford: Blackwell, 1982), p.25.
11. Michael Ignatieff, in Appignanesi and Maitland, op.cit., p.251.
12. Shabbir Akhtar, in Appignanesi and Maitland, op.cit., p.240.
13. Richard Rorty, *Contingency, Irony, and Solidarity* (Cambridge: Cambridge University Press, 1989), p.xiv.
14. Bernard Williams, 'Morality and the Emotions', in *Problems of the Self* (Cambridge: Cambridge University Press 1973), p.227.
15. Ibid.
16. Joseph Raz, *The Morality of Freedom* (Oxford: Clarendon Press, 1986), p.391.
17. Richard Rorty, op.cit., p.xvi.

Index